# OUR DAILY BREAD
## FOR
# KIDS®

**365** Meaningful Moments with God

Written by
Crystal Bowman & Teri McKinley

Illustrated by Luke Flowers

**Discovery House®**
from Our Daily Bread Ministries

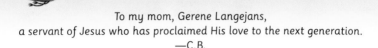

To my mom, Gerene Langejans,
a servant of Jesus who has proclaimed His love to the next generation.
—C.B.

In loving memory of my father-in-law, Terry McKinley,
who wanted all people to know Jesus.
—T.M.

To Owen, Lydia, and Naomi, my little lights that shine brightly with the love of the Lord.
May you continue to grow brighter with His Word.
—L.F.

With special thanks to Andrew, Paul, Miranda, Kris,
and the Discovery House team for their excellent work.

*Our Daily Bread for Kids*
© 2014 by Crystal Bowman and Teri McKinley
Illustrations by Luke Flowers and © 2016 by Discovery House
All rights reserved.

Discovery House is affiliated with Our Daily Bread Ministries, Grand Rapids, Michigan.

Requests for permission to quote from this book should be directed to:
Permissions Department, Discovery House, P.O. Box 3566, Grand Rapids, MI 49501,
or contact us by e-mail at permissionsdept@dhp.org

Design by Kris Nelson/StoryLook Design
ISBN of the paperback edition: 978-1-62707-656-2

**Library of Congress Cataloging-in-Publication Data**
Bowman, Crystal.
    Our daily bread for kids : 365 meaningful moments with God /
Crystal Bowman and Teri McKinley ; illustrations by Luke Flowers.
        p.  cm
    ISBN 978-1-62707-332-5
    1.  Devotional calendars--Juvenile literature.  I. Flowers, Luke, illustrator. II. Title.
BV4870.B6955 2014
242'.62--dc23                                                   2014037748

Printed in the United States of America
First printing of this edition in 2016

# INTRODUCTION

**One day Jesus' disciples asked Him how they should pray.**
Jesus taught them a prayer that has become famous all over the world. It's often called **"The Lord's Prayer."** This is how Jesus prayed:

> "Our Father in heaven,
> hallowed be your name, your kingdom come,
> your will be done, on earth as it is in heaven.
> Give us today our daily bread.
> And forgive us our debts,
> as we also have forgiven our debtors.
> And lead us not into temptation,
> but deliver us from the evil one."
>
> MATTHEW 6:9–13 NIV

Did you notice those three words, **"our daily bread"**? What do they mean?

Throughout the Bible God shows that He loves people by taking care of their needs every day. One of our biggest needs is food—actual bread for our bodies and spiritual "bread" for our souls. God fed His chosen people, the Israelites, by sending bread called manna to their campsites every morning. In the New Testament, Jesus calls himself our "bread of life."

This book is all about our spiritual food. The readings in Our Daily Bread for Kids will help you get inside the Bible every day. They were written to explain Bible stories and ideas, and they will always point you to what God says in Scripture. Every day you can read one of these devotionals and your Bible. If Scripture is the bread that feeds our souls, this book is like the plate that serves the bread. Keep it right next to your Bible!

This is not a Bible storybook, so the 365 readings do not follow the order of Scripture. Some readings are about Jesus or other people in the New Testament, some are about stories from the Old Testament, and some are about Bible verses that might have a special meaning for you. If you come across words you don't understand, look them up in the glossary at the back. If you want to read about a certain topic, check out the index of topics. If you come across anything you don't understand, just keep reading. Don't give up! The more you read and study the Bible, the more you will understand the big story God has for us.

You can read this book by yourself, or have your parents or grandparents read it with you. You might want to use this book at mealtime or at bedtime. However you use Our Daily Bread for Kids, we hope you like it. But more importantly, we hope you learn that Jesus loves you so much that He's given you a chance to become a part of God's family.

As you use this book, we pray you will have many meaningful moments with God.

Crystal and Teri

> Then the LORD God formed a man. He made him out of the dust of the ground. He breathed the breath of life into him. And the man became a living person.
>
> **GENESIS 2:7 NIRV**

# A Special Creation

**In the beginning there** was nothing but water and darkness. The earth was empty. It had no shape. But God was there before everything else, and He had a plan to create a world.

God is so powerful that all He had to do was speak to fill the world with good things. First He said, "Let there be light." And there was light. Then He told the water to separate from the sky—so it did. Then God said, "Let the waters be gathered into one place." And that is exactly what happened. God told trees and plants to appear on the land—so they did. Then God created the sun, moon, and stars and put them in the sky. He told birds to fly in the sky and fish to swim in the seas. God told the land to bring forth different kinds of animals—and it did. God liked everything He made because it was good.

## I am created by God.

On the last day of creation, God decided to make a man. But God didn't say, "Let there be a man." Instead of using words, God did something different. He formed a man from the dust of the earth. Then God breathed His own breath into the man, and the man became a living person.

People are different from the rest of God's creation. He made us so we can talk to Him, love Him, and know Him in a real and personal way. God created you and gave life to you too. You are a special part of His creation, just like the first person He created.
—C.B.

## READ MORE

Read Genesis 2:21–22.
Who was the second person God created?
How did God create her?

## FUN FACT

Did you know that water covers most of the earth? Only about one-fourth of the earth is dry land.

> Ever since the world was created it has been possible to see the qualities of God that are not seen. I'm talking about his eternal power and about the fact that he is God. Those things can be seen in what he has made.
>
> **ROMANS 1:20 NIRV**

# Can You See It?

**You cannot see the wind,** but you can see what it does. You can watch trees wave back and forth as the wind blows their branches. You can watch a boat glide across a lake as the wind pushes its sails. You can watch a kite soar high into the sky as the wind carries it along. And you can watch an umbrella turn inside out on a windy, rainy day. If someone said, "I don't believe in the wind because I cannot see it," that would be silly. We know the wind is real because we can see everything it does.

Just like the wind, we can't see God either—but we can see what He does. We can look at the nighttime sky and see the moon and stars He created. We can see His power in the waves of a mighty ocean. We can watch a flock of geese fly south for the winter as God guides them along. And we can see His artwork when He paints colorful sunsets and rainbows.

God wants us to know He is real. That is why He reveals himself to us through His creation. If you want to see God, just look around at all He does. God's work is everywhere! —C.B.

## I can see what God does everywhere.

### FUN FACT

The strongest hurricanes, called "Category 5," have winds over 155 miles an hour. That's more than twice as fast as cars on the highway.

### READ MORE

What does Psalm 19:1–6 tell us about God's creation?

# Just Ask!

**Kids who get the best grades** in school often win awards. It is good to study hard and be smart, but it is also important to be wise.

A person who is smart knows many things. But a person who is wise knows how to make good choices. Wise people understand how to treat others with kindness and respect. They understand what is right and wrong. They choose to live the way God wants them to.

> If any of you needs wisdom, you should ask God for it. God is generous. He enjoys giving to all people, so God will give you wisdom.
>
> **JAMES 1:5 ICB**

The Old Testament tells us about a wise man named Solomon. He became king of Israel after his father, David, passed away. God spoke to Solomon in a dream and said He would give Solomon whatever he wanted. Many people would ask for money or popularity or a long life. But Solomon asked for wisdom. God was very pleased with that choice. God told Solomon that because he asked for wisdom, he would also get riches and honor.

Ask God for wisdom.

**God will give me wisdom. All I need to do is ask.**

In the New Testament, James tells us that if we ask God for wisdom He will give it to us. Many times, we get wisdom from God's Word, the Bible. When we read the Bible, God helps us to understand what is right and wrong. He helps us understand how He wants us to live.

You don't have to be grown-up to be wise. You can ask God for wisdom right now. It's a wise thing to do! —C.B.

**READ MORE**

Read Proverbs 2:1–11.
What are the rewards of wisdom?

**FUN FACT**

The word wisdom appears in the Bible more than two hundred times.

> He will cover you
> with his wings.
> Under the feathers
> of his wings you
> will find safety.
> He is faithful.
> He will keep you
> safe like a shield
> or a tower.
>
> **PSALM 91:4 NIRV**

# Wings of Safety

**A mother hen is very protective** of her chicks. She begins to care for her babies when they are just eggs. She pays close attention to the eggs' temperature. She pecks at other birds or animals that come near the nest. When the chicks finally break out of their eggshells, the mother hen continues to watch them carefully. Any time the hen senses danger, she makes a clucking noise and spreads her wings. The babies run underneath her wings to hide. There the chicks are safe and warm. They can even walk around underneath the shelter of their mother's wings.

## I can run to God when I am in danger.

Psalm 91 says that God protects you like a mother hen protects her chicks. When you think of God guarding you, imagine a hen spreading her wings. When you are afraid, God wants you to run to Him for safety. You can always depend on Him to be your shelter.

But how do we run to God? We can run to Him anytime by praying to Him and asking Him to help us.

Whether it's daytime or nighttime, you can stay close to God. When you are close to Him, God covers you with His wings of safety. —T.M.

### FUN FACT

A hen's wings stretch twenty to thirty inches (fifty-one to seventy-six centimeters). That means about twelve chicks can fit under her wings at one time.

### READ MORE

Read Psalm 17:8.
Use this as a prayer asking God to keep you safe.

# Dinner on the Mountainside

**Imagine trying to feed** five thousand people. That would take a lot of food!

The Bible says Jesus fed five thousand hungry people on a mountainside. And that number doesn't even include the women and children who were there! There wasn't a store on the mountain where Jesus could buy food. There wasn't a barn full of food nearby. But there was a young boy in the crowd who had five small loaves of bread and two little fish. And he was willing to share with Jesus.

> Then Jesus took the loaves and gave thanks. He handed out the bread to those who were seated. He gave them as much as they wanted. And he did the same with the fish.
>
> **JOHN 6:11 NIRV**

Jesus' disciples didn't think the boy's lunch would help thousands of hungry people. But Jesus performed a miracle. First He told the people to sit down. Then He thanked God for the food and began to hand it out. He turned a small lunch into a huge dinner for all those people! There were even leftovers for the disciples.

## Jesus can use what I have, no matter how big or small.

The Bible doesn't tell us the name of the boy. We don't know anything else about him. It seems he was a regular kid. But Jesus showed His own greatness because a boy was willing to share the small amount he had.

Like that boy, we all can give what we have. It doesn't matter what it is. What matters is that we are willing to share what we have with others.

When you give, Jesus can do great things through you too. —T.M.

### READ MORE
Did you know God performed a similar miracle in the Old Testament? Read about it in 2 Kings 4:42–44.

### FUN FACT
The average loaf of bread has about twenty slices. Without Jesus' miracle, it would have taken around 250 loaves of bread just to give everyone in the crowd a single slice.

> Two people are better than one. They can help each other in everything they do.
>
> **ECCLESIASTES 4:9 NIRV**

# Let's Work Together

**It's fun to play catch** on a sunny afternoon. But have you ever tried to play catch by yourself? It is not very easy to do alone! You need a friend to catch the ball when you throw it. And you need someone to throw the ball back when it's your turn to catch.

Chores might not be as much fun as playing catch. But have you noticed that chores are easier with two people? Making a bed by yourself can take a long time. Straightening the sheets and fluffing the pillows is a lot of work! But with another person's help, you can get the work done much more quickly.

The Bible says two people can do more together than one person alone. It is good to remember this when we serve God too. Just as playing catch and doing chores are better with friends, Christians accomplish more when they work together. And remember that God is the one who gives you the strength to work!

Think about all the people you see serving at church. The pastor preaches a message to the people, but many others serve too. Sunday school teachers, greeters, musicians, and other helpers all work as a team so people can worship together and learn about God.

## Two are better than one.

Can you think of ways you can work with others at home, at church, or at school? You will get more done and have more fun! —T.M.

### FUN FACT

The world record for one person running a mile is three minutes and forty-three seconds. But the world record for a relay team running the same distance is much better—only two minutes and fifty-four seconds!

### READ MORE

Read Mark 6:7.
How did Jesus send out His disciples?

# A Big Assignment

**God created a perfect world.** But when people disobeyed God, they ruined His perfect world. The people were sinful and didn't care about God. God was sorry that He had made people to live on the earth. He wanted to start over.

> **Noah did everything exactly as God commanded him.**
> GENESIS 6:22 NIRV

But there was one man who still loved God, and his name was Noah. God had a big assignment for Noah!

God told Noah to build a giant boat—called an ark—big enough for his family, two of every animal, and lots and lots of food. Noah would build the ark of cypress wood and cover it with tar inside and out. It was big—450 feet long (about 137 meters), 75 feet wide (about 23 meters), and 45 feet high (about 14 meters). God told Noah that He was going to send a flood to destroy the earth, but He would keep Noah and his family safe inside the ark.

## God wants me to obey Him, even when others don't.

The Bible doesn't say how long it took Noah to build the ark, but it may have taken a hundred years! Some people probably laughed at Noah for building the ark. But Noah did everything God told him to do because he trusted God. When the flood came, Noah and his family were safe in the ark while the rest of the world was destroyed.

It's not always easy to obey God. It may be hard if your friends are not doing the right things. They might even laugh. But God is pleased when you let Him work through you. And He may even give you a big assignment someday! —C.B.

## READ MORE
Read Genesis 8:6–12.
How did Noah know the
flood water was finally going down?

## FUN FACT
The world's largest ship today is called the *Prelude*. It is 1,601 feet long (488 meters), more than three times the length of Noah's ark!

> How you made me is amazing and wonderful. I praise you for that. What you have done is wonderful. I know that very well.... God, your thoughts about me are priceless. No one can possibly add them all up.
>
> **PSALM 139:14, 17 NIRV**

# Amazing and Wonderful

**Did you know** that no two snowflakes are exactly alike? Each snowflake has its own special pattern and design. The same is true for people—not even identical twins are alike in every way.

Every person God creates is unique. That means there is no one else exactly like you. From your laugh to your freckles to the color of your hair—God made you, and He knows all about you.

Think about the things you like to do and the things you're really good at. Not only does God know your interests and talents, He's the one who gave them to you. He thought about you before you were even born. He planned your smile and the color of your eyes. He knew what would make you laugh and what subjects you would like in school. He gave you your own voice and your own personality.

## I am a wonderful part of God's creation.

Every part of God's creation—including you—is amazing and wonderful! In the book of Psalms, King David thanks God for making him in such an amazing and wonderful way. He praises God for thinking about him so much.

David says that God's thoughts about him are priceless. God's thoughts about you are priceless too. You have great value because God made you amazing and wonderful.
—T.M.

### FUN FACT

Your fingerprints are unique to you. They are on your fingers when you're born, and stay the same throughout your whole life.

### READ MORE

Read Psalm 139:1–6.
What does God know about you?

# Kids Can Make a Difference

> There was no king like Josiah either before him or after him. None of them turned to the LORD as he did. He followed the LORD with all his heart and all his soul. He followed him with all his strength. He did everything the Law of Moses required.
>
> **2 KINGS 23:25 NIRV**

**There are many kings** in the Bible—some were good, and others were very bad. The Bible tells us that King Josiah was one of the best. He did what was right in the eyes of God.

The Bible says something very interesting about Josiah. Are you ready for this? He was only eight years old when he became king! Josiah had some adult helpers, of course, but he was the leader.

Some of the kings before Josiah were evil, and God's people began worshipping other gods which weren't even real. Josiah knew that was wrong! So when he was twenty-six years old he destroyed all the places where people worshipped other gods. He got rid of the statues of the fake gods the people had made. Josiah took away everything else the Lord hated in the land. That was a big job for a young king, but he did it because he loved God, and he wanted the people to love God too.

## I can make a difference no matter how old I am.

Have you ever thought you're too young to make a difference? That's not true. There are many things that kids can do to serve God. Maybe you could be a friend to a lonely kid at school or in your neighborhood. Maybe you could invite other kids to church or Sunday school so they can learn more about God. By being a good friend, you can make a difference in another person's life.

With God's help, you can make a difference—even if you're not a king! —C.B.

## READ MORE

King Josiah promised to do something very important. Read 2 Kings 23:1–3 to find out what it was.

### FUN FACT

Alfonso XIII of Spain was declared king as soon as he was born in 1886.

Fix your thoughts on what is true, and honorable, and right, and pure, and lovely, and admirable. Think about things that are excellent and worthy of praise.

**PHILIPPIANS 4:8 NLT**

God is good!

# Something to Think About

**What do you think** about when you go for a walk? How blue the sky is? How the sun feels on your face? Why the squirrels run away as you get close to them? God loves it when we think about good things.

But thinking those good thoughts can be hard when bad things happen around us. And bad things do happen. Kids have problems just like grown-ups do. That's why God tells everyone to think about things that are good and worthy of praise. He wants us to remember that He is in control. He wants us to trust Him and believe that He will take care of us.

*When I think about good things, I will thank God.*

Today's Bible verse says to think about what is "true, and honorable, and right." Things like this: God loves you and cares about you. God wants what is best for you. God has a special plan for your life. God will always be with you.

The verse also says to think about what is "pure, and lovely, and admirable." You could think about pure snowflakes and lovely butterflies. You could think about the people in your life who you admire.

When you do something nice for another person, don't you enjoy being thanked? So does God! Thank Him for giving you so many good things to think about. —C.B.

**FUN FACT**

Our brains think anywhere from twelve thousand to fifty thousand thoughts every day!

**READ MORE**

What does Psalm 105:1–8 tell us to do?

# Why Me, God?

**Moses was an Israelite.** That means he was one of God's special people. One day, when he was guarding a flock of sheep, Moses saw a bush that was burning with fire. But it never burned up! So Moses walked over for a closer look.

Suddenly God's voice came from the bush. "Moses, Moses," God said. "Take off your sandals for you are standing on very special ground."

God told Moses that He had heard the cries of the Israelites, who were living in Egypt as slaves. God wanted Moses to lead His people out of Egypt. But Moses didn't think he was the right person for the job.

Moses gave God all kinds of excuses. But God kept telling Moses that He would help. God even showed Moses miracles to prove His power. Still, Moses tried to say "no."

> **But Moses said to God, "Who am I that I should go to Pharaoh and bring the people of Israel out of Egypt?"**
>
> EXODUS 3:11 GW

*I will say "yes" to God when He wants to use me.*

"I'm not a good speaker," Moses said.

"I will help you speak," God told him.

Finally, Moses told God to send someone else! Moses was looking at his own weakness rather than God's power. God could have taken His people out of Egypt by himself, but He wanted to use Moses for the job.

You know what? God still uses people to do His work. Whenever God chooses people, He gives them the ability to do the job He has for them. When we say "yes" to God, He will do great things through us. —C.B.

## READ MORE

Moses became a great leader for the children of Israel. Read Exodus 14:10–31. How did God use Moses in this story?

## FUN FACT

"Burning bush" is the name of a shrub that turns fiery red and orange in the fall. The shrub got its name from the Bible story.

# What Is God Like?

> The LORD your God . . . is gracious. He is tender and kind. He is slow to get angry. He is full of love. He takes pity on you.
>
> JOEL 2:13 NIRV

**Video chats are fun.** It's great to be able to see and hear a person who lives far away. Maybe you have a relative or friend in another city, or even another country. With the right computer or phone, you can see that person's smile and hear her laugh!

When you can see and hear someone else, it's easier to know what that person is like. Being face-to-face makes you feel closer to others.

But you can't see God face-to-face, and He doesn't talk to you out loud. Sometimes you might wonder what God is like, or feel like He's far away. That's why He gave us the Bible. His Word shows us what He is like.

The Bible says God is loving and cares about you. He is tender and gentle. God is kind. He doesn't get angry easily. God loves you a lot. He understands how you feel when you are sad or having a bad day. Everything about God is good.

You can't talk to God over video chat. But when you want to know more about Him, your Bible will tell you everything you need to know. The verses you read will help you understand just what God is like. —T.M.

## Reading the Bible will help me know about God.

**FUN FACT**

The telephone company AT&T created a "Picturephone" as early as 1964.

**READ MORE**

What does Micah 7:19 tell us about God?

# Moving Day

But Ruth replied, "Don't try to make me leave you and go back. Where you go I'll go. Where you stay I'll stay. Your people will be my people. Your God will be my God."

**RUTH 1:16 NIRV**

**Moving can be scary!** Whether you move to a new school or church or city, it can be difficult to make new friends. It might be hard to find where you need to go. And everything is just different. Sometimes people have to move even when they don't really want to.

The Bible tells the story of a woman named Ruth, who chose to move—even though she didn't have to. Ruth was from a country called Moab. She met her husband when his family came to Moab in search of food. There was a famine—a time when food is hard to find—in their hometown of Bethlehem.

Ruth lived with her husband and his family in Moab for ten years, but then something terrible happened. All the men in the family died! Ruth's husband, his brother, and the men's father were gone. Three women were on their own. Ruth's mother-in-law, Naomi, decided to move back to Bethlehem. She hoped God would help her there.

## Wherever I go, I know God will be with me.

Ruth's sister-in-law, Orpah, went to her own family in Moab, but Ruth followed Naomi. Ruth left the place she had always lived to go to Naomi's town. Naomi told Ruth to stay in Moab. She even tried to talk Ruth out of going to Bethlehem.

But Ruth knew it was right to help her mother-in-law, so she moved anyway. Because of Ruth's courage, God blessed both women. He provided food for them and gave Ruth a new husband.

Before long, Ruth had a baby—and that baby became the grandfather of King David!

Ruth's story shows that God will be with us wherever we go. If you ever have to go somewhere new, remember this: God will go with you. —T.M.

### READ MORE

Read Genesis 12:1–4.
Who did God tell to move to another country?

### FUN FACT

In the Hebrew language, the name *Bethlehem* means "house of bread."

# Marked by the Owner

[God] put his Spirit in our hearts and marked us as his own. We can now be sure that he will give us everything he promised us.

2 CORINTHIANS 1:22 NIRV

*If you ever see a cow* up close, you might notice some letters or a colored tag on its body. A farmer will often put a mark on his animals. He does this to show that the animals belong to him. Farmers choose a special way of marking their animals that is different from the other farmers' marks. Then, if the animal gets lost, it can be returned to its owner. Everyone knows who the animal belongs to because of its mark.

Did you know the Bible says God marks people too? You can't see the mark, but it's there. The Bible tells us that when we believe in Jesus the Holy Spirit comes into our hearts. The Holy Spirit is God's mark on us. It means we belong to Jesus!

When we belong to Jesus, we receive all of God's promises. He will be with us. He will protect us. He will provide for us. He takes care of His people, just like a farmer watches over his animals.

Once we ask Jesus to forgive our sins, we will always be His. No one can ever take His love away from us or pull us away from Him. Even if the world seems scary, Jesus is watching over everyone who carries His mark. —T.M.

## Jesus marks those who belong to Him.

### FUN FACT

The ancient Egyptians were probably the first people to mark their animals.

### READ MORE

Read Ephesians 1:13.
How does this verse explain how Christians are marked?

# Daniel Prayed Anyway

**Have you ever heard** the story of Daniel and the lions' den? Do you know why Daniel spent a night with the lions?

Daniel was a man who lived far from home. He worked in the palace of a king named Darius. The king wanted to put Daniel in charge of everything because Daniel was trustworthy. The other men who worked with Daniel were jealous and wanted to get rid of him.

Daniel was faithful to God. Three times each day, he went to his room and prayed to God. Daniel's enemies tricked Darius into signing a law that said everyone had to pray to the king. If anyone prayed to someone else, that person would be thrown into a den of lions.

> When Daniel heard that the new law had been written, he went to his house. He went to his upstairs room. The windows of that room opened toward Jerusalem. Three times each day Daniel got down on his knees and prayed. He prayed and thanked God, just as he always had done.
>
> **DANIEL 6:10 ICB**

When Daniel heard about the law, he continued to pray to God three times a day, just like before. Though Daniel worked for King Darius, he worshipped God. So Daniel prayed only to God—and no law was going to change that.

The lions' den was dangerous, but Daniel trusted God. When Daniel was thrown into the den, God kept him safe by sending an angel to shut the lions' mouths.

## Praying to God is always the right thing to do.

Some people don't want us to pray, but we can pray anyway. It doesn't have to be out loud. You don't have to get on your knees. You can pray in your mind and in your heart. You can be faithful to God just like Daniel was! —C.B.

### READ MORE

King Darius made another law. Read Daniel 6:26–27 to find out what it was.

### FUN FACT

A grown-up male lion eats about fifteen pounds of meat per day. That would be sixty quarter-pound hamburgers!

> "As long as the earth lasts, there will always be a time to plant and a time to gather the crops. As long as the earth lasts, there will always be cold and heat. There will always be summer and winter, day and night."
>
> **GENESIS 8:22 NIRV**

# Always the Same

**When you wake** up in the morning and see the sun, you know it's the beginning of a new day. You know it will be light for many hours. When you go to bed at night, you know it will be dark for a long time so you can sleep. Then it will be morning again. You never wake up in the morning to find out that it's suddenly nighttime.

The same is true of the seasons. Though seasons change, they always follow the same order. Spring always follows winter, and summer always comes after spring. Fall always follows summer, and winter always comes after fall. It would be crazy if one year fall came after winter, or summer followed fall. Farmers wouldn't be able to plant their crops or harvest them at the right time. Birds wouldn't know when to fly north or south for the season!

## God always stays the same.

God is a God of order. He created the sun and moon to mark the days and seasons. The earth obeys His orders, and that will never change. God never changes either. You can always count on Him to be with you.

When you wake up in the morning, God is there—just like the sun. When you go to bed at night, God is with you—all through the hours of darkness. Every hour, every day, every season, every year, God loves you. And that will never change. —C.B.

## FUN FACT

One of the hottest days on earth was July 10, 1913, when it was 134° F (56.7° C) in Furnace Creek, California. One of the coldest days ever was July 20, 1983, when it was −128.6° F (−89.2° C) in Antarctica.

## READ MORE
Read Hebrews 13:8.
What does this verse tell us about Jesus?

# Best Buddies

**Having a best friend** is special. It's more fun to play hide-and-seek with someone you like. It's nice to have a friend to build a fort with. Eating ice cream is even sweeter when you can share it with a friend. God gives friendship as a gift. And He can use it to do great things!

> Jonathan and David became close friends. Jonathan loved David just as he loved himself.
>
> **1 SAMUEL 18:1 NIRV**

The Bible tells us about two best friends. Their names were David and Jonathan. Jonathan was the son of Saul, the first king of Israel. Saul liked Jonathan's friend David for a while, but then he became jealous. Saul knew that David was going to be the next king—and he wasn't happy about that. Saul tried to keep David from becoming king and even tried to hurt David.

*Friendship is a gift from God.*

But no matter what, Jonathan was loyal to David. Even though Jonathan could have been the next king, he never became jealous of David. Jonathan talked honestly with David and helped him escape when Saul wanted to hurt him. The Bible says Jonathan "loved David just as he loved himself." That means he did what was best for David, even when it was hard.

Jonathan is a great example of a good friend, just like Jesus is a good example for us. A good friend helps out and puts his friends' feelings ahead of his own. At church, at school, and in your neighborhood, you can show God's love by being a good friend!
—T.M.

## READ MORE

Read 1 Samuel 19:4.
What did Jonathan tell King Saul to do?

## FUN FACT

The name *David* means "loved." David was loved by his friend Jonathan.

# Beautiful Feet

> It is written,
> "How beautiful are
> the feet of those who
> bring good news!"
>
> ROMANS 10:15 NIRV

**Feet are not always** pleasant. They can be sweaty and stinky! When you walk outside without shoes your feet can be covered in dust or sticky mud.

But the Bible says people who take the good news about Jesus to others have beautiful feet. It doesn't matter what their feet look like—or even how they smell. Feet can be beautiful because they carry people out to preach the good news about Jesus.

A missionary is a person with beautiful feet. Missionaries have a special job because they tell others about God's love. They tell others about God's Son, Jesus. Did you know you can be a missionary right now? You can take God's Word to people right where you are! People all around you are ready to hear about Jesus.

Maybe you have family members who are still learning about God. Maybe you have a friend at school who wants to know more about the Bible. You can teach them and encourage them to love Jesus. You can take the good news about Jesus to anyone. It doesn't matter how old you are or where you go. When you tell other people about God, your feet are beautiful! —T.M.

My beautiful feet take me to tell others about God.

## FUN FACT

Some health experts say people should try to take ten thousand steps per day. That means you would walk about 115,000 miles in a lifetime!

## READ MORE

To read a Bible story about feet, look up John 13:1–17.

# Lots of Names

**Do you know** why your parents chose your name? Some kids are given a name because of what the name means. Sometimes they're named after someone else in their family. And sometimes they're given a name just because their parents like it. Our first name is usually what people call us, and our last name tells others what family we belong to. Names are important!

The prophet Isaiah lived a long time before Jesus was born. But he wrote down many special names for Jesus. God told Isaiah about things that were going to happen in the future. The prophet wrote those things down in the Old Testament book of Isaiah. One thing Isaiah wrote was that God's Son would be born as a baby.

> For a child is born to us, a son is given to us. The government will rest on his shoulders. And he will be called: Wonderful Counselor, Mighty God, Everlasting Father, Prince of Peace.
>
> **ISAIAH 9:6 NLT**

*Jesus has many wonderful names.*

About seven hundred years later, an angel visited a girl named Mary and told her she was going to be the mother of God's Son. The angel told Mary to name her baby Jesus.

But Isaiah had said that Jesus would be called by other names too. People would call him "Wonderful Counselor" because He would be a teacher of truth. They would call Him "Mighty God" because He would have God's power. He would be called "Everlasting Father" because He came from His Father in heaven and would live forever. He would be called "Prince of Peace" because He would bring peace to everyone who believes in Him as Savior. Jesus has many special names because He is the most special person of all!
—C.B.

## READ MORE

In Matthew 16:13–16, Jesus asked one of His disciples who people thought He was. How did Peter answer Jesus?

## FUN FACT

Since the year 912, there have been forty-seven kings and world rulers named Henry!

> He remembers
> his covenant forever,
> the promise he made,
> for a thousand
> generations.
>
> **PSALM 105:8 NIV**

# Promises, Promises

**God gives us** a lot of promises in the Bible. Some of them can be found in the Old Testament, and others are in the New Testament. We don't know for sure how many promises are in the Bible, but some people have counted more than three thousand!

What kinds of promises does God make? He promises to take care of us and watch over us. He promises to give us what we need. He promises to comfort us when we're sad. He promises to lead us and guide us if we ask Him to. He promises to help us with our troubles. He promises to give us wisdom and power. He promises to listen when we pray to Him. God doesn't promise that our lives will be easy—but He promises that He will always be with us. The best promise of all is that we can live forever with Him when we believe in Jesus as our Savior.

## God keeps His promises.

People make promises too. But people don't always keep their promises. Sometimes we forget what we had promised. Sometimes we find that other people or things get in the way. And even though it's wrong, sometimes we just change our minds.

But God is never like that. He doesn't forget. He doesn't get confused. He doesn't change His mind. God does what He says He will do. He will always keep His promises—all three thousand of them! —C.B.

## FUN FACT

Other words with
meanings similar to
"promise" are covenant,
pledge, vow, and oath.

## READ MORE

Read Matthew 28:20.
What promise did Jesus give
to His disciples before going back to heaven?

# Prayer Power

**Prayer is talking** to God. We can pray to thank God for our dinner. We can pray to tell God when we're sad or scared. We can pray to ask God for things we need.

Prayer can be powerful. Sometimes when we pray, God will do things that seem impossible.

After Jesus was taken to heaven, Peter and the other disciples were telling everyone about Him. The king didn't like that. He arrested some of the disciples and did terrible things to them. Then he arrested Peter and put him in prison. While Peter waited to learn what the king would do to him, the church was praying hard for Peter. And God heard their prayers.

In the middle of the night, Peter was sleeping between two soldiers. He had chains around his wrists. Suddenly, an angel appeared. "Hurry!" the angel said. "Get up!" And guess what? The chains fell off Peter's arms!

> So Peter was kept in prison. But the church prayed hard to God for him.
>
> **ACTS 12:5 NIRV**

## My prayers are powerful.

The angel led Peter out of prison. Peter was so confused he didn't think what was happening was real. But it was real. The angel walked Peter past the guards and led him to the city gate. The big metal gate opened all by itself! Once Peter was safe, the angel left, and Peter realized he was not having a dream. So he went to the house where his friends were praying. They were amazed when he told them what happened.

No matter what you pray about, God hears you. Sometimes, He answers in amazing ways! —T.M.

## READ MORE

Did you know this wasn't the only time God sent an angel to rescue people from prison? Read Acts 5:17–20 to discover another time God helped His followers.

## FUN FACT

Many cities in Bible times were protected by thick walls. A city gate was an opening in the wall that could be closed at night to keep out enemies.

> The LORD and King gives me strength. He makes my feet like the feet of a deer. He helps me walk on the highest places.
>
> HABAKKUK 3:19 NIRV

# Run like a Deer

**Did you know** that deer can take their first steps about half an hour after they're born? At first, their legs are wobbly, but when deer are grown, they can run very fast and jump very high.

A deer's long legs are built for strength and speed. Because they can run fast and jump high, deer can often escape other animals that try to attack them. When a deer runs at high speed, it can leap over fallen trees or large rocks. Deer are also graceful animals with good balance. They can walk on steep rocks and hills without stumbling.

In the Bible, a prophet named Habakkuk used the example of deer to help us understand that God is our strength. When we love God and spend time learning more about Him, He gives us the strength we need to run away from trouble. When we get our strength from God and His Word, He will keep us from stumbling into sin.

Sometimes kids can find themselves in hard situations. If someone wants you to do something that you know is wrong, imagine a deer running at high speed. Just say no. Turn and walk away from that temptation. God can give you strength to run from danger and find a place that is safe. —C.B.

## God will help me to run from danger.

### FUN FACT

White-tailed deer can run at a top speed of about thirty-six miles per hour (about fifty-eight kilometers per hour). They can jump about eight feet high (about two and a half meters) and thirty feet long (about nine meters).

### READ MORE

Psalm 42:1 is another verse about deer. What does this verse says about being thirsty?

Even though you
planned evil
against me, God
planned good
to come out of it.

GENESIS 50:20 GW

# Good Instead of Bad

**Joseph had eleven brothers.** Their father, Jacob, liked Joseph best and gave him a colorful coat.

Joseph's brothers were jealous of him. They were mean and they picked on him. One day when all the brothers were in a field, they decided to get rid of Joseph for good. They met some travelers passing by and sold Joseph to be their slave. Joseph's brothers thought they would never see him again. But they were wrong.

Even though Joseph's brothers did mean things to him, God was with Joseph. He helped Joseph succeed in everything he did. After a few years, Joseph became an important official in Egypt!

God told Joseph that Egypt was going to run out of food. He gave Joseph wisdom to prepare for the famine so that all the Egyptians would have enough to eat.

## When others are unkind, I know God is in control.

When the famine came, Joseph's brothers traveled to Egypt to buy food. They didn't recognize him, but Joseph knew who they were. When Joseph told them who he was, they were sorry for all they had done to him. Joseph could have been angry. He could have punished his brothers. Instead, he told them that when they did bad things to him, God used it for good.

Maybe there is someone who is unkind to you. Maybe you know a bully who makes fun of you. Maybe someone has taken something from you. No matter what, God is in control! You can choose to act like Joseph. You can be nice to others even when they aren't nice to you. —T.M.

### READ MORE

Not only did Joseph forgive his brothers, he also took care of them when they needed help. Read Genesis 45:9–11 to find out what he did.

### FUN FACT

Joseph was only thirty years old when he started ruling over Egypt. He lived for eighty more years, until he was 110!

# Let It Show

> Love is patient.
> Love is kind. It does
> not want what
> belongs to others.
> It does not brag.
> It is not proud.
>
> **1 CORINTHIANS 13:4 NIRV**

**What is the nicest** thing you can say to someone? How about "I love you"?

Parents say "I love you" to their children, and children say it back to their parents. Grandmas and grandpas tell their grandkids "I love you." Aunts and uncles and other relatives may say "I love you." When you love someone, it means you care about them. We can tell people we love them, but we can also show it by the way we act.

Love is more than just words. You can show your love for others by being kind. Do you share your games or books with your friends? That's showing love. Have you helped a brother or sister or parent with chores? That's showing love too!

When you love others, you're happy when good things happen to them. If your friends get a new bike or video game, you can be happy for them. If your brother or sister gets an A on a test, you can say, "Good job!"

When Jesus lived on earth, He showed His love for others in many different ways. He fed people who were hungry. He healed people who were sick. And He died on the cross to take the punishment for our sins.

## Love is more than words can say.

It's important to tell others that we love them. But let's be like Jesus and show our love too! —C.B.

### FUN FACT

There are different kinds of love: friendship, kinship (or family love), romantic love (between a man and woman), and divine love. Divine love is God's love and is also called agape (uh-GAH-pay) love.

### READ MORE
What does 1 Corinthians 13:13 say about love?

# Don't Be Afraid

**After Moses died,** Joshua became the leader of the people of Israel. God told Joshua to take the people into the land that God had promised to them.

But they couldn't just march in and set up camp. First they had to cross the Jordan River—which was flooded. And there was another problem. The people who already lived in the land didn't want to share it. They did not want a million Israelites moving in.

But Joshua trusted God and obeyed Him. He was ready to do whatever God said, and God told Joshua to be strong and brave. God did not want Joshua to be afraid. God promised Joshua that He would go with him wherever he went.

> "Remember that I commanded you to be strong and brave. So don't be afraid. The Lord your God will be with you everywhere you go."
>
> JOSHUA 1:9 ICB

God is with me—so I will not be afraid.

So Joshua told the people to get ready to cross the river and enter the land. Then a miracle happened! When the very first people, the priests, stepped into the Jordan River, God stopped the water from flowing. Everyone crossed the river on dry ground! God was with Joshua, just as He had promised.

You can be strong and brave too. You can trust and obey God, just like Joshua did. You may never lead a million people across a flooded river, but there will be things in your life that make you afraid. Talk to God about them, and ask Him to help you. God will be with you just like He was with Joshua. He doesn't want you to be afraid. —C.B.

## READ MORE

Did you know Jesus did something important at the Jordan River too? To learn more, read Matthew 3:13–17.

## FUN FACT

The Jordan River is about 156 miles (251 kilometers) long.

## JANUARY
## 26

> "We should remember the words that the Lord Jesus said, 'Giving gifts is more satisfying than receiving them.'"
>
> ACTS 20:35 GW

# Be a Giver

**Everyone loves** getting presents!

Isn't it fun to open a box on your birthday and get a new toy or video game? Have you ever snooped under the Christmas tree to see if any of those beautiful packages are for you? Sometimes you might even get a gift for no special reason. Surprise gifts are especially exciting!

But it can be just as exciting to give a gift. Maybe you made something special for your mom or picked out a brand-new toy for a friend's birthday. It's fun to see the smiles on other people's faces and the joy they get from receiving something you picked out for them.

## It's better to give than to receive.

You may have heard someone say, "It's better to give than to receive." Did you know that saying comes from the Bible? Jesus is the one who said it! He was saying that we can be happier when we give things than when we get things. When you give, God uses you to make others happy.

And it's not only presents. You can give to others by speaking a kind word, helping someone out, or sharing food and clothes with people who need them. Giving to others shows your love for Jesus. Giving gifts is really better than receiving them! —T.M.

## FUN FACT

The tradition of giving gifts at Christmas began with the wise men who brought gold, frankincense, and myrrh to Jesus.

## READ MORE

Read James 1:17.
Where do good gifts come from?

# Grapes and Grapevines

**Do you like** to eat grapes? Whether they're red or purple or green, grapes are juicy and delicious. They grow on plants called grapevines which grow upward along a fence. The leaves are connected to the vine by branches. The branches connect to the trunk, which connects to the roots underground. All of the parts work together to give the grapes what they need to grow.

> "I am the vine; you are the branches. If you remain in me and I in you, you will bear much fruit; apart from me you can do nothing."
>
> JOHN 15:5 NIV

Jesus once told His friends that He was a grapevine and they were the branches. As His time on earth grew short, Jesus wanted His disciples to know that His spirit would be with them even after He had gone to heaven. Jesus said that if His disciples stayed connected to Him, like the branches on a grapevine, His power would flow into them and they would grow fruit. But Jesus didn't mean grapes. The fruit He meant was love and joy and peace, and other good things that make people more like Jesus.

## I will stay connected to the vine.

When Jesus went to heaven, His disciples continued the work Jesus had started. Because they were connected to Jesus like branches to a grapevine, they became more like Him. They preached about God with boldness and did miracles to help people.

Jesus wants us to stay connected to Him too. How do we do that? By reading the Bible and praying. By loving Jesus and obeying what He tells us to do. When we stay connected to Jesus—the vine—our lives will be "fruitful" for Him! —C.B.

## READ MORE

How does Acts 3:1–10 show that Peter and John were becoming more like Jesus?

### FUN FACT

China, the United States, Italy, France, and Spain are the countries that grow the most grapes.

> "Again, the kingdom of heaven is like a trader who was looking for fine pearls. He found one that was very valuable. So he went away and sold everything he had. And he bought that pearl."
>
> **MATTHEW 13:45–46 NIRV**

# Treasure Hunt

**What's the most** valuable thing you have? For some people, it's a computer or tablet. Others have an old coin that's been in the family for years. Maybe it's fancy jewelry that used to belong to a grandmother or great-grandmother.

When you have something valuable you take good care of it. You might keep it in a special box or hide it somewhere so no one else can find it. But what if you lost it? That would be upsetting! You would search very hard until you found it. You might even stay up past your bedtime.

In the book of Matthew, Jesus told His disciples that God's kingdom was like a treasure. Jesus told a story about a businessman searching for a pearl—an expensive and precious jewel. When the man found the perfect pearl, he knew it was worth a lot of money. So he sold everything he owned to get money to buy it.

## I can search for God's kingdom like it's a treasure.

Jesus came to earth searching for us and gave up all He had to be with us. His love is the most valuable thing we can have. As He helps us understand His love for us, we can show our love for Him. When we give up everything else to put Him first, we're like the man who bought the pearl.

Learning all about Jesus and His kingdom is like hunting for treasure. If we spend time searching, we will find something priceless. —T.M.

## FUN FACT

The largest pearl ever discovered weighs over fourteen pounds (six kilograms) and is worth millions of dollars!

## READ MORE

Read Proverbs 2:1–5.
What else should we search for like a treasure?

# Important Advice

**There's an old familiar** saying that goes like this: "If at first you don't succeed, try, try again."

What does it mean to "succeed"? To succeed, or to find "success," is to have things turn out the way you want them to. Success for many people is being popular or having lots of money and things. But real success comes from obeying God and doing what He wants you to do.

King David ruled God's people, the Israelites, for forty years. When he was old and about to die, David gave his son Solomon some important advice. David told Solomon to obey God and follow His commands. He said that if Solomon wanted to be successful, he needed to do everything that God expected him to do.

David's advice is for us too! To be successful, we need to trust and obey God. He will guide us and help us to do what He wants us to do. Remember that success isn't just having a lot of money or being popular. Success means loving God and caring for other people.

Do you want to be successful? Then listen to the important advice of King David: "Do everything the LORD your God requires." —C.B.

> "Do everything the LORD your God requires. Live the way he wants you to. Obey his orders and commands. Keep his laws and rules. Do everything that is written in the Law of Moses. Then you will have success in everything you do. You will succeed everywhere you go."
>
> **1 KINGS 2:3 NIRV**

## Success comes from obeying God.

### READ MORE
Look up 2 Chronicles 9:22. What does it say about King Solomon?

### FUN FACT
The great inventor Thomas Edison tried hundreds and hundreds of times to make a working light bulb. When someone asked him, "How did it feel to fail one thousand times?" Edison answered, "I didn't fail one thousand times. The light bulb was an invention with one thousand steps."

# Follow the Leader

Godly people are careful about the friends they choose. But the way of sinners leads them down the wrong path.

**PROVERBS 12:26 NIRV**

**Have you ever** played the game "Follow the Leader"? When you're the leader, everyone else has to do whatever you do. If you jump on one foot, all the others have to jump on one foot. If you sing a silly song, everyone else sings it too. When another person becomes the leader, you have to copy whatever she does.

Kids (and grown-ups too) often copy the things their friends do—even when they're not playing a game. That's why it's so important to choose good friends. When we "follow the leader," we want to be like friends who love God and do what's right. We are wise when we choose friends who know it's right to obey parents and respect teachers. We become better people when we play with friends who are kind to others and share and take turns. But following someone who often gets into trouble might get us into trouble too.

When Jesus was living on earth, He invited some men to follow Him. They are known as Jesus' "twelve disciples." Many of them became His good friends as they followed Jesus and did the things He told them to do.

Jesus still asks people to follow Him today. How can we do that? By learning more about Him from the Bible. God's Word tells us how Jesus wants us to live and what He wants us to do. You'll never follow a better leader than Jesus! —C.B.

## I will choose to follow good friends.

### FUN FACT

Sheep "follow the leader." They follow the sheep that is in front of them. If the lead sheep goes somewhere it shouldn't, the rest of the flock often go there too!

### READ MORE

Read Matthew 4:18–22 to learn about the first four disciples who followed Jesus. What were their names?

# A Brave Choice

**Do you know** someone who is brave? Is it your dad because he catches the spiders in your house? Is it an older brother or sister who isn't afraid of the dark? Kids often think the biggest and strongest people seem the bravest. It can be hard to be brave when you are young. But with God on your side, you can choose to be brave even when you're afraid.

> "What if you don't say anything at this time? . . . It's possible that you became queen for a time just like this."
>
> **ESTHER 4:14 NIRV**

Esther was a beautiful young woman who lived in Old Testament times. She was brought to the king of Persia's palace for a beauty contest to decide who would be the next queen. Out of all the girls in the contest, Esther won! Everyone in the palace loved her. But Esther had a secret that no one else in the palace knew. She was Jewish.

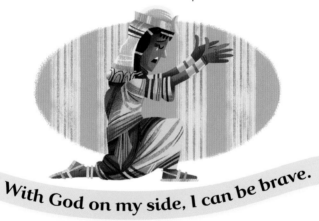

With God on my side, I can be brave.

One of the king's top officials hated the Jewish people and wanted the king to kill them. So Esther had a tough choice to make. Her cousin Mordecai told her to talk to the king. But Esther knew if she went to the king without permission, she could be killed. Mordecai told her it was the right thing to do, and Esther decided to do it. When Esther went to see the king, he was pleased. He listened to her and agreed to save the Jewish people!

Esther's story shows how God uses people for His special plans. God gave Esther the courage to do what He wanted her to do. And He will give you courage when you need it too. —T.M.

## READ MORE

Read Daniel 3 to learn about three other people who made a brave choice.

**FUN FACT**

Esther and the other girls in the beauty contest went through a whole year of beauty treatments! (See Esther 2:12.)

# Do-over

Anyone who
believes in Christ
is a new creation.
The old is gone!
The new has come!
**2 CORINTHIANS 5:17 NIRV**

**Have you ever been given** a do-over when you messed up? Maybe you got a bad grade on a test and your teacher let you retake it. Maybe you kicked the ball the wrong way and your coach let you try again. Do-overs are great! It's nice to be able to start over when something doesn't go right the first time.

People who believe in Jesus get a great big do-over. God's Word tells us that anyone who believes that Jesus is the Son of God is a "new creation." That means the bad

## Christians are a new creation.

choices they made before they trusted Jesus are not held against them. Their sins have all been forgiven. They can now live a life that pleases God.

When God looks at people who believe in Jesus, He doesn't see their mess-ups and sins. He sees Jesus! Do you know what that means? Because Jesus never, ever sinned, God sees His perfection instead of what we have done wrong.

Even after we've become Christians, we sometimes still mess up. But when we do, God gives us more do-overs. When we're sorry for our sins and ask God to forgive us, Jesus wipes those sins away. He's just like a teacher erasing words from the board at school. Now that's a great do-over! —T.M.

**READ MORE**
What does God tell us in Isaiah 43:18–19?

**FUN FACT**
A do-over in the game of golf is called a mulligan.

> Godly people are careful about the friends they choose. But the way of sinners leads them down the wrong path.
>
> **PROVERBS 12:26 NIRV**

# Keep Good Company

**Do you know what it means** to "keep good company"? It means to spend time with the right kind of people. Having the right kind of friends is important.

Abram was a man who obeyed God. He had a nephew named Lot. One day they decided it was time to move away from each other. They needed more space for their animals and families. Lot made a bad choice. He moved close to the cities of Sodom and Gomorrah. The people who lived in those cities did not obey God. Lot moved even closer until he was living right inside Sodom. He did not keep good company.

Before long, Lot was in trouble. The kings of Sodom and Gomorrah got into a big fight with seven other kings. During the battle, Lot and his family were kidnapped!

*It's important to choose good friends.*

When Abram heard about it, he built an army of more than three hundred men. The army divided up into groups and made a surprise attack. Abram was able to bring back everything the enemy had stolen, including Lot.

You might think that Lot would have learned a lesson. But he went back to live in the city of Sodom, where the people were still disobeying God. And one day, Lot lost everything he had.

Always choose good friends, and be sure to keep good company! —C.B.

## FUN FACT

A famous poet in Greece more than two thousand years ago said, "Every man is known by the company he keeps."

## READ MORE

Read Genesis 14:22–24.
Why did Abram decide not to keep anything from Sodom?

# Bird Watching

"Aren't two sparrows sold for only a penny? But not one of them falls to the ground without your Father knowing it. He even counts every hair on your head! So don't be afraid. You are worth more than many sparrows."

MATTHEW 10:29–31 NIRV

**You've probably seen** sparrows. They are small brown birds that like to live near people. Sparrows are one of the most common birds in the world, found in Africa, Europe, North and South America, and parts of Asia. Because they're so common, sparrows don't get a lot of attention. Even in Bible times, they were not worth very much.

One time, Jesus told His disciples not to be afraid of the people who were against them. Jesus knew that some people might treat His disciples badly. But He reminded them that God is always watching over them and always caring for them. He told His disciples that God watches over and cares for the sparrows. If He does that, God will certainly watch over and care for His people.

## God watches the sparrows—and He watches me.

God loves sparrows because He created them. He helps them find food to eat and places to rest. He knows if even one of those little birds falls to the ground. And do you know what? God loves you the same way! He created you. He gives you food to eat, clothes to wear, and a place to live. He even knows how many hairs you have on your head.

That's why Jesus tells us, "Don't be afraid." God cares about little brown sparrows, and you are worth much, much more than sparrows. —C.B.

## READ MORE

Jesus talked about birds another time.
Read Matthew 6:25–27. What did He say?

## FUN FACT

House sparrows are almost everywhere—from high up on New York City's Empire State Building to deep in a mine in Yorkshire, England.

# Old Enough

> Don't let anyone look down on you for being young. Instead, make your speech, behavior, love, faith, and purity an example for other believers.
>
> 1 TIMOTHY 4:12 GW

**Has anyone ever told you,** "You're not old enough to do that"? When you're young, it can feel like you're not allowed to do many things. You have to be a certain height to ride a roller coaster. You can't stay up as late as your mom or dad. You can't ride your bike too far away from home.

You might even feel like people don't listen to what you say because you're young. When that happens, you may want to grow up quickly so people will respect you more.

The Bible tells us about a young man named Timothy. He studied God's teachings under the apostle Paul and went on missionary trips with him. Timothy loved God. Even though he was young, he was grown-up in his faith. Timothy became a pastor in the city of Ephesus. Paul wrote a letter telling Timothy to stay strong in his faith and be a good example, even though he was young.

You can be a good example too—even to people older than you. The way you act can show others that you love God. When you say please and thank you, others will see you're respectful. When you help clean up a neighbor's yard, people will see that you serve others. When you pray before a meal or read a Bible verse out loud, others will see that you want to be close to God. Even young children can show others that God is great! —T.M.

*I can be a good example, no matter how old I am.*

## READ MORE

Read John 13:13–17 in your Bible. How does Jesus set an example for us?

# Keep the Lights On

**It's hard to see** in the dark. If you're in a dark room, you want to switch on the lights. If you're outdoors at night, you want to carry a flashlight. If a storm knocks out power to your house, you want to have candles or a lantern to be able to see.

> This is the message we heard from Christ and are reporting to you: God is light, and there isn't any darkness in him.
>
> **1 JOHN 1:5 GW**

Being in the dark can be dangerous. If you can't see, it's easy to trip and fall or bump into things. And can you imagine what it would be like if cars didn't have headlights? Drivers couldn't see where they were going and might crash into other cars or trees or buildings.

## God is light.

Sin is a kind of darkness. When we choose to do wrong, it's like bringing darkness into our lives. It's a dangerous way to live and bad things can happen.

But the Bible tells us that God is light. When we believe in God and learn how He wants us to live, it's like turning all the lights on. God helps us to see what is right and wrong. He helps us to see how much He loves us and cares for us. He helps us to see all the things that can hurt us.

With God there is no darkness. God not only gives us light, He is the light. And God's light never goes out!
—C.B.

### FUN FACT

Because of the way the earth is tilted, people who live near the Arctic Circle may not see the sun for many days or weeks. At other times of the year it may be light for a very long time.

### READ MORE

**Read Genesis 1:14–19 to learn about the lights God created. Why did He create these lights?**

> Simon answered, "Master, we've worked hard all night and haven't caught anything. But because you say so, I will let down the nets."
>
> **LUKE 5:5 NIV**

# Because You Say So

**One night Jesus' disciples** were out fishing. But they didn't catch anything. So they rowed back to shore and began washing their nets. Jesus came along and talked to Simon Peter, one of His disciples. Jesus told Simon Peter to row back into the deep water and drop his nets again. Simon Peter was probably very tired. He had fished all night without catching anything. He didn't feel like going back out with the nets he had just cleaned. But Peter obeyed, because Jesus said so.

Do you know what happened next? The disciples caught so many fish that their nets began to break! They had to shout for their friends to help them drag all the fish to shore!

The disciples were amazed. They knew Jesus had performed a miracle. Then Jesus told them they would start fishing for men. Just like the disciples had caught a lot of fish, Jesus wanted them to bring many people to Him to become His followers.

## Jesus knows best.

This story shows us what trust in Jesus looks like. Simon Peter did something just because Jesus said so. Jesus responded to that trust by performing a miracle and giving Simon Peter a new job: fishing for people!

You can trust Jesus like that too. You can invite your friends to church or pray with them or share your things with them, just because Jesus says so. When you trust Him, He will respond to your trust. —C.B.

## FUN FACT

Early Christians used a fish picture to stand for their faith. Those Christians spoke the Greek language. When they took the first letters of the words for "Jesus Christ, Son of God, Savior," they spelled the Greek word for "fish": ΙΧΘΥΣ.

## READ MORE

Before Jesus went back to heaven, He said other things about bringing people to Him. Read Mark 16:15–20 to see what He said.

# A Shepherd's Love

**A shepherd is** someone who takes care of sheep. Depending on where you live, you might never see a shepherd working in a field. But when the Bible was being written, shepherds were very common. Because people in ancient Israel knew shepherds well, the Bible writers often used shepherds as an example of God's love.

> The LORD is my shepherd. I am never in need.
> **PSALM 23:1 GW**

Shepherds' duties include keeping their flock together, guiding the sheep where they need to go, and protecting the sheep from other animals that could hurt them. King David, who was also a shepherd, wrote Psalm 23, one of the best-known psalms in the Bible. It explains how God is our shepherd.

Just like a shepherd takes care of his sheep, God takes care of us. Shepherds lead their sheep to green fields when they need to lie down to rest. God gives us times of rest and sleep when we're tired. A shepherd uses his voice or a special stick to guide the sheep where they need to go. God guides us and speaks to us through the Bible. When sheep travel through a dangerous area where they might be attacked, the shepherd is there to protect them. God does the same for us—He is right beside us when we face scary things, and He protects us from harm.

Sheep need a lot of help. So do we! God promises to meet all of our needs, just like a shepherd takes care of his sheep. —T.M.

The Lord is my shepherd.

## READ MORE
What does the prophet Isaiah say about Jesus in Isaiah 40:11?

### FUN FACT
The wooden stick a shepherd carries is called a staff. It can be used to guide the sheep on the path or to fight off animals that attack the sheep.

When Jesus came to the tree, he looked up and said, "Zacchaeus, come down! I must stay at your house today."

LUKE 19:5 GW

# Jesus and Zacchaeus

**When Jesus was passing through** the city of Jericho, many people rushed to see Him. Zacchaeus wanted to see Jesus too, but he was a short man. Poor Zacchaeus couldn't get a glimpse of Jesus above all the people standing around him!

That's when Zacchaeus got an idea. He ran ahead of the crowd and climbed up into a sycamore tree. Zacchaeus knew he would be high enough above the crowd to see Jesus as He passed by. But Zacchaeus didn't expect what happened next.

When Jesus came near the tree, He looked up and said, "Zacchaeus, come down! I must stay at your house today." Zacchaeus was excited! He quickly climbed down the tree and welcomed Jesus to his home.

Some people weren't happy about Jesus visiting Zacchaeus's house. Zacchaeus was a tax collector—his job was to take money from people in the town. And he wasn't always honest when he asked for their money. Sometimes Zacchaeus cheated the people. That's why they didn't like him. They were surprised that Jesus would spend time with a dishonest man.

## Jesus helps people change from the inside out.

But Jesus didn't judge Zacchaeus the way others did. Jesus knew Zacchaeus could change. After spending time with Jesus, Zacchaeus realized that he had been treating other people badly. He told Jesus he would pay back everyone he cheated. Zacchaeus became a generous person.

Jesus knows people can change. He's not looking for perfect people. All Jesus asks is that we believe in Him and love Him. Then others will see the change in our lives. —T.M.

### FUN FACT

The type of tree that Zacchaeus climbed can reach a height of about fifty feet (fifteen meters). It grows a kind of fruit called figs.

### READ MORE

Read Acts 9:1–18 to find out about another man who changed from the inside out.

# Don't Give Up

**"I'm bored!"** How many times have you said that? It's easy to get bored after you've done the same thing for a while. Did you ever get a toy or video game that looked really fun? When you first get something new, it's really exciting. But after a while it doesn't seem so interesting. It's normal to get tired of doing the same thing over and over—even if it's something we like.

> So let's not get tired of doing what is good. At just the right time we will reap a harvest of blessing if we don't give up.
>
> **GALATIANS 6:9 NLT**

The Bible tells us we should never get tired of doing good things. The apostle Paul, who wrote the book of Galatians, seemed to understand that people can get bored doing the same things over and over. That's why he told us not to give up. When it comes to helping others and doing good, it's important that we don't get bored or quit before we're finished.

*I won't get tired of doing what is good.*

Continuing to do good things and choosing to follow God's rules isn't always easy. Sometimes your friends might not understand why you serve God. At other times you may not feel like doing the right thing. But God uses people who love Him to accomplish His plans for the world. Continue to do good things and don't give up, because God is worthy of it. And He promises to bless those who obey and serve Him! —T.M.

### FUN FACT

Mother Teresa, famous for caring for the poor and sick of India, started doing good for others in 1948. Her first year was very hard and she almost gave up. By the time she died in 1997, her work had spread to more than one hundred countries!

### READ MORE

What does 1 Corinthians 15:58 tell us about doing God's work?

> As long as Moses held his hands up, the Israelites would win the fight.
>
> **EXODUS 17:11 ICB**

# Helping Hands

**After the Israelites left** Egypt, they lived in a desert for many years. One day they were attacked by people called the Amalekites. Moses told Joshua to choose men to fight against the Amalekites. While Joshua and his men went out to fight, Moses went to stand on top of a hill to watch.

Moses took his brother, Aaron, and a man named Hur with him. Moses held up his hands, and the Israelites started to win the battle. But whenever he lowered his hands, the Amalekites would begin to win. After a while, Moses' arms got tired. So Aaron and Hur found a rock for Moses to sit on, then each man held up Moses' hands until the Israelites won the fight. After the battle, Moses built an altar to God. He named it "The Lord Is My Banner." Moses said, "I lifted my hands toward the Lord's throne."

## I will reach out to God for help.

Moses lifted his hands to God because he knew his help came from God. And when Moses got tired, his friends were there to lift him up. Just like Moses, we can raise our hands to God for help. But we can also bow our knees to pray. There is no wrong way to ask God for help! Whether we sit or stand or kneel or lie down, God wants us to come to Him for help. He hears our prayers. He is strong and mighty. Reach out to Him! —C.B.

## FUN FACT

In many churches, the service ends with a blessing called a benediction. The pastor reads a blessing such as Numbers 6:22–27 as he raises his hands to God.

## READ MORE

Lamentations 3:41 tells us something else we can lift to the Lord. What is it?

# Vocabulary Words

**Do you get lists** of vocabulary words at school? You have to learn how to spell the words as well as learn what the words mean. And you'll probably have to take a test on them at some point!

Learning vocabulary words helps us to understand what we read. And what we read helps us understand the world around us. Grace, mercy, and peace are three words that are found in the Bible. They can be your vocabulary words for today.

> Grace, mercy, and peace, which come from God the Father and from Jesus Christ—the Son of the Father—will continue to be with us who live in truth and love.
>
> 2 JOHN 3 NLT

Grace is help and love God gives us even though we don't deserve it. It's like a teacher giving you an A on a test after you got all the answers wrong. None of us are perfect, but God loves us anyway. He gives us many blessings that we do not deserve. When we believe in Jesus and turn away from the wrong things we do, we are saved by God's grace.

*Grace, mercy, and peace are gifts of God's love.*

Mercy is God's gentle forgiveness. If you disobey your parents and they decide not to punish you—that's mercy. Because of God's mercy we are not punished for our sins. We deserve to be punished, but Jesus took that punishment for us when He died on the cross.

Peace is a calm feeling we have inside because we know God loves us and will care for us no matter what. Peace is the opposite of worry. When things in life don't go well for us, we can still have peace by trusting in God.

Grace, mercy, and peace are all gifts from God. They're also good vocabulary words! —C.B.

## READ MORE

**Read Ephesians 2:4–8.
What do these verses tell us about God's grace and mercy?**

### FUN FACT

Most three-year-old kids have a vocabulary of about two hundred words. By age five, they know up to two thousand words!

So the Lord caused
them to spread out
from there all over the
whole world.

**GENESIS 11:9 ICB**

# Confusion in the City

**Do you remember** the flood God sent in Noah's time? After the flood, Noah's sons had many children. Their families grew and grew. God told all those people to go to different parts of the earth. But the people didn't want to live in different places. They didn't listen to God.

At that time everyone spoke one language. They said to each other, "Let's make some bricks. Let's build a city with a tower that reaches into the sky. We will become famous and we won't become scattered all over the earth."

So they made their bricks and began to build their fancy tower. When God saw what the people were doing, He decided to stop it. God confused the people's language so they could no longer work together. When the people realized they were speaking different languages, they stopped building the tower. They spread out across the land the way God wanted them to. The place where the people tried to build the tower was called Babel.

These people learned that God was much stronger than they were. When God wants something to happen, it will happen. God wants His people to obey Him—but when they don't obey, He will still do what He knows is best.

## No matter what, God will always have His way.

Today there are many people who are famous, smart, or important. Some people act as if they don't need God. But that's not true. Everyone needs God, and no one will ever be greater than He is. —C.B.

### FUN FACT

There are close to seven thousand languages in the world. The complete Bible has been translated into about five hundred languages, and the New Testament has been translated into nearly thirteen hundred languages.

### READ MORE

What does Isaiah 55:10–11 tell us about the words that God speaks?

# One Way

**We often need directions** to find our way to a new place. We might use a map. We might use the Internet or a GPS unit, or we might even ask another person. If you asked a friend how to get to his house, you'd want him to give you the clearest directions possible. If he said, "Well you can take Third Street and then turn right on Maple Avenue, or you can take Tenth Street and then turn left on Fourth, or if you want to go another way, you can go down Main Street and then turn left on Meadow Street," that would be confusing and frustrating! If you want to get somewhere, you need clear directions!

One day Jesus told His disciples that He was making a place for them in heaven. Thomas asked, "How can we know the way?" Jesus didn't give a bunch of different answers. He told Thomas the only way to heaven is through believing in Him. "I am the way!" Jesus said.

> Jesus told him, "I am the way, the truth, and the life. No one can come to the Father except through me."
>
> JOHN 14:6 NLT

## Jesus is the way to heaven.

When we believe that Jesus died to save us from our sins—when we ask Him to be our Savior—we will go to heaven when we die. Jesus is the way to God the Father. You don't need to find another way, because Jesus is the only way. If your friends ask you how to get to heaven, you can give them good directions. You can say, "Believe in Jesus as your Savior. He is the way!" —C.B.

## FUN FACT

GPS stands for "Global Positioning System." It uses twenty-four satellites, floating in space above the earth, to help people find their way. GPS was first used by the military but is now available for anyone to use.

## READ MORE

While they were in prison, Paul and Silas gave directions to someone. Read Acts 16:23–34 to find out what happened.

> Dear friends, let us continue to love one another, for love comes from God. Anyone who loves is a child of God and knows God.
>
> 1 JOHN 4:7 NLT

# Love Is from God

**Have you ever** given a valentine to a friend or to someone in your family? On Valentine's Day many people give cards or flowers or candy to show their love. The Bible says that love comes from God. If we are God's children, we need to love others the way that God loves them.

Jesus talked a lot about loving our neighbors. But He didn't mean only the people who live on our street. One time Jesus told a story to help people understand who their neighbors really are. Jesus said, "A man was traveling down a road when some robbers attacked him. They tore his clothes, beat him up, and left him on the side of the road. Another man came along and saw the hurt man, but didn't stop to help him. Then another man walked by and didn't stop to help him either. A third man came by and stopped to help the man who was hurt. He put the man on his donkey and brought him to an inn. He paid the innkeeper to take care of the man, and even offered to give the innkeeper more money if he needed it."

*I will show love the way God wants me to.*

Then Jesus asked which of the three men in the story showed love to the man who was hurt. The people knew the answer—it was the third man, who stopped to help the person who was hurt. Jesus said, "That's right. Now go and do the same thing."

Valentine's Day is fun, but showing love to others is better than any valentine card!
—C.B.

### FUN FACT
Around the world, approximately one billion Valentine cards are sent each year.

### READ MORE
What does 1 Corinthians 13:1–7 tell us about love?

> "Rahab and all those who are with her in her house must be spared. That's because she hid the spies we sent."
>
> JOSHUA 6:17 NIRV

# A Faithful Woman

**God told the Israelites** to take over the city of Jericho. He wanted His people to live there. Israel's leader, Joshua, told the Israelites to destroy everything in the city as an offering to God.

Before the Israelites attacked Jericho, they sent two spies into the city. While they were in Jericho, the spies stayed at the house of a woman named Rahab. The king of Jericho heard there were spies from Israel searching his city. He wanted to capture them. But Rahab hid the spies from the king when his men came looking for them.

Rahab had heard stories about God's miracles. She knew how God had helped the Israelites escape from Egypt. Rahab could see that God was on the side of the Israelites and that He had helped them defeat many enemies. She believed that the God of the Israelites was the true God of the universe.

## We are saved by faith.

Rahab asked the spies to protect her when the Israelites took over Jericho. The spies told her to hang a red rope out her window as a sign to the soldiers. When they saw the rope, they would save Rahab and her whole family.

On the day the Israelites attacked Jericho, Rahab and her family were the only people who were saved. Because of Rahab's faith, God saved her and blessed her. She became the great-great grandmother of King David—which means she was a relative of Jesus!

Rahab did not live in a city where the people believed in God. But because she had faith in the one true God, she was saved. —T.M.

## READ MORE

Read Ephesians 2:8–9.
Where does salvation come from?

### FUN FACT

Jericho is known as "the city of palm trees." It has many streams of water, which is why people have wanted to live there for thousands of years.

Praise the Lord for the glory of his name. Bring your offering to him. Worship the Lord because he is holy.

1 CHRONICLES 16:29 ICB

# Praise the Lord!

**When David was king** of Israel, he wanted the people to praise God with instruments and songs. He chose a man named Asaph to be the worship leader. Asaph played the cymbals while others played harps and lyres. There were also two priests who blew trumpets. Asaph and his team had the job of singing praises to God.

In our churches today, there are people like Asaph. They have the responsibility to lead others in praise and worship. When we sing songs of praise to God, it shows that we love Him. Singing praises is one way we worship God. Our songs can help us remember how great and holy God is. They might remind us of how much God loves us— and how much we love Him. Singing songs of praise to God can help us feel close to Him.

## I can praise God anytime and anywhere.

God loves to hear your songs of praise. It doesn't matter if you're a good singer or not. You can sing to God anywhere—you don't have to be in church to praise Him. You can sing songs you learned at church, or make up your own. Our songs of praise please God! So sing out loud and let God hear your praises! —C.B.

### FUN FACT

A lyre is a stringed musical instrument that was used in ancient Greece. The sound box was usually made from a turtle shell. The lyre was often used to provide music for singing.

### READ MORE

Psalm 150 tells us how to praise the Lord with music. How many different instruments are mentioned in this Psalm?

# Two Builders

**Everyone likes to hear** a good story! Stories are fun to listen to—and sometimes they teach us a good lesson.

When Jesus taught the people who followed Him, He often told stories. His stories are called parables. Jesus told parables to help people understand more about God. Some people understood the parables, but others didn't.

> "Anyone who listens to my teaching and follows it is wise, like a person who builds a house on solid rock."
>
> MATTHEW 7:24 NLT

One day Jesus told the story of two men who built their houses on different foundations. A foundation is the base or bottom part of a house that holds up the rest of the house.

In Jesus' parable, a wise man built his house on rock. It was a solid foundation. When the rain came down, the wind blew hard, and the water rose, the house stood firm. But a foolish man built his house on sand. Sand is not a good foundation and will not support a house for very long. When the rain came down, the wind blew hard, and the water rose, the foolish man's house tumbled down!

Jesus said that anyone who listens to His teaching and does what He says is like the wise man who built his house on a rock. Like the person who builds a house on a solid foundation, we can build our lives on Jesus. When trouble comes, we will be strong.

Since you're young, this is a perfect time to build your life on a solid foundation. Jesus is the rock! —C.B.

## Jesus is my foundation.

**FUN FACT**

The world's largest tree house is located in Crossville, Tennessee. It is ten thousand square feet in size—almost four times larger than most American homes!

**READ MORE**

What does Psalm 18:1-2 tell us about God?

# Call on Jesus

> **Because Jesus experienced temptation when he suffered, he is able to help others when they are tempted.**
> HEBREWS 2:18 GW

**Have you ever wanted** to keep something that wasn't yours? Imagine finding a brand-new ball on the playground. Though you know it belongs to someone else, you still want to keep it. When we want to do something we know is wrong, it's called temptation.

Some people are tempted to lie or steal. Kids can be tempted to cheat on a test at school. You can even be tempted to say something mean to another person.

The very first people God made were tempted. Adam and Eve lived in the Garden of Eden. God told them they could eat the fruit from any tree in the garden, except for one. When they were tempted to disobey God, they gave in to that temptation. They sinned against God and brought much trouble into the world.

Did you know that Jesus was tempted too? But Jesus never gave in to temptation. He knew what was right, and He always chose to do the right thing. But Jesus understands how hard it is when we face temptation. He wants to help us be strong and do the right thing.

It is not a sin to be tempted. But it is a sin to do the wrong thing after we are tempted. When we are tempted to do wrong, we can call out to Jesus for help. And we can ask God to keep us from being tempted. God will help us to live the right way.

And if you ever find a brand-new ball on the playground, you can take it to the lost and found. —C.B.

## When I am tempted, I will call on Jesus.

### FUN FACT

France was home of the first lost-and-found office in 1805. The emperor Napoleon told police to start the office as a place to collect things found on the streets of Paris.

### READ MORE

**Do you know how Jesus handled temptation? Read Matthew 4:1–11 to find out what Jesus did.**

# Contest on a Mountain

**Elijah was a prophet** who served the one true God. One day God sent Elijah to see Ahab, an evil king who ruled the people of Israel. King Ahab had turned the people away from God, and they began worshipping a false god.

Elijah told King Ahab to send the leaders of the false religion to the top of a hill called Mount Carmel. Then Elijah challenged King Ahab and his men to a contest. It was Elijah all by himself against 450 leaders on the other side. Elijah told them to build an altar. He told them to ask their god to send fire to their altar.

The 450 men prayed and cried out to their god all day long. But nothing happened. There was no fire, not even a spark. Then Elijah told all the people to come over to his side. As the people watched, Elijah rebuilt the altar of the Lord that had been torn down. He asked men to pour four big jars of water over the altar. Then he told them to do it again. And then he told them to do it a third time!

> "O LORD, God of Abraham, Isaac, and Jacob, prove today that you are God in Israel and that I am your servant. Prove that I have done all this at your command."
>
> **1 KINGS 18:36 NLT**

## I will worship the one true God.

When everything was ready, Elijah asked God to show that He was the real God. Elijah asked God to change the people's hearts. And God heard Elijah's prayer. He sent fire from heaven that burned up the altar and even the water around it! When the people saw that, they shouted, "The Lord is God! The Lord is God!"

Elijah believed in God's power, and we can too. Even when others don't understand our faith, we know that we worship the one true God. —T.M.

## READ MORE

Read James 5:17–18.
What else did Elijah ask God to do to show His power?

## FUN FACT

The altars the Israelites built to God were usually made from one of three materials: dirt, stone, or a yellowish-brown metal called bronze.

> He who watches over
> you won't get tired . . .
> or go to sleep.
>
> PSALM 121:3–4 NIRV

# Up All Night

**Have you ever** stayed up late? Maybe your mom or dad let you stay up until midnight on New Year's Eve. Or maybe you had a friend spend the night, and you told stories and giggled way past your bedtime. But no matter how late you stayed up, eventually you did go to sleep.

We all have to sleep at some point. We can't skip our sleep because our bodies need rest. Sleep helps us to have strength and energy for the next day.

It isn't like that with God, though. The Bible tells us that God never sleeps. He never even gets tired! It's hard to imagine having never-ending strength and energy—but God does. That's another example of His greatness. Every second of the day and night, God is watching over all His creation. He's always taking care of everything. And that includes you.

Did you ever wake up at night and notice your parents were still awake? Somehow, the house feels safer when you know someone is still up. But even after your parents go to sleep, you can still feel that safe because God stays up all night watching over you. Daytime or nighttime, God is awake—and He is taking care of you. —T.M.

God is always watching over me.

## FUN FACT

In 1964, a seventeen-year-old named Randy Gardner stayed awake for eleven days and twenty-four minutes. Many believe that's a world record!

## READ MORE

Read Exodus 12:31–42 to learn about an important event that happened during the night.

# Time Stands Still

**The king of Jerusalem** was afraid. He heard that Joshua and the Israelites had taken over Jericho and defeated a city called Ai. Both of these cities were large and strong.

The Israelites had made peace with an important city called Gibeon. Because Gibeon was on Israel's side, the king of Jerusalem was even more scared. He knew if the Israelites and Gibeon worked together, they could take over his kingdom. So he called together other kings from around Jerusalem. They agreed to attack Gibeon and take it over. That way they would all be protected from the Israelites.

The people of Gibeon sent a message to Joshua asking for help. They wanted Joshua to come and fight for them. God said He would be with Joshua and help him defeat the evil kings. So Joshua and his army marched all night to Gibeon. At daylight, they began to fight. God made the Israelites strong in this battle and helped them win. God also dropped big hailstones on the enemy armies.

> So the sun stood still. The moon stopped. They didn't move again until the nation won the battle over its enemies. . . . The sun stopped in the middle of the sky. It didn't go down for about a full day. There has never been a day like it before or since.
>
> JOSHUA 10:13–14 NIRV

*God can do great things for His people.*

As the day went on, Joshua prayed an amazing prayer. "Sun, stop over Gibeon," he said. "Moon, stand still over the Valley of Aijalon." God listened to Joshua's prayer! He held the sun in place for almost a whole day so Israel could finish the fight. God fought for His people and gave them victory!

Nothing is too hard for God. He is faithful to those who trust Him. If God can stop the sun and the moon in the sky, He can help you with your problems too. —T.M.

## Read More
Read 2 Kings 20:8–11.
What did Isaiah ask God to do? Did God do it?

### FUN FACT
A solar eclipse happens when the moon moves between the sun and earth. During a solar eclipse, the earth is in the moon's shadow.

A joyful heart
makes a
cheerful face.

PROVERBS 15:13 GW

# From the Inside Out

**Have you ever** heard someone say, "It's what's on the inside that counts"? That means it doesn't matter what you look like. The most important part of a person is what's in her heart.

The way we treat people shows what we're like on the inside. The words we say let others know who we really are. If there's joy in your heart, it will show in the way you live your life.

God is the one who gives us joy. When you love God, He puts joy in your heart. With God's joy inside you, you can have peace even when things aren't going the way you'd like them to. When you have joy in your heart, it's hard to keep it inside. It will bubble out of you like fizz from a bottle of soda!

Joy in your heart puts a grin on your face. You can smile at the people you pass on the sidewalk. You can encourage a friend who is having a bad day. Sharing your joy with others is a great way to show God's love.

Just like it's tough to smile when you feel sad, it's hard to feel hopeless when you have God's joy and peace in your heart. God wants that joy and peace to be on display to everyone around you. So let it flow from the inside out! —T.M.

## God puts joy in my heart.

### FUN FACT

Some people believe kids smile much more than adults. Kids smile as many as four hundred times a day. That's a lot of joy you can share with your friends and family!

### READ MORE

What does Proverbs 17:22 say about being cheerful?

God is able to do far more than we could ever ask for or imagine. He does everything by his power that is working in us.

**EPHESIANS 3:20 NIRV**

# Keep Pouring

**Elisha was a prophet** of God who continued the work of Elijah. One day a poor widow came to Elisha for help. She had two sons to care for, and all she owned was a little olive oil. When that was gone, she would have nothing.

Elisha told the woman to ask her neighbors for empty jars. He told her to get as many as she could, then start pouring her oil into the empty jars. The widow didn't ask questions. She trusted Elisha and did what he told her to do.

When the widow filled a jar with oil, her sons would bring her another jar to fill. She poured and poured and poured until every jar was full! When she filled the last jar, the oil from her own jar stopped flowing. With all the oil she now had, she could sell the jars and have enough money to take care of her sons.

## God can do more than I can imagine.

This is one of many amazing stories that we read in the Bible. It's another example of how God can do impossible things. The Bible doesn't tell us how many empty jars the widow brought to her house. Do you think if she had borrowed even more jars, that those jars would have been filled too?

God can do much more than we can imagine. When we trust and obey God, His blessings pour over us like oil that doesn't stop. —C.B.

## READ MORE

1 Kings 17:1–16 tells us a story about a widow who fed the prophet Elijah. Read the story to find out about another miracle.

## FUN FACT

Olive oil is made by squeezing olives. Almost all of the olive oil in the world comes from countries around the Mediterranean Sea.

> For this reason we must pay closer attention to what we have heard. Then we won't drift away from the truth.
>
> **HEBREWS 2:1 GW**

# Drop Anchor

**Have you ever seen** a big, heavy anchor on the side of a ship? Anchors are made of metal and sink fast to the ocean floor when they're thrown over the side of a boat. Do you know what an anchor is used for? If a ship's captain wants to keep the boat in a certain place, he drops the anchor on a long chain into the water. The anchor digs into the sand on the ocean floor and keeps the boat from drifting. When the waves start rolling and the wind starts blowing, the boat stays where it should.

The Bible is like an anchor in our lives. It shows us the teachings of Jesus and helps us to know how we should live. When we obey Jesus' words and do what He says, it's like throwing an anchor over the side of a boat. It holds us right where we need to be. It keeps us from being pushed and pulled in the wrong direction.

## Jesus is my anchor.

There may be times when other people want you to do something you know is wrong. Sometimes you might want to hide when others make fun of your beliefs. But if we stay anchored to Jesus and do what He tells us to do, we'll be right where He wants us. We won't drift away. —T.M.

## FUN FACT

Some boats use a "mushroom anchor." It was given this name because it's shaped like an upside-down mushroom. This kind of anchor is used where the ocean bottom is very soft.

## READ MORE

What does Hebrews 6:18–19 say about anchors?

# Walking on Water

> So Peter went over the side of the boat and walked on the water toward Jesus. But when he saw the strong wind and the waves, he was terrified and began to sink. "Save me, Lord!" he shouted.
>
> MATTHEW 14:29–30 NLT

**Peter and the other disciples** had had a long day. Crowds of people followed the disciples as they traveled with Jesus. Jesus spent the day teaching and even performed a miracle to feed five thousand people who were listening on a mountainside. When the long day was over, Jesus sent the disciples ahead of Him on a boat to cross the Sea of Galilee.

As the disciples sailed into the night, the wind started to blow and waves crashed against the boat. Suddenly, the disciples saw someone walking on the water toward them! They thought they were seeing a ghost—and they were afraid. But Jesus called out, "Don't be afraid. I am here."

Peter said, "Lord, if it's really you, tell me to come to you walking on the water." Jesus told Peter to come, so Peter got out of the boat. He placed his feet on the water.

## I can keep my thoughts fixed on Jesus.

He took a step. Then he took another. Peter was walking on the water to Jesus! But then Peter noticed the strong wind and the big waves. He took his eyes off of Jesus—and he quickly began to sink. Peter cried out to Jesus for help, and Jesus reached out His hand to save Peter.

Sometimes, like Peter, we think about things around us instead of thinking about Jesus. When we take our thoughts off Him, we can get scared and forget that He is always there to help us. When you're facing hard things, you can know that Jesus is with you. Keep your attention on Him, and He will help you. —T.M.

### FUN FACT

The Dead Sea lies on the border of Israel and Jordan. It is one of the saltiest bodies of water in the world. Because of how salty the Dead Sea is, people float very easily—but they can't walk on it!

### READ MORE

Read Luke 8:22–25 to learn about another time Jesus rescued the disciples on the water.

# Waiting for Good Things

The LORD is good to those who wait for him, to anyone who seeks help from him.

**LAMENTATIONS 3:25 GW**

**"Good things come** to those who wait" is a common saying that has been popular for many years. It reminds us of the importance of being patient.

God promised that Abraham would be the father of a great nation. He told Abraham to go outside and look at the sky. "There are so many stars you cannot count them," God said to Abraham. "In the same way, your descendants will be too many to count."

Abraham was about seventy-five years old when God promised to give him and his wife, Sarah, a son. But Abraham and Sarah waited another twenty-five years before their child was born! Abraham was one hundred years old and Sarah was ninety when they had their baby. His name was Isaac.

Kids have to wait for good things too. You have to wait for special days like your birthday or Christmas. You have to wait for your permanent teeth to grow in! Have you ever had to wait for a visit from your grandma and grandpa? It can be hard to wait, but good things come to those who wait.

## I will wait for good things.

God is pleased when you wait patiently for good things. You don't have to wait for His love, because you already have that! But sometimes you have to wait for God to work out His plans as you grow up. God's timing is always right, so you can trust Him as you wait for the things you hope for.

Always believe that God will show you the good things He has for you. Remember that God's good things are worth waiting for. —C.B.

### FUN FACT

A mother elephant has to wait more than a year and a half for her baby to be born! It takes about ninety-five weeks for an unborn elephant to develop inside its mother. That's more than twice as long as a human baby.

### READ MORE

What is the greatest thing that Christians wait for? Read John 14:1–3 to find out.

# Say Thank You

**Think of all the times** you could say thank you. When someone gives you a gift, saying thank you is the right thing to do. You should also say thank you when someone pays you a compliment or helps you out. Do you remember to say thank you to your mom or dad for making a delicious dinner? Do you thank your grandma when she sends you a birthday card? When you pray, do you thank God for your home and your family? When you say thank you, it shows that you are grateful.

> Give thanks no matter what happens. God wants you to thank him because you believe in Christ Jesus.
>
> **1 THESSALONIANS 5:18 NIRV**

It's easy to be thankful for good things. But the Bible tells us to be thankful all the time—no matter what! Bad things can happen in anyone's life. People we love get sick. Friends move away. Parents can lose their jobs. We don't have to be thankful for the bad things themselves, but we can be thankful that God is with us during our hard times.

*I will thank God all the time.*

Anyone who believes in Jesus is a child of God. Good parents don't want to see their children sad or hurt, and God doesn't want that either. He wants you to depend on Him to help you through bad times. No matter what happens, you can be thankful that you have a God who loves you and cares about everything that happens in your life.

In good times and bad times, say thank you to God for loving you. —C.B.

## READ MORE

Read Psalm 118:28–29.
Why should we give thanks to God?

## FUN FACT

"Thanks" is the most popular one-word message typed on mobile phones. "Thank you" is the most popular two-word message!

> "If a man has a hundred sheep and one of them gets lost, what will he do? Won't he leave the ninety-nine others in the wilderness and go to search for the one that is lost until he finds it?"
>
> **LUKE 15:4 NLT**

# The Lost Sheep

**If you have a pet,** you know how you would feel if you lost it. You would stop everything you were doing and go out to find it. You wouldn't worry about how far away you had to look or how long it took. You'd keep looking until you found your pet. You'd do everything you could to get it back.

When Jesus taught lessons about the kingdom of God, He often used parables. One of Jesus' parables talks about losing a sheep.

Jesus told the story of a shepherd who had one hundred sheep. One of those sheep got lost, so the shepherd left the ninety-nine others to go find the one that was missing. When he found the lost sheep, the shepherd picked it up and carried it home. He was so happy to find his sheep, he invited his friends and family to celebrate with him.

## Jesus wants everyone to follow Him.

### FUN FACT

The American Society for the Prevention of Cruelty to Animals did a study on dogs and cats that are lost. It learned that more than eight of ten lost pets are found again!

Jesus told this story to show how God feels about His people. God loves everyone—even the people who run away from Him. God will look for lost people just like the shepherd searched for his lost sheep. And when someone turns to God and becomes a Christian, there is much celebrating in heaven!

If you ever know someone who is running away from God, pray for that person. Always remember that God wants everyone to become a Christian. —T.M.

### READ MORE

Jesus told another parable about something that was lost and found. Do you know what it was? Find out in Luke 15:8-10.

# All Over the World

**Did you know** that when you wake up in the morning, other kids are getting ready for bed? It can be morning in one part of the world and nighttime on the other side of the earth. So when you're getting ready for bed at night, other kids are just starting their day. As the sun is setting in the sky where you live, it is rising someplace else.

> From where the sun rises to where the sun sets, the name of the LORD should be praised.
>
> **PSALM 113:3 GW**

It seems like the sun circles the earth, but it's the other way around. The earth "revolves"—or goes around—the sun, one time each year. But the earth also "rotates"—or spins—making one complete turn every day. As the earth revolves and rotates, the sun shines on different parts of the world.

*I will praise the name of the Lord.*

The Bible verse for today says that God's name should be praised from wherever the sun rises to wherever the sun sets. That means everywhere. And it means all the time.

God is so great—He is the one who created the sun and the earth and the heavens. He's the one who put the moon and the stars in the sky. He created the planets and set them in motion. God is the only one who could have done that.

The whole universe shows the glory and greatness of God. He is worthy of our praise. Everyone, everywhere, at every time can praise the name of the Lord. —C.B.

## FUN FACT

It takes the earth a little more than 365 days to go around the sun. Each year actually takes an extra six hours. That's why, every four years, we add a "leap day"—February 29— to the calendar.

## READ MORE

Read Psalm 113:1–6. How great is God's glory?

> When God's people are in need, be ready to help them. Always be eager to practice hospitality.
>
> **ROMANS 12:13 NLT**

# Practice, Practice, Practice

**Have you ever heard** the saying, "Practice makes perfect"? It means that when you do something over and over, you can learn to do it well. If you want to play the piano, ride a bike, or write stories, you have to practice. The more you practice, the better you get.

We can also practice to become better Christians. The more we read the Bible and do what it says, the better we live the way God wants us to. One thing God wants us to do is "practice hospitality." That means to be kind to others and help people in need. Hospitality can mean inviting another person into your home for a meal or a place to stay.

The apostle Paul and his friend Silas traveled many places to tell others about Jesus. They often had to eat and sleep in other people's homes. On one of their trips they met

## I can practice hospitality.

a woman named Lydia. Her business was selling purple cloth. Lydia worshipped God and listened closely to the words Paul said about Jesus. After listening to Paul, Lydia and her family believed in Jesus and were baptized. Lydia invited Paul and Silas to stay in her home so she could show them hospitality.

You can practice hospitality just like Lydia did. If your family knows people who need a meal or a place to stay, invite them over. When you practice hospitality, you'll get really good at it! —C.B.

### FUN FACT

In Bible times, purple cloth was made from a dye that came from a kind of shellfish. It took lots of shellfish to make the dye, so purple cloth was very expensive. People who wore purple were the "rich and famous" of their time.

### READ MORE

Luke 24:13–35 tells what happened when two travelers invited another traveler to stay with them. Who was the third traveler?

For we are God's
masterpiece.
He has created us
anew in Christ Jesus,
so we can do the good
things he planned for
us long ago.

EPHESIANS 2:10 NLT

# God's Masterpiece

**The Mona Lisa** is a famous work of art by Leonardo da Vinci. It may be the most famous work of art in the world.

Every year, millions of people visit the Louvre Museum in Paris, France, to see the Mona Lisa. People come every day to see this painting of a woman because it is considered a masterpiece. Do you know what a masterpiece is? A masterpiece is a person's greatest work or accomplishment. It is the best thing a person can possibly make.

Like an artist, God has created many beautiful things. He formed the oceans and colored them with pretty shades of blue and green. He made the mountains with pointy peaks and capped them with snow. He shaped silky flowers in every color of the rainbow. He thought up millions of creatures and designed each one to look different from the others. All of these things are wonderful and show God's skill.

## I am God's masterpiece.

But in all creation, what is God's masterpiece? The Bible says people are God's masterpiece—and that includes you! You are more valuable than all the amazing things God created in this world.

We were made to be God's masterpiece so we can do the good things God planned for us a long time ago. When we do those things, we display our Creator's greatness to the world—just like the Mona Lisa hanging in a fancy museum! —T.M.

### FUN FACT

The Mona Lisa was stolen in 1911. It was missing for two years before the police finally caught the thief and returned the painting to the museum.

### READ MORE

Read Psalm 139:13–18.
What does this verse say about how you were created?

# Seven Dips in the River

**A man named Naaman** was commander of an army. God helped him win a battle against his country's enemies. He was very important and brave—but he had a terrible skin disease called leprosy.

So Naaman went down to the Jordan River. He dipped himself in it seven times. He did exactly what the man of God had told him to do. Then his skin was made pure again. It became clean like the skin of a young boy.

**2 KINGS 5:14 NIRV**

Naaman's wife had a servant girl from Israel. The girl told Naaman's wife that if Naaman went to see God's prophet in Samaria, he could be healed from his disease. But Naaman went to see the king of Israel first. The king was angry because he knew he couldn't help Naaman. But when the prophet Elisha heard about Naaman, he told the king to send Naaman to see him.

Elisha knew God could heal Naaman. So Elisha told the commander, "Go wash yourself in the Jordan River seven times. Then your skin will be healed."

Naaman was upset. He thought Elisha would pray and wave his hand and heal Naaman right away. The commander thought it was silly to take a bath in the Jordan River. He figured he could bathe in a river closer to his home!

## God's way is always the right way.

But Naaman's servants encouraged him. They believed in Elisha's orders and told Naaman to obey the prophet. So Naaman went to the Jordan River. He dipped himself in the water seven times, just like Elisha said. And when he came out of the water, he was healed! His skin was pure again.

Just like Naaman, we often want God to fix our problems easily. But God's way of doing things isn't always our way. If we obey what He tells us to do, we will receive His blessings. Even when we don't understand God's way, it's still right. —T.M.

### READ MORE

Read Isaiah 55:8–9. According to this verse, how much higher are God's ways than our ways?

## FUN FACT

The Jordan River is mentioned about two hundred times in the Bible. The name Jordan comes from a Hebrew word which means "descender" (something that goes down). The river flows from the heights of Mt. Hermon to the Dead Sea, which is the lowest spot on land in the whole world.

> He heals the
> brokenhearted
> and bandages
> their wounds.
>
> PSALM 147:3 NLT

# Fixing Broken Hearts

**When people say** they have a "broken heart," it means they're hurting inside. They're talking about their feelings rather than the actual heart that beats in their chest. Hearts "break" when we're disappointed with someone or hurt by other people. When families split apart, hearts are broken. When people we love die, our hearts break. When friends say mean things to us, our hearts can be broken too.

The good news is that broken hearts can be fixed. You don't have to see a doctor or take extra vitamins. If you ask Him to, God will fix your broken heart. When you're feeling hurt or sad, you can always talk to God. You can read your favorite Bible stories or listen to songs that praise God. You could even ask God to help you find a friend or grown-up who understands how you feel. Just like broken bones can heal, broken hearts can get better too. God can make your heart happy again. It just takes time.

Do you have friends or family members with broken hearts? If you do, pray for them. Be kind and loving to them. When you show care for people who are sad, it's like putting a big Band-Aid on their heart. God can use you to help others be happy again! —C.B.

## God heals hurting hearts.

**READ MORE**

Psalm 34:17–18 gives hope to people with broken hearts. What do these verses say about God?

Even when I walk through the darkest valley, I will not be afraid, for you are close beside me.

PSALM 23:4 NLT

# Victory in the Valley

**Israelite soldiers** were gathered on a hill. Enemy Philistine soldiers were on another hill. The Valley of Elah was between them.

One of the Philistine soldiers was a giant named Goliath. Every day Goliath dared the soldiers of Israel to send someone out to fight him. When the Israelites saw Goliath, they were afraid and ran to hide. But David, a shepherd boy, wanted to fight Goliath. God had helped David fight off both a lion and a bear while he was watching his sheep. David knew God would help him fight Goliath too.

King Saul agreed to let David try. First, Saul dressed David in the king's coat of armor and helmet. Then David strapped on the king's sword. David walked around in the armor, but it made him uncomfortable. So he took it all off.

Instead, David grabbed his shepherd's staff and walked to a stream in the valley. He picked up five smooth stones and put them in his bag. Then David took his sling and went to fight the giant. Goliath laughed when he saw David coming.

## God will help me face my giants.

But David wasn't laughing. "You are coming to fight me with a sword," David shouted, "but I'm coming in the name of the Lord. He is the God of Israel. He's the one you have dared to fight!"

As Goliath moved in to attack, David reached into his bag. He put a stone in his sling and whirled it around. Then he let the stone fly. It hit Goliath on the forehead and he crashed to the ground. David had won!

David beat Goliath because he trusted in God to help him. When you have giant-sized problems, remember David's story. God is with you too. —C.B.

### **FUN FACT**

Shepherds often carried a bag made of animal skins. It was slung over their shoulders, and large enough to carry a day's worth of supplies.

### **READ MORE**

Read Ephesians 6:10–18 to learn about another kind of armor. What is "the sword of the Spirit"?

# Amen

> Then all the people said amen and praised the LORD.
>
> 1 CHRONICLES 16:36 GW

**Whether you pray** out loud or quietly by yourself, you probably say amen at the end of your prayer. In church, pastors often say amen at the end of their prayers too. Sometimes pastors finish their prayers by saying, "And all God's people said . . ." Then everyone in the room can say amen together.

Do you know why we say amen at the end of a prayer? People have done that for thousands of years, since the days of the Old Testament. Today's Bible verse is part of a prayer that ends with amen. It's the first time in the Bible that happens!

King David led this prayer when the Israelites set up a place of worship to God. When David finished the prayer, the people said amen and began praising God. The word amen means "so be it." That's a fancy way of saying, "We hope what was just said is what happens." It means we agree with what was prayed.

When someone says something that you think is true or exciting, you might yell out, "Yeah!" or "That's right!" Saying amen at the end of a prayer means the same thing. It means we agree with God's goodness and His ability to answer our prayers. It's like ending your prayer with an exclamation point!

So when you finish talking to God, let out a big amen to show you believe all the things you said. —T.M.

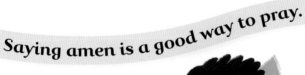

**Saying amen is a good way to pray.**

## FUN FACT

A popular gospel song is called "Amen." It was written by Jester Hairston and was first recorded in 1963. The song uses the word amen thirty-five times!

## READ MORE

Many people also end their prayers by saying, "In Jesus' name, amen." Find out why by reading John 16:23–24.

# Planting Seeds

**If you've ever planted seeds,** you know it takes a lot of work to make something grow. The soil has to be just right—not too dry or too wet. The seeds need warmth from sunlight and protection from weeds. You'll need to water your seeds with a hose or sprinkler. But with the right conditions and care, a seed will grow into a healthy plant.

Jesus said that telling others about Him is like planting seeds. Sometimes people hear about Jesus and don't understand. That's like a seed that falls on the hard soil of the road. Then a bird eats the seed. The bird is Satan taking the truth away from someone's heart. That seed doesn't even have a chance to sprout.

Sometimes people are excited to hear about Jesus—but when they run into problems they give up on God. That's like a seed planted in rocky ground. There isn't enough soil for good roots. Other people hear about Jesus, but they love the world more than they love Him. That's like a seed planted in a thorny soil. The seed can't grow because the thorns choke it.

> "The seed that fell on good soil represents those who truly hear and understand God's word and produce a harvest of thirty, sixty, or even a hundred times as much as had been planted!"
>
> MATTHEW 13:23 NLT

*Telling others about Jesus is like planting a seed.*

But some people hear about Jesus and understand what He did for them. They accept Him and become strong Christians. They are like seeds planted in good soil. These seeds produce a crop that just keeps growing!

When you share Jesus with others, you may not know what kind of "soil" they are. But you can trust God to care for the seeds you plant. When the time and conditions are right, the seeds can sprout into something beautiful. —T.M.

## READ MORE

Read Isaiah 55:10–11.
What is the seed in this verse?

## FUN FACT

Acorns are the seeds that come from oak trees. Some oak trees don't produce acorns until they are fifty years old.

> Let us, then, feel free to come before God's throne. Here there is grace. And we can receive mercy and grace to help us when we need it.
>
> HEBREWS 4:16 ICB

# Feel Free

**When someone says** to you, "Feel free to come over anytime," it means you don't need an invitation to visit. People who are close friends, good neighbors, or loving relatives know each other well. They feel free to go to each other's houses whenever they need to. If your mom needs some eggs for a recipe, she might go to a neighbor's house to borrow some. If your grandma lives nearby and you want to visit her, you can stop in anytime you want. That's the way it is with people who know each other well.

But it's different with people you don't know. If you want to talk to someone who doesn't know you—maybe a very important person—you might have to ask permission or make an appointment. You wouldn't stop in just because you needed something.

## I can always feel free to talk to God.

God is more important than anyone. But because He knows you well, He wants you to feel free to talk to Him anytime. You don't need to ask permission or make an appointment. He's always happy for you to come to Him!

And you can feel free to talk to God about anything. You can tell Him about your problems or just tell Him you love Him. If you feel badly about doing something wrong, you can tell God you're sorry and He will forgive you.

God is full of love and kindness. Feel free to talk to Him anytime. —C.B.

## FUN FACT

Long ago the Israelites built a "tabernacle"—a special tent—for their place of worship. At one end was a place called the "holy of holies" where a priest would meet with God one time each year. It was separated by a curtain and nobody else was allowed to enter.

## READ MORE

Psalm 100 talks about ways we can come before God. What are some of those ways?

# Forever King

**Countries and nations** have rulers. Some are ruled by kings and queens. Others are led by presidents or prime ministers. Some rulers are voted into office, while others become rulers because they belong to a royal family. Presidents hold their jobs for a certain amount of time, called a "term." Sometimes, if the people vote to keep them, presidents lead for more than one term. Kings and queens usually rule until they die; then another family member takes over. But even though there are many kinds of rulers, they all have one thing in common—they will not rule forever.

> "The Lord God will give him the throne of King David, his ancestor. He will rule over the people of Jacob forever. His kingdom will never end."
>
> LUKE 1:32–33 ICB

King David was leader of the Israelites, God's chosen people. Old Testament prophets announced that the Messiah would come from the family of David. One day, an angel told a young Israelite woman named Mary that she was going to be the mother of God's Son.

### Jesus is my King.

The angel said that her son, Jesus, would rule forever. When Jesus was born, some Israelites thought He would be a king in Jerusalem. They wanted Jesus to defeat the Romans who were ruling over Israel. But Jesus said, "My kingdom is not of this world."

Jesus' kingdom is the kingdom of heaven, and His rule will last forever. Everyone who believes in Jesus as Savior belongs to the kingdom of heaven. If you believe in Jesus, He is your King. And He will be your King forever! —C.B.

### FUN FACT

King Herod the Great ruled in Jerusalem when Jesus was born. But he was not related to the Israelites. The Roman Empire made him a king.

### READ MORE
Read Daniel 6:26–27 to find out what King Darius said about God.

# A New Family

You have received the spirit of God's adopted children by which we call out, "Abba! Father!"

ROMANS 8:15 GW

**Do you know** anyone who is adopted? Adoption is a very special act of love. When parents adopt a child, they welcome someone who is not related to them into their family. Those parents might choose a special first name for the child, but they all share the same last name. This shows that the child belongs to his new family. Parents take care of an adopted child and love him just like a child that comes into a family by birth. An adopted child can call his new parents "Mom" and "Dad."

The Bible says that Christians have been adopted into God's family. Before we become Christians, we are not in God's family because our sins keep us from belonging to God. But when we believe in Jesus, our sins are forgiven. God welcomes anybody into His family after their sins are forgiven.

We aren't born into God's family naturally. We become part of His family when we believe in His son, Jesus. And when we believe, we get a new name, too. We are now called "child of God"!

God knows us and loves us like we were always part of His family. He takes care of us and provides for us, just like good parents do for their kids. We can even call God Father because we are His children. And guess what? There's always room for more children in God's family! —T.M.

## I can be a child of God.

### FUN FACT

About 120,000 children are adopted each year in the United States. About 7,000 of those kids are from countries around the world. Every year, millions of people around the world are adopted into God's family by becoming Christians.

### READ MORE

Read John 1:12.
What right is given to people who believe in Jesus?

# A Comforting Friend

**Isaac's mother, Sarah,** had a special life. God told her husband, Abraham, that He would build His nation through their descendants. Even though Abraham and Sarah were very old and didn't have children, God performed a miracle. He gave them a child when Abraham was one hundred and Sarah was ninety. Sarah lived to be 127 years old.

> She became his wife, and he loved her. So Isaac was comforted after his mother died.
>
> **GENESIS 24:67 NIRV**

After Sarah passed away, Abraham knew it was time for Isaac to get married. Abraham wanted Isaac to find a wife who did what was right. He didn't want Isaac to marry someone who wasn't following God.

In those days parents chose the person their child would marry. So Abraham sent out a servant to find a wife for Isaac. The servant asked God for help—and God brought him the right woman. Her name was Rebekah, and she agreed to leave her family and go to live with Isaac and his family.

## God gives friends to comfort me.

When Isaac saw Rebekah coming to meet him, she covered herself with a veil. That was a way to show respect for Isaac. As soon as Rebekah reached Isaac's camp, they got married. Rebekah's love comforted Isaac after his mother died.

Everyone faces sad times. When we go through hard things, God is with us. And He puts other people in our lives to comfort and encourage us. If you are facing a sad time right now, you can ask God to give you a special friend or family member to help you. And if you know of someone else who is sad, ask God to help you comfort that person in a special way. —T.M.

## READ MORE

Read Genesis 24:1–27.
How did Abraham's servant know that
Rebekah was the right wife for Isaac?

## FUN FACT

Isaac's father, Abraham, lived to be 175 years old!

# The Animals Know

"But ask the animals what God does. They will teach you. Or ask the birds of the air. They will tell you. Or speak to the earth. It will teach you. Or let the fish of the ocean educate you. Are there any of those creatures that don't know what the powerful hand of the LORD has done? He holds the life of every creature in his hand. He controls the breath of every human being."

JOB 12:7–10 NIRV

**Have you ever seen** a flock of geese fly overhead in the shape of a V? Have you ever watched a squirrel gather nuts before the cold weather comes? Did you know that bears eat a lot of food before they curl up in their dens for a long winter snooze? These behaviors are known as "animal instincts." Because of their instinct, geese know when it's time to fly south. Squirrels know when it's time to gather nuts. Bears know when it's time to fill their bellies with food so they can sleep for several months.

God created the animals. He made them with instincts so they know what to do at certain times of the year. Since the time of creation, God has been caring for the animals—from the birds that soar high above, to the fish that swim in the depths of the sea. God makes the wind that carries an eagle through the sky. He helps a robin find twigs to build a nest. He leads a thirsty deer to drink from a stream. He guides the squirrel to gather acorns. And He helps lions, elephants, polar bears, and duck-billed platypuses do whatever they do!

## God's creatures are in His hands.

Animals know what to do and where to go. They know how to travel, when to sleep, and where to find food. God made them that way! He not only created them, but He holds them in His hands. —C.B.

### FUN FACT

Every year the Arctic tern flies from the far north of the world to the far south, and then back again. That's a trip of about twenty-two thousand miles (thirty-five thousand kilometers), the longest migration of any bird in the world.

### READ MORE

What does Psalm 50:10–11 say about animals?

# Heavy Loads

**Have you ever tried** to carry something very heavy? Maybe you moved a stack of books to the closet to help your teacher. Or maybe you had a big suitcase to lug around when you traveled. If you've tried to carry a heavy load, you know it can be exhausting. After a while, you just want to set it down and take a break. Our bodies aren't meant to carry heavy things all day.

> "Come to me, all who are tired from carrying heavy loads, and I will give you rest."
> **MATTHEW 11:28 GW**

Since he was a carpenter, Jesus probably carried heavy pieces of wood. And He used the idea of carrying heavy stuff to help us understand something very important. Sometimes we "carry" things on the inside, and they make us tired. When you have problems at school or in your family, it almost feels like you're holding a heavy weight. Struggles can wear us down, just like a heavy backpack would.

*Jesus gives me rest from my worries.*

But Jesus says we can bring our heavy loads to Him. We can talk to Him about the things that weigh us down. And do you know what happens when we do that? He will give us rest! When we talk to Jesus about the hard things in our lives, it's like setting down a heavy stack of books. Jesus gives rest to our souls. That means He'll give us peace and a feeling of comfort inside. It's almost like our body says "ahh" from the inside out.

Jesus can handle all of our problems and worries. Nothing is too heavy for Him to hold! —T.M.

## READ MORE

Read Isaiah 40:29–31 to find out how you can have strength instead of feeling tired.

## FUN FACT

A shekel was a measure of weight used during biblical times. One pound equals forty shekels.

> No power in the sky above or in the earth below—indeed, nothing in all creation will ever be able to separate us from the love of God that is revealed in Christ Jesus our Lord.
>
> **ROMANS 8:39 NLT**

# Can't Separate It

**Have you ever heard** of "separating" an egg? That means dividing the yellow yolk from the gooey "egg white." It isn't easy to separate an egg, but it can be done.

But some things are not meant to be separated. You wouldn't want the tires to separate from your bicycle unless you were fixing a flat. You wouldn't want your laces to separate from your tennis shoes unless you were washing them. And you wouldn't want the oars to separate from your rowboat if you were out in the middle of a lake!

Did you know there is one thing you can never separate? It's God's love for you! If you love Jesus, God's love will always be with you. You can travel anywhere in the world and God's love will be with you. You can fly high in the sky in an airplane or go scuba diving deep in the ocean, and God's love will be with you. In the middle of a thunderstorm or a blizzard or even a typhoon, God's love is with you.

### Nothing can separate me from God's love.

Whether you are happy or sad, alone or with your family, enjoying the sunshine or afraid of the dark, nothing can separate you from God's love. He loves you now. He will love you forever. —C.B.

### FUN FACT

Cooks say cold eggs are best for separating. When the eggs are cold, the yolks and egg whites hold their shape better and separate more easily.

### READ MORE

What does Psalm 103:11 say about God's love?

# Finishing the Wall

**The Israelites** had been away from their hometown of Jerusalem for a long time. But they weren't on vacation. A group of people called the Babylonians had forced them to leave their homes.

After many years, though, the Israelites were allowed to move back to Jerusalem. When they got home, they had a lot of work to do. The big wall that went around the city had been destroyed and needed to be built again. Nehemiah was in charge of this project.

As the wall grew taller and more sturdy, the Israelites' enemies started to get concerned. Two men kept picking on Nehemiah as he worked. But Nehemiah didn't pay any attention to them. So they tried to trick Nehemiah. They told him they wanted to have a meeting with him.

But Nehemiah was wise. He knew that if he came down from his work the two men would hurt him. Instead of falling for their trick, Nehemiah sent a message back. He said, "I am carrying on a great project and cannot go down."

> So I sent messengers to them with this reply: "I am carrying on a great project and cannot go down. Why should the work stop while I leave it and go down to you?"
>
> **NEHEMIAH 6:3 NIV**

## It's good to finish what I start.

He also gave swords to his workers so they could protect themselves against anyone who tried to stop their project.

Nehemiah is an example of someone who didn't give up. Sometimes, when you're working hard toward an important goal, people may discourage you. Others might try to stop you from doing what you know you are supposed to do. When that happens, you can be like Nehemiah. With God's help, stay focused on your project. Don't quit until you finish what you started.
—T.M.

### FUN FACT

The longest wall in the world is the Great Wall of China. The main part of the wall is 2,150 miles (3,460 kilometers). Construction of the wall began about two hundred years before Jesus was born.

### READ MORE

Read Nehemiah 6:15–16.
Who helped the Israelites finish building the wall?

# A Strong Tree

**Trees are tall,** beautiful examples of God's work. Their size can remind us of God's greatness.

But trees don't grow strong without help. You don't see many trees in the desert because there isn't enough rain. The soil is dry and lacks the nutrients that trees need. The sun is so hot it can wilt the leaves.

But in the right place, with the right amount of sunlight and water to grow, a tree can become all that God designed it to be. Some, like orange trees, produce fruit for people to eat. These trees are so strong and healthy, they are able to grow things for people to enjoy.

## A person who loves the Bible is like a strong tree.

The first psalm teaches us about the Bible by using the example of a tree. It says that a person who finds happiness in Scripture and obeys it is like a fruitful tree. As we read the Bible and do what it says, it's like taking vitamins for our hearts. When we follow the commandments of the Bible, it's like a big drink of water that gives us spiritual energy. And like a tree full of oranges, we show the fruit of the Spirit growing in us.

Reading, loving, and obeying the Bible will help us grow stronger in our faith. We can be strong like a big, healthy tree. —T.M.

## FUN FACT

The largest species of trees is the giant redwood. Trees in this family grow almost 380 feet tall (about 85 meters) and up to 26 feet around (8 meters). They grow in the northwestern United States.

## READ MORE

Read Galatians 5:22–23.
What kind of "fruit" do Christians produce?

# Bread from Heaven

> Jesus replied, "I am the bread of life. Whoever comes to me will never be hungry again. Whoever believes in me will never be thirsty."
>
> JOHN 6:35 NLT

**After the Israelites escaped** from Egypt, they spent many years living in the wilderness. It was a hard, wild place, and the people often complained to Moses because they were hungry.

One day God told Moses that He would send bread from heaven. The bread was called manna. It would settle on the ground like dew. Every morning, people would gather as much manna as they needed for the day. The manna would fill people when they ate it. But, as with any food, they would need more the next day.

The New Testament shares another story about bread. Jesus performed a miracle when He used five small loaves of bread to feed more than five thousand hungry people. After that miracle, many people followed Jesus around. He knew that some of those people were following Him because they were hungry again. They were just hoping for more food!

Jesus told the people that God had sent Him from heaven, just like God had sent the manna many years before. Jesus told the people that He was the "true bread." He said that anyone who believed in Him would never be hungry. But the people didn't understand that Jesus was talking about spiritual hunger.

## The bread from Jesus lasts forever.

Everyone has an emptiness inside that needs to be filled. Some people try to fill that emptiness by having lots of money or being popular. But nothing in this world can fill our emptiness inside. It's a spiritual hunger that only Jesus can satisfy.

When we choose to follow Jesus, He takes care of our spiritual hunger. The "bread" that Jesus gives us is life that lasts forever. —C.B.

## READ MORE

Moses gave the people specific instructions about gathering the manna. Read Exodus 16:19–20 to see what happened when some of the people didn't listen.

## FUN FACT

For people in Bible times, bread was the main source of nourishment. Usually, women made the bread. It took about three hours every day to make enough bread for a family of five.

# Amazing Grace

> "One thing I do know.
> I was blind but
> now I see!"
>
> JOHN 9:25 NIV

**"Amazing Grace"** is considered the most famous Christian song in the world. It was written by John Newton in the late 1700s. One part of the song says:

I once was lost, but now I'm found

Was blind, but now I see.

Did you know these words are based on the Bible? While Jesus was on earth, He healed many people. Some of them were very sick. Some couldn't hear or walk. One day Jesus and His followers passed by a man who had been born blind. To show God's grace—His help and love that we don't deserve—Jesus stopped and did what only He could do. First, He spit on the ground and made mud. Then He put the mud in His hands and wiped the mud on the blind man's eyes. Finally, Jesus told the blind man to wash off the mud in a nearby pool. When the man did the things Jesus told him to, he could see for the first time! He was no longer blind.

## Jesus can do the impossible.

The people and leaders of the town thought it was impossible for a blind man to be healed. They had a hard time believing that Jesus could give sight to a man who couldn't see. So the leaders brought the man into a meeting to ask him questions about what had happened and who had done it. The man couldn't answer all of the questions, but he knew one thing for sure. He said, "I was blind but now I see."

Jesus can do anything—even things that seem impossible. When He performs a miracle, it shows His amazing grace. —T.M.

### FUN FACT

God's "amazing grace" really changed John Newton. At one time, he was the captain of a ship that carried slaves from Africa to England. But after John Newton became a Christian, he realized how wrong slavery was, and he worked to stop slavery in England.

### READ MORE

Read Mark 7:31–35 to find out about another man who Jesus healed. How did Jesus heal this man?

# No Other Gods

**While the Israelites** were living in the wilderness, Moses would talk to God at a place called Mount Sinai. One day when Moses was on the mountain, God reminded Moses of the laws He wanted the people to obey. God told Moses to write the Ten Commandments on two flat pieces of stone, called tablets.

Moses was on the mountain with God for a long time. The people thought he wasn't coming back, so they went to Moses' brother, Aaron. They told Aaron they wanted a god they could see. So Aaron asked for all their gold jewelry. He melted the gold and made an idol in the shape of a calf. Then the people danced and celebrated in front of the golden calf.

As Moses came down the mountain, he heard the celebration and saw the golden calf. He was so angry that he smashed the stone tablets on the ground. Moses was angry that the people had turned away from God so quickly. He was angry at his brother for being a bad leader. Moses ground up the golden calf and mixed the powder into the people's drinking water!

"I am the LORD your God. I brought you out of Egypt. That is the land where you were slaves. Do not put any other gods in place of me. Do not make statues of gods that look like anything in the sky or on the earth or in the waters."

**EXODUS 20:2–4 NIRV**

## I will obey and worship God.

God was angry too. He was the one who had helped the people escape from Egypt. He was the one who had sent the people bread from heaven. God sent a kind of disease called a plague on the people because they had worshipped the golden calf. Many people died because of their disobedience.

God is Creator of all and wants to be our only God. He is worthy of all of our worship. He doesn't want us to put any other thing ahead of Him. When we choose to obey God and follow leaders who obey Him, He is pleased. —C.B.

### FUN FACT

An enemy of Israel, the Philistines, once put a statue of their false god Dagon in front of God's ark of the covenant. In the morning, the statue had fallen on its face and broke into pieces!

### READ MORE

What did God tell Moses to do in Exodus 34:1–4?

# Be Still

> "Be still, and know that I am God! I will be honored by every nation. I will be honored throughout the world."
>
> PSALM 46:10 NLT

**The world can be a busy,** noisy place. We listen to music, click the keys on the computer, and turn on the television. Motorcycles roar, cars honk their horns, and trains blow their whistles. Kids have school and sports and friends and chores. The sound and activity never end!

But in the middle of our noisy busyness, God is there. He wants us to take time to be still. He wants us to spend time thinking of Him.

It can be hard to think about God with so much noise and busyness. That's why it's so important to turn off the sound and "unplug" for a while. Turn off the television, the music, and the computer. Open your Bible or a Bible storybook and read in a quiet place. Talk to God and tell Him everything that's going on in your life. Praise Him and thank Him for all He does for you. Then be quiet and listen.

*I will take time to be still with God.*

You might hear some sounds from God's creation, things you don't usually notice. You might hear the wind rustling through the trees or a bird chirping or the gurgling of a stream. Let those quiet sounds remind you how close God is to you. He is always nearby, but when you're busy, it's easy to forget.

You can be busy with good things. But the best thing is being still with God. —C.B.

## FUN FACT

The bush cricket in Colombia, South America, is one of the noisiest insects in the world. The male cricket can chirp as loud as a power saw when it rubs its wings together.

## READ MORE

Psalm 119:97–105 lists some of the blessings that come from reading God's Word. Read the verses to find out what they are.

# Pick Me

**Sometimes during class,** a teacher will ask for a volunteer. She might need help with the lesson, or she might want someone to join her in passing out treats. When it's something exciting that all the students want to do, they wave their hands in the air and say, "Pick me! Pick me!" It's fun to be selected for a special assignment!

> Then I heard the voice of the Lord. He said, "Who will I send? Who will go for us?" I said, "Here I am. Send me!"
>
> ISAIAH 6:8 NIRV

Isaiah was a man who was selected for a very special assignment. He became God's messenger to tell the Israelites about the coming birth of Jesus. Isaiah was very close to God and even saw visions of heaven. God spoke to Isaiah and said He was looking for a volunteer. God wanted someone to be His messenger— and Isaiah said with excitement, "Send me!" Isaiah could have asked God to send someone else, but he wanted to be picked. Isaiah wanted to be obedient.

## I can choose to be a part of God's work.

God gives all Christians an opportunity to be part of a special assignment. When we have believed in Jesus as our Savior, God asks us to share the good news about Jesus with others. Just like a teacher asking for a volunteer in a classroom, God loves it when His followers reply with excitement.

When God asks you to be part of His work, you can respond like Isaiah. With joy you can say, "Pick me!" —T.M.

### READ MORE

Read Matthew 4:18–22.
How did Peter, Andrew, James, and John respond when Jesus invited them to be a part of his work?

### FUN FACT

The United States and Brazil send out the most Christian missionaries each year. And both countries receive the most Christian missionaries, too!

# When I Grow Up

Trust in the LORD with all your heart; do not depend on your own understanding. Seek his will in all you do, and he will show you which path to take.

**PROVERBS 3:5–6 NLT**

**One day a mother asked** her three-year-old son, "What do you want to be when you grow up?" He thought for a minute and said, "A daddy!"

What do you say when people ask you that question? Do you want to be a teacher or a scientist? Would you like to work with computers? Some kids want to be doctors or nurses or missionaries. Maybe you'd like to be a construction worker and build schools and hospitals. Police officers and firefighters have jobs that protect people. If you like music, you might want to be a songwriter or a worship leader.

It's fun to imagine what you will be someday. But you don't have to decide right now. Most kids figure that out when they get older. And you don't have to worry about it! If you love God and keep learning about Him and obeying Him, He will show you what He wants you to do.

Teacher?
Scientist?
Builder?

**God will help me know what He wants me to be.**

God created you for a special purpose. And He will help you to know what that purpose is. Maybe it will become clear when you are in high school or college. Sometimes you might not know God's purpose until later. Even after adults choose a job, God sometimes leads them to do something else. Someone might go to school to become a teacher and end up being a writer. Another person might study to be a lawyer, then become a pastor.

The important thing is to ask God to show you what He wants you to do. Let Him guide you. He will help you to decide. —C.B.

## FUN FACT

One of the world's fastest growing jobs is software developer. People in this job create video games and the computer programs that run on cell phones.

## READ MORE

What does Proverbs 16:9 say about God and your future?

> "The LORD does not look at the things people look at. People look at the outward appearance, but the LORD looks at the heart."
>
> **1 SAMUEL 16:7 NIV**

# God Looks Inside

**Do you know** someone who is good-looking? Sometimes people admire others who are good-looking. But God says there's a much better way to see people.

Samuel was a prophet and judge of Israel. God told Samuel to see a man named Jesse, because one of Jesse's sons was going to be the next king of Israel. When Samuel went to Jesse's house, he met seven of Jesse's sons. Samuel thought the young men were tall and handsome. But none of these men were God's choice to be the next king.

God knew what Samuel was thinking. So God told Samuel not to look at the outside of a person. That's not what God looks at! God knows what is in a person's heart, and that is what matters to Him.

*It's what's in my heart that matters to God.*

Samuel asked Jesse if he had any more sons. So Jesse told Samuel about his youngest son, David, who was out taking care of sheep. When David came in, God told Samuel that this was the man He had chosen. Samuel anointed David—that means he poured oil on David's head—to show that someday David would be king.

God didn't choose David because he was the strongest or tallest or most handsome. David was chosen because he loved God. That is how God looks at people. He doesn't care how tall you are or what color eyes or hair you have. When you love God, He sees what's in your heart. And that is what matters to Him. —C.B.

## FUN FACT

In Exodus 30:22–25, God gave Moses a recipe for making a special "anointing oil." It included several spices, like cinnamon, blended with olive oil.

## READ MORE

What does Isaiah 53:2–3 say about Jesus' looks while He was on the earth?

> "So you must go
> and make disciples of
> all nations. Baptize
> them in the name of
> the Father and of
> the Son and of the
> Holy Spirit."
>
> MATTHEW 28:19 NIRV

# Three in One

**Before Jesus went** back to heaven, He told His disciples to travel all over the world to tell people about Him. He told the disciples to baptize believers in the name of the Father, the Son, and the Holy Spirit. Those are three names that refer to God.

There is only one God, but there are three "persons" to God. This is called the Trinity. If that's hard to understand, it's okay! The Trinity can be confusing because we have human minds that can't fully understand what God is like.

When Jesus lived on earth He said that He was the Son of God. He also said, "I and the Father are one" (John 10:30). We know that Jesus is the Son of God, but Jesus also is God. Then Jesus told His followers that after He went to heaven, God would send a helper called the Holy Spirit. The Holy Spirit is the third "person" of God, the one who lives inside us when we accept Jesus as Savior. After Jesus went to heaven, the Holy Spirit gave the disciples power to continue the work of Jesus.

## I believe in the Trinity.

God wants us to have faith in Him. Faith is believing in something even when it's hard to understand. And since there are some things we cannot fully understand about God, we need faith!

Even though it's hard to understand or explain the Trinity, we can believe it by faith. We can know in our hearts that is it true. —C.B.

### FUN FACT

Pentecost is the day that God sent the Holy Spirit to fill the hearts of believers (see Acts 2:1–4). Each year, Pentecost Sunday comes fifty days after Easter Sunday. The name Pentecost comes from the Greek word for "fifty."

### READ MORE

Read Matthew 3:16–17 to find out what happened when Jesus was baptized.

# Hosanna

**Do you enjoy parades?** One time, Jesus and His disciples traveled down a busy street while people all around them cheered. We remember this exciting time every year on Palm Sunday.

Jesus and His disciples were going to Jerusalem to celebrate Passover. As they got close to the city, Jesus gave two of His disciples a job. "Go to the village ahead of you," Jesus said. "As soon as you get there, you will find a donkey tied up. Her colt will be with her. Untie them and bring them to me. If anyone says anything to you, say that the Lord needs them."

The disciples did what Jesus said. They brought the donkey and colt to Jesus and placed their coats on the animals' backs. Then Jesus sat on the colt and rode it into the town.

As a way to show respect, Jesus' followers spread their coats on the ground in front of Him. They cut down branches from palm trees and spread them on the road too. They began shouting, "Hosanna to the Son of David! Blessed is the one who comes in the name of the Lord!"

When Jesus entered Jerusalem, people in the city heard the cheering. "Who is this?" they asked. The crowd answered, "This is Jesus. He is the prophet from Nazareth in Galilee. Hosanna in the highest heaven!"

> Some of the people went ahead of him, and some followed. They all shouted, "Hosanna to the Son of David!" "Blessed is the one who comes in the name of the Lord!" "Hosanna in the highest heaven!"
>
> **MATTHEW 21:9 NIRV**

## I can praise Jesus by saying "Hosanna!"

The word hosanna means, "Hooray for salvation! It's coming! It's here!" The people honored Jesus that day as their Savior. Every year we celebrate Palm Sunday the week before Easter. We too can praise Jesus by saying, "Hosanna!" —T.M.

### READ MORE

Read Zechariah 9:9. Zechariah wrote this verse five hundred years before Jesus was born. What did he say the coming king would do?

### FUN FACT

A male donkey is called a jack. A female donkey is called a jenny, and a baby donkey is called a foal.

> Let us not give up
> meeting together.
> Some are in the habit
> of doing this. Instead,
> let us cheer each
> other up with
> words of hope.
>
> **HEBREWS 10:25 NIRV**

# Let's Go to Church!

**Do you get excited** about going to church? Some churches have special programs just for kids. In other churches, families sit together during the service. Churches come in all different sizes. Some are really big, some are small, and many are in between.

After Jesus went to heaven, His followers began to meet in homes to share meals, to pray together, and to talk about Jesus. This was the beginning of "going to church." As the number of Christians grew, they needed more places to meet and began putting up church buildings.

Did you know there are places in the world where Christians are not allowed to meet for church? Sometimes, when people from other religions become Christians, they are rejected by their families. They can be put in prison or even killed for their faith. So in some of these countries Christians meet in secret places. They pray together, read the Bible, and talk about Jesus in hidden places where no one will see them.

## I will be glad when I can go to church.

Meeting for church is a freedom that many people don't have. So if you can go to church without fear of being punished, be thankful! Church is a place to join other Christians in praising and worshipping God. It's about reading the Bible together and learning more about how God wants us to live.

When it's time to go to church, get excited and be glad! It's a very special place.
—C.B.

## FUN FACT

The Sistine Chapel is a famous church in Rome, built in the 1400s. Millions of people visit the chapel every year to see paintings on the ceiling done by an artist name Michelangelo.

## READ MORE

1 Corinthians 16:19 tells us about two people who had church in their home. Read the verse to find out who they were.

# What Do You Want?

**Have you ever** wanted something really badly? Maybe you saw an exciting new game or a great pair of shoes, and you couldn't think of anything else. When you finally got what you wanted, you enjoyed it for a while. But then you got a little bored playing your game, or it got broken. Your new shoes got scuffed and dirty, or you just outgrew them. That's the way it is with things. They don't last very long. And then we want something else.

> "Seek the Kingdom of God above all else, and live righteously, and he will give you everything you need."
> MATTHEW 6:33 NLT

Jesus told the story of a young man who came to Him with a question. To show respect to Jesus, the man fell on his knees. Then he asked, "Good teacher, what must I do to get eternal life?"

The man told Jesus that he had kept all of God's commandments. But Jesus told the man he needed to do one more thing. Jesus told the man to sell everything he had, give the money to the poor, and follow Him.

## I want to put God first.

The young man turned and walked away. He was sad because he was very rich. He thought he needed things more than he needed Jesus. He hoped that being good would earn him eternal life.

It is good to be good. But that's not enough to get eternal life. Only Jesus can give us eternal life. When we love Him more than we love anything else, we'll have everything we want. —C.B.

## READ MORE
What does Matthew 6:19–21 tell us about the things we treasure?

### FUN FACT
When kids are six to ten years old, their feet grow almost a half inch (twelve millimeters) in length each year. That's why your shoes get tight!

> Why should the nations wonder where our God is? Our God is in heaven, and he does whatever he wants.
>
> PSALM 115:2–3 ERV

# One Living God

**During the time** of the Old Testament, many nations worshipped false gods. They made idols from gold and silver. Some were made of wood or stone. They made their gods with their own hands and prayed to them. At times, even the Israelites turned away from God to worship false gods.

There is only one true, living God, and He is in heaven. People did not make Him. He made us! Psalm 115 shows how silly it is to worship a man-made idol. Idols are not alive. They have mouths but they can't talk. They have eyes and ears but they can't see or hear. They have noses but they can't smell. They have hands but they can't feel. They have feet but they can't walk. They can't think or understand. They can't answer prayers or help anyone—because they are just lumps of metal or wood or stone.

## My God is alive.

Our God in heaven is the only God. He can see us and hear us. He knows what we need, and He listens to our prayers. He loves us and cares for us. He protects us and blesses us. That's because He is alive!

Aren't you glad you can believe in a God who is real? God is the only one who deserves our praise and worship. There is no other God besides Him. —C.B.

## FUN FACT

In the New International Reader's Version of the Bible, God is called "the living God" twenty-nine times!

## READ MORE

Read Psalm 115:12–13.
Whom will the Lord bless?

# It's Your Choice

**After Moses died,** Joshua was the leader of Israel. Joshua always obeyed God, and he led the people into the promised land.

> "Then choose today whom you will serve. . . . But as for me and my family, we will serve the LORD."
>
> JOSHUA 24:15 NLT

After many years, Joshua gathered the Israelites together at a place called Shechem. He reminded the people of everything God had done for them. Joshua was disappointed that many of the people had worshipped other gods. He told them it was time to make a choice.

Joshua said the people could choose to worship false gods, or they could throw away their idols and serve the Lord. Then he told them his own choice. Joshua made it clear that he and his family would serve the Lord.

The Israelites said they wanted to serve the Lord too. So Joshua wrote that down as a reminder. Then he placed a large stone by an oak tree as another reminder that the people had made a choice to serve the Lord.

*I will choose to serve the Lord.*

We all make choices every day. You might choose what clothes to wear or what snacks to eat. Many of our choices are small, but others can be very important, like choosing the right friends and the right activities.

Of all the choices you make in your life, the most important one is to love and serve God. When we ask Him, God will help us to make good choices and live the way He wants us to live. —C.B.

## FUN FACT

When Abraham left his home and traveled to the land of Canaan, the first city he came to was Shechem. Abraham built an altar to the Lord in Shechem, and God said He would give this land to Abraham's descendants.

## READ MORE

Genesis 35:1–4 tells another story of someone who made a good choice and went to Shechem. Read the verses to find out who it was.

# Special Clothes

As God's chosen people, holy and dearly loved, clothe yourselves with compassion, kindness, humility, gentleness and patience.

COLOSSIANS 3:12 NIV

**What kind** of clothes do you like to wear? If you live where it's warm, you probably wear shorts and T-shirts. If you live where it's chilly, you might wear long pants and a jacket. If you live where it's cold and snowy, you need to wear coats, warm hats, and mittens.

There are many different types of clothes. Some kids like clothes with bright colors. Others wear bold stripes or designs. And some kids wear uniforms for school. The uniforms show what school the children belong to.

Did you know the Bible talks about special clothes to wear? It doesn't mean pants or T-shirts. It's talking about how we act as God's children. We can show people we are God's children by the way we treat others.

When you say kind words to someone who is sad, it's like wearing a T-shirt that says, "I care about you." When you're humble about getting a good grade on a test, it's like wearing a hat that says, "God helps me to do my best."

When you dress yourself in the morning, you are getting ready for the day. At the same time, put on the "clothes" that the Bible talks about. You can be kind and caring. You can be patient and humble. When you put on that kind of clothing, you will truly be ready for whatever the day brings.

Just like a school uniform, your "spiritual clothes" will show others who you belong to. —C.B.

*I will clothe myself with the right things.*

## FUN FACT

People in the Bible wore clothes made from wool, linen, and animal skins. They wore sandals made from wood and leather.

## READ MORE

The Bible tells us that fine clothing does not make us beautiful. Where does 1 Peter 3:3–4 say our beauty comes from?

# No Talking

**John the Baptist** was a special part of God's plan. He was born to prepare the way for Jesus.

John's birth was a miracle. That's because his parents, Zechariah and Elizabeth, had been unable to have a baby. They both loved God very much and prayed that they would have a child.

Zechariah was a priest who served in God's temple. One day he saw an angel, and he was very afraid. But the angel, whose name was Gabriel, told Zechariah good news. Gabriel said, "Don't be afraid, Zechariah! God has heard your prayers. Your wife, Elizabeth, will have a son, and you will name him John." Gabriel told Zechariah that John would be a great man who would bring many people back to God.

> "But because you didn't believe what I said, you will be unable to talk until the day this happens. Everything will come true at the right time."
> LUKE 1:20 GW

## I will trust what God says.

Zechariah could hardly believe what he heard. So he asked Gabriel how he could be sure the news was true. Gabriel answered, "God sent me to tell you this good news. But because you didn't believe me, you will not be able to talk until these things happen." So God took away Zechariah's voice. He wasn't able to talk until baby John was born.

We can always believe what God says. Many things may seem impossible to us, but nothing is impossible for God. When you trust God's Word, it shows you have faith. You know that God will always do what He promises. —T.M.

## READ MORE

Read Genesis 18:9–15.
How did Sarah respond when she heard that she and Abraham would have a baby?

**FUN FACT**

Zechariah got his voice back shortly after his baby was born. As soon as Zechariah wrote, "His name is John," he could speak again!

> The Spirit who
> lives in you is greater
> than the spirit who
> lives in the world.
>
> 1 JOHN 4:4 NLT

# True or False

**In many countries,** the first day of April is April Fools' Day. It's a day when family members and friends play tricks on each other. One person tries to fool another by saying something that is not true. For example, your mom might say, "Guess what? You don't have school today." You might get excited and say, "Really?" Then she would say, "April fool!"

That's just a silly game people play every year on April 1. But on any day of the year, some people will say things that aren't true. When Jesus went back to heaven, His disciples received the Holy Spirit as Jesus had promised. The disciples taught about Jesus wherever they went. Many more people believed in Jesus and became Christians. But there were also false teachers who did not tell the truth. They tried to confuse Christians into believing things that were wrong. Jesus' disciple John reminded Christians that they have the Holy Spirit in them. John said that God's Spirit was

## The Holy Spirit will help me know what is true.

greater than any false teacher. God's Holy Spirit would help believers understand what was true and what was false.

When you become a Christian, you have the Holy Spirit in you too. You can ask the Spirit to help you understand what is true or false. Always remember that every word in the Bible is true. Nobody who believes the Bible is foolish!
—C.B.

### READ MORE
Read Psalm 119:160.
What does this verse say about God's Word?

**FUN FACT**
April Fools' Day is celebrated in Europe, Australia, and the United States. It became popular in the 1800s.

# All She Had

**Have you ever given** away something valuable? One day Jesus sat near the offering box in the temple as people brought their gifts of money. Rich people wanted everyone to see that they put in lots of money. But then a poor widow came in. She dropped two small coins in the money box. Together, they weren't even worth a penny!

Jesus saw what the woman had done, and He was pleased. He told His followers, "This poor widow gave only two small coins. But she gave more than the rich people gave." Then Jesus explained that even though the rich people gave a lot of money, they gave only what they didn't need. The poor widow had only two coins. She gave God all she had.

God is pleased when we give generously. He loves it when we give from our hearts—because that's how He gives. The Bible says that when we give generously, God will bless us. He will bless us with the good feeling we get from helping others. But God may bless us in other ways too.

You may not have a lot to give, but that's okay. If you get an allowance, you can put some of it into the offering at church. You could give some of your toys or clothes to a mission. You could volunteer your time to help other people.

Everything you have comes from God. Whenever you give back, God will bless you. —C.B.

## God will bless me when I will give.

### FUN FACT

In Jesus' time, metal coins were a common kind of money. Paper money didn't come into use until about a thousand years after Jesus. The Chinese were the first to use paper money.

### READ MORE

God made a promise to the Israelites if they would give Him one tenth of their crops. Read Malachi 3:10–12 to find out what God promised them.

> "In the same way
> let your light shine
> in front of people.
> Then they will see the
> good that you do and
> praise your Father in
> heaven."
>
> MATTHEW 5:16 GW

# Shine Your Light

**Lights are easy** to spot in the dark. A city at night is full of light. If you are driving into a city at nighttime, you can see its lights shining from far away. The city can't be hidden because the light shows everyone where it is.

At home in the evenings, you've probably turned on a light when you walked into a room. Lamps take away the darkness. If you turn on a lamp, you don't hide it under something and cover up the light. The reason you turned it on in the first place was so the light would shine in the room!

Jesus said that Christians are like a city built on a hill, or like a lamp in a dark room. Since Christians are filled with God's love, He wants us to display His love for everyone else to see. Just like the lights of a city shine at night, the love of God should shine

## I can shine my light.

through us. Just like a lamp removes the darkness from a room, the joy of God in our lives brightens the world around us.

God doesn't want us to hide His love and joy. He wants us to let them shine through our lives! When you are filled with God's Spirit, you can let His light show. You can help your friends pick up their toys. You can tell your parents how much you love them. You can thank your teachers for guiding you.

Jesus says others will see the good you do and praise God in heaven. It's good to shine your light! —T.M.

## FUN FACT

Polaris is one of the brightest stars in the northern sky. It is also called the North Star. Long ago sailors used this star to help them find their way as they traveled across the ocean.

## READ MORE

Read Isaiah 60:19. This verse says a time will come when the sun and moon are no longer needed. Where will the light come from instead?

# A Talking Donkey

> The donkey said to Balaam, "I'm your own donkey. You've always ridden me. Have I ever done this to you before?"
>
> NUMBERS 22:30 GW

**Balak, the king** of Moab, was worried. The Israelites had moved into his territory after defeating another country in battle. Balak was afraid the Israelites would do the same thing to his army.

So Balak sent messengers to a man named Balaam who lived nearby. Balaam was a prophet, and Balak wanted Balaam to curse the Israelites. Balak thought Balaam's words would hurt the Israelites and protect his own army.

But God told Balaam not to speak against the Israelites. Balaam was allowed to talk to Balak, but Balaam was only supposed to say what God told him.

The next day Balaam got his donkey ready for the journey to Moab. God was upset by something in Balaam's heart, so He sent an angel to stop Balaam. Balaam didn't see the angel, but his donkey did. One time the donkey tried to turn around, but Balaam became angry and forced the animal to keep going. The next time the donkey saw the angel, it moved off the road and squeezed Balaam's foot against a wall. The third time the donkey saw the angel, it just lay down on the road.

Then God did something amazing to get Balaam's attention. He made the donkey speak! After Balaam heard the donkey talk, his eyes could finally see the angel. God allowed Balaam to go to Moab, but God used Balaam to bless the Israelites rather than curse them.

## God's Word tells me the right way to go.

God wants us to obey Him. When we're going the wrong way, He will let us know. Then we can choose to turn around and go the right way.
—T.M.

### FUN FACT

Most species of parrots can be taught to say words in the language of their owners. The Congo African grey parrot is one of the best birds for speech.

### READ MORE

Look up Genesis 28:10–15 to read about another traveler who saw angels.

# Focus Your Eyes

> Keep your eyes focused on what is right. Keep looking straight ahead to what is good. Be careful what you do. Always do what is right.
>
> PROVERBS 4:25–26 ICB

**In many sports,** people use a ball to play the game. From soccer to baseball, from tennis to basketball, and from football to golf, balls are kicked, smacked, bounced, and thrown during games. Coaches tell their players to "keep your eyes on the ball." When players lose their focus and become distracted, it can mean the difference between winning and losing.

The book of Proverbs is known as one of the Bible's "wisdom books." In Proverbs 4, God gives us many wise instructions. Just like a coach tells his players to keep their eyes on the ball, God tells us to keep our eyes focused on what is right. If we look away from what is right and good, we can become distracted. We can also be tempted to sin.

Many things can pull our eyes from what is right. Satan will use the things of this world to distract you. He wants to get you to look away from God. That's why it's so important to be careful in everything you do.

*I will keep my eyes focused on what is right.*

You are careful when you choose good friends and good activities. You are careful when you stay close to God by reading His Word and praying every day. And you are careful when you keep your eyes away from anything that would displease God.

The instructions in Proverbs are written to help us understand the wisdom of God. When we listen to God's wisdom, we can avoid the pain of bad decisions. —C.B.

## READ MORE

What other words of wisdom are found in Proverbs 4? Read verses 20 through 24 to find some.

### FUN FACT

The earliest rubber balls were developed by the Mayans about sixteen hundred years before Jesus was born. The Mayans, who lived in Central America, combined the sap from the rubber tree with the juice of morning glory vines.

# Live for Jesus

For to me, living means living for Christ, and dying is even better. But if I live, I can do more fruitful work for Christ. So I really don't know which is better.

**PHILIPPIANS 1:21–22 NLT**

**What do you think** it would be like to be in prison?

The apostle Paul spent a lot of time in prison, but not because he had done bad things. He was locked up for preaching about Jesus! When he wrote his letter to Christians in a city called Philippi, he wasn't sure what was going to happen to him. Many Christians were being killed because of their faith in Jesus. And Paul knew the Roman emperor might kill him too.

Instead of being afraid, though, Paul had courage. He knew that if he died, he would be with Jesus. That was an exciting thought! But Paul also knew that as long as he lived, he could keep working for God. He could spend his time telling others about Jesus and teaching them how to become Christians.

God had given Paul a very special job. Paul knew he was supposed to carry the good news of Jesus to all kinds of people. Paul encouraged people who were already following Jesus. He told everyone he met what Jesus had done for him. He even talked to his own prison guards about Jesus! Paul lived every day for God's work.

Just like Paul, you can use each day to live for Jesus. Think of your life as a special job. You can tell others about the great things God does for you, and ask them to follow Him too. When you live for Jesus, every day is important! —T.M.

## I can live for Jesus.

**FUN FACT**

Some people think Paul spent about six years in prison for preaching about Jesus. But he never stopped praising God or telling those around him how to be saved from their sins.

**READ MORE**

Read Acts 16:16–34 to learn about a jailer who guarded Paul in prison. What did the jailer learn from Paul?

# No Paybacks

**It's hard when** people hurt us. When someone does something unkind, it's easy to want to get even with that person. You might think it would feel good to say something mean in return. Or maybe doing something unkind would even the score. Many times, fighting back feels like the only way to win.

> Don't pay people back with evil for the evil they do to you. Focus your thoughts on those things that are considered noble.
>
> ROMANS 12:17 GW

But the Bible tells us to do something totally different. Instead of adding your unkind words to their unkind words, God tells us to be noble. That means we do what is honest and right and honorable. When people do things that hurt us, we can choose to respond kindly. We can even pray for them! None of this means we say that what they did was okay. It just means we choose to forgive them.

*I can choose to be kind.*

People did a lot of unkind things to Jesus. They called Him names and said mean things about Him. They made fun of Him. Before He was nailed to the cross, Jesus was beat up and spit on. But He never did or said anything hurtful to those who were hurting Him. Jesus knew it wasn't His place to punish those who were unkind. That was up to God. Jesus always lived His life in obedience to God, doing the right thing.

We can follow Jesus' example. Repaying unkindness with kindness can be very hard to do. But God will give us the strength to do it if we ask Him for help. When we choose to be kind, we honor God.
—T.M.

## READ MORE

Look up Luke 6:27–28 in your Bible. What does Jesus say we should do to those who are mean to us?

## FUN FACT

Some people have set up special times to remind everyone to be kind. There's a "Random Acts of Kindness Week" in February. And "World Kindness Day" is held in November.

# Can't Run Away

But Jonah got up and went in the opposite direction to get away from the LORD.

**JONAH 1:3 NLT**

**God told a prophet** named Jonah to go to a city called Nineveh. The people in Nineveh were doing many evil things, and God wanted Jonah to preach to them.

But Jonah didn't want to go to Nineveh. Instead of obeying God, Jonah got on a ship going to Tarshish. It was heading in the opposite direction!

Jonah thought he could run away from God. But while Jonah was on the ship, God sent a strong wind which made the sea very rough. Even the sailors were afraid they were going to drown. When the sailors figured out that God had sent the rough seas because of Jonah, Jonah told them to toss him into the water. They did what Jonah said and the sea became calm. The sailors were amazed at God's power. But something even more amazing was coming.

God sent a huge fish to swallow Jonah! He was in the belly of the fish for three days and nights, and he prayed to God. So God made the fish spit out Jonah onto the shore.

Once again, God told Jonah to go to Nineveh. This time Jonah obeyed. He preached to the people, and they were sorry for what they had done wrong. When they cried out to God, He forgave them.

Sometimes God gives us a job that seems big or scary. But if we trust Him, He will always give us the power to do whatever He asks. —C.B.

When God wants to use me, I will obey.

### FUN FACT

Some people think that the sperm whale or the great white shark might be the "great fish" of Jonah's story. They're both big creatures that swim in the Mediterranean Sea.

### READ MORE

How did Jesus compare himself to Jonah in Matthew 12:40–41?

# Beautiful Music

**An orchestra** is made up of many different instruments. The violin, cello, and bass are some of the stringed instruments. The woodwinds include the flute, clarinet, and oboe. The brass family has trumpets, French horns, and tubas. The percussion family has a long list of instruments including drums, chimes, and xylophones. Each instrument makes its own special sound, but when they all play together, there is beautiful music.

> In his grace, God has given us different gifts for doing certain things well.
>
> **ROMANS 12:6 NLT**

People are sort of like those different instruments. God created us to have our own special talents and abilities. He wants us to work together and help each other out. Because we're all different, we need each other. Together, we're better than we can be all by ourselves.

I will use my talents to help others and serve God.

If you sing or play the piano, you can use your talents to help others praise God. If you are good at math, you can help a friend with her homework. If you have an eye for design, you can use your skills to create posters for school. If you are good at sports, you can help others practice so they can get better. Or maybe your talent is being kind to someone who just needs a friend.

Whatever gift or ability you have, God gave it to you to use. And when we all use our talents together, it's like a beautiful symphony. —C.B.

### READ MORE

Read 1 Corinthians 12:4–7 to find out where our gifts and talents come from.

## FUN FACT

A boy named Curtis Elton, from London, England, began playing the piano when he was three. By the time he was nine years old, he was the youngest person to earn a college-level music diploma.

> Without faith it is impossible to please God, because anyone who comes to him must believe that he exists and that he rewards those who earnestly seek him.
>
> HEBREWS 11:6 NIV

# Pleasing God

**The Old Testament** tells the story of a man named Enoch. He was the great-grandfather of Noah and lived before the great flood God sent on the world.

We don't know much about Enoch. But we do know that he loved God. The Bible says Enoch "walked faithfully" with God. That means he believed in God and obeyed Him. Enoch kept his faith in God at a time when many people on earth were turning away from God.

We learn a little more about Enoch in the New Testament. The eleventh chapter of Hebrews is sometimes called "The Faith Hall of Fame." It lists people from the Old Testament who were known for their faith in God. Hebrews 11:5 says that Enoch was known as a person who pleased God. He is listed with famous people of faith like Noah, Abraham, Isaac, Jacob, Joseph, and Moses.

## My faith pleases God.

The Bible says that without faith we cannot please God. But people who have faith and look for God will be rewarded. Because of his faith, Enoch pleased God—and Enoch was rewarded. God didn't let Enoch die! Enoch lived for 365 years, walking faithfully with God. Then he disappeared because God took him away.

We live in a time when many people are turning away from God. But you can please God like Enoch did. Have faith in God and look for Him every day! —C.B.

### FUN FACT

A hall of fame is a building, room, or hallway that displays plaques, pictures, and other items in honor of famous people. Halls of fame honor people like pilots, athletes, musicians, actors, and even circus performers!

### READ MORE

Read 2 Kings 2:6–14 to learn about another man of faith who never died. How did God take this man to heaven?

# Train like an Athlete

**Did you know** that sporting events like the Olympic Games go all the way back to Bible times?

Just like today, sports were popular around the time Jesus lived. And just like today, athletes had to train very hard. They committed their whole lives to get ready for a few sporting events. They got their hearts pumping with exercises like jumping jacks and running. They worked to strengthen their muscles. They even had their own trainers to help them get into shape for the games. Athletes did all of this work hoping to become the best and win their events. Winners were given crowns made of leaves or red ribbons to wear around their heads.

In the Bible, the apostle Paul wrote about athletes. He said that Christians should follow their example. Just like athletes spend time and energy to train for the games, Christians should spend time and energy to live well for God.

When you spend time reading God's Word, you can grow stronger as a Christian. When you listen to Sunday school teachers and pastors, you can learn to understand God's truth. The more you "train," the more prepared you'll be to tell others about Jesus and the great things God has done. —T.M.

> All who take part in the games train hard. They do it to get a crown that will not last. But we do it to get a crown that will last forever.
>
> **1 CORINTHIANS 9:25 NIRV**

## I can train like an athlete for God.

### READ MORE
Read 2 Timothy 2:5.
Besides training hard, what else does an athlete have to do to win a crown?

### FUN FACT
Olympic gymnasts train up to forty hours per week. That's like a full-time job.

# Sad Sisters

> "This sickness will not end in death. No, it is for God's glory. God's Son will receive glory because of it."
>
> JOHN 11:4 NIRV

**A man named Lazarus** was very sick. He lived in a town called Bethany with his two sisters, Mary and Martha. They were all friends of Jesus.

Mary and Martha sent a message to Jesus, asking Him to come and heal their brother. But Lazarus died before Jesus got to Bethany. When Martha heard Jesus was nearby, she went out to meet Him. "If you had been here sooner," she said, "my brother would not have died."

"Your brother will live again," Jesus told Martha. She thought Jesus was talking about a day in the future when all believers will rise from the dead. But that's not what Jesus meant.

Then Mary came to see Jesus too. When Jesus saw how sad Mary and Martha were, He was sad. Jesus asked the sisters to take Him to Lazarus's grave. The body had been put into a cave, with a heavy stone rolled across the opening.

## Jesus did amazing things because He's the Son of God.

Jesus ordered the stone to be taken away. He had planned something exciting!

Jesus prayed to God the Father out loud, so everyone would hear Him. He wanted the people to know that God was going to show His power. Then Jesus said, "Lazarus, come out!" And just like that, Lazarus came out of the grave. He was alive again!

Many people had come to comfort Mary and Martha. When they saw Jesus' miracle, they put their faith in Him. God put stories like this into the Bible so we could have faith in Jesus too. When we believe in Him, we get a new life too—eternal life. —C.B.

## FUN FACT

Lazarus is a boy's name that comes from the Hebrew language. It means "God is my help."

## READ MORE

Matthew 28:1–7 tells about another stone that was rolled away from a grave. How did the stone move? What happened to the person who'd been in the grave?

# Lifeguard on Duty

**Going swimming** at the beach or in a pool can be lots of fun! When you know how to swim, it's fun to jump in and splash around—especially if the water is nice and warm.

Where does my help come from? My help comes from the LORD. He is the Maker of heaven and earth.

**PSALM 121:1–2 NIRV**

If you have ever been swimming at a public beach or pool, you may have seen a sign that says Lifeguard on Duty. The sign lets swimmers know that if they need help, someone is nearby to rescue them. When the lifeguard sees swimmers struggling, he will dive into the water and save them.

God is like a lifeguard for our everyday struggles. Psalm 121 tells us that God gives us help. He is always on duty to rescue us when we need it. If you face a hard test in school, God is there to help you through it. When you get sick or hurt, God is there to rescue you. Maybe you are having problems with your friends or family. God is there to help you through those problems, too.

*My help comes from God.*

God made heaven and earth. Nothing is too hard for Him. Ask God for help whenever you need it because He is always listening. When things are difficult, you can ask yourself the question from today's verse: "Where does my help come from?" The answer is God!

No matter what you may need help with, remember that God is your helper. He is always there. —T.M.

## READ MORE

Read Psalm 121:1–8. According to verse 8, how long will God watch over us and guard us?

## FUN FACT

Many people around the world have joined lifeguard clubs that volunteer to protect swimmers in the oceans. In Australia, lifeguards for surfers are called clubbies.

# Role Models

**Have you heard of Titus?** He was one of the apostle Paul's closest friends, and he led a church on an island called Crete.

Paul told Titus that it was important for younger Christians to have role models. Paul gave Titus many instructions about leading the church and teaching people how to help others. Paul told Titus, "Teach the older women to train the younger women to love their husbands and children and take care of their homes. The older women should be examples of how to be wise and pure."

Paul told Titus to teach the older men to have self-control and be worthy of respect. They needed to be good examples to younger men by having strong faith and being filled with love and patience. Paul knew that if the adults were good role models, the younger people would learn to be better Christians. Then everyone would become stronger in their faith. The church would be a place where people would grow to be like Jesus.

The same thing is true today. It is good to have role models in the church and in your home. Do you know someone who sets a good example for you to follow? Do you have someone to look up to? Maybe your role model is a parent, a grandparent, or a teacher. If you know some older people who love Jesus, you can learn from their example.

And you don't have to wait until you're a grown-up to be a role model to others. If you have younger friends or siblings, ask God to help you be a good example right now. —T.M.

## It's good to have someone to look up to.

### FUN FACT

A study of students in the United States asked teenagers who they have as a role model. Most of the students said it was a family member!

### READ MORE

Read 1 Timothy 5:1–2.
How does the Bible say we should treat those who are older or younger than we are?

> "But the gate is
> small and the road
> is narrow that lead
> to life. Only a few
> people find it."
>
> MATTHEW 7:14 NIRV

# A Narrow Road

**If you've ever gone hiking,** you know what it's like to stay on a path. You follow the trail wherever it goes.

Sometimes the path is wide and flat. It's easy to walk on that kind of path. Other times the path becomes very narrow. It can become tricky when the path winds its way up a hill or mountain. As the trail gets steeper, you have to be very careful with every step you take. You have to stay focused and really watch where you're going. But if you stick with it, there's often a beautiful view at the end of the trail.

Jesus told His disciples that following Him was like walking a narrow path or roadway. It isn't always easy. Sometimes it's hard to stay focused on what you're doing. A lot of people give up. Sometimes it seems easier not to follow Jesus, just like it's easier to take a wide and flat path.

*Following Jesus is like walking a narrow road.*

But when we choose to accept God's forgiveness, we become His children. He gives us the strength to follow Him. No matter how hard the path of following Jesus may seem, it's worth it! Just let Him lead you one step at a time. —T.M.

### 🌸 READ MORE
Read Psalm 119:105.
What can we use to "light" the path of our lives?

### FUN FACT
The Caminito del Rey trail in Spain is considered one of the most dangerous paths in the world. It's a walkway built onto the sides of steep cliffs. The Caminito del Rey is only three feet wide (one meter) and hangs 330 feet (one hundred meters) in the air.

# Nobody's Perfect

Everyone has sinned.
No one measures up to
God's glory.
ROMANS 3:23 NIRV

**Have you ever gotten an A+** on a test because you answered all the questions right? In some sporting events where judges give points, a 10 is a perfect score. It's a good feeling to do something perfectly! When we say something is perfect, we mean that it's exactly right.

God is perfect and He created a perfect world. He did everything exactly right. But the world did not stay perfect for long. Adam and Eve, the first people God made, brought sin into the world when they disobeyed Him. But it wasn't just Adam and Eve who did something wrong. The Bible says everyone sins. Even good people have sin in their lives. Sometimes we sin with our words or our thoughts. Sometimes we sin in the things we do. No one can be perfect like God. Our sin keeps us away from Him.

Jesus can make me perfect before God.

That's why God sent Jesus to earth. Because He is God's Son, Jesus is the only person who could live a perfect life. Jesus never, ever sinned! But when He died on the cross, He took the punishment for all the wrong things we do. And Jesus can bring us close to God.

When we believe that only Jesus can save us, God accepts Jesus' payment for our sins. God forgives us. Even though we are still not perfect, God sees us that way. It's like we get an A+ on a test. God is our judge and gives us a perfect 10 because of Jesus. —C.B.

### FUN FACT

In 1976, Nadia Comăneci became the first female gymnast to earn a perfect score of 10 in an Olympic gymnastics event. Nadia, who was from Romania, was only fourteen years old!

### READ MORE

What does Psalm 32:1–5 tell us about having our sins forgiven?

> Imitate God, therefore, in everything you do, because you are his dear children.
>
> **EPHESIANS 5:1 NLT**

# Imitate God

**Kids like to** imitate grown-ups. Little girls play with dolls and pretend they are moms. Little boys play with fire trucks and pretend they are firefighters. Many kids try to be like their parents. If a mom plays the piano, her kids often want to play the piano too. If a dad likes to go fishing, his kids will want to go fishing. Children learn from watching their parents, and imitating their words and actions.

When Jesus was on earth, He was God in a man's body. He taught people what it means to be like God. He set an example for us to imitate. Jesus treated others with love and kindness. It didn't matter if they were young or old or rich or poor. Jesus showed love and kindness to everyone. He talked to people who weren't popular and even ate meals with them. In everything He did, Jesus showed us how to be like God.

## I want to be more like God.

The Bible tells us that we should imitate God. He is our Father and He loves us—and kids love to imitate their parents! Since God is perfect and holy, we can't be exactly like Him. But we can treat others with love and kindness the way Jesus did.

The more we know about God, the more we will be able to be like Him. —C.B.

## READ MORE

Read Romans 12:1–2 to learn how we can become more like God.

### FUN FACT

Most of a baby's learning comes by watching and imitating what other people do.

# Listen and Do

> Do what God's
> teaching says;
> do not just listen
> and do nothing.
>
> JAMES 1:22 ICB

**When your parents** tell you to do something, you hear what they say. But if you don't do what they tell you, they might say you didn't listen to them. Obedience is both hearing and doing.

Abraham is a great example of obedience. He loved his son Isaac. Isaac was the miracle baby that God had given to Abraham and his wife, Sarah. Abraham believed God's promise that Isaac's family would one day become a whole nation. But then God asked Abraham to sacrifice Isaac. God told Abraham to kill his own son!

Can you imagine how Abraham must have felt? How could God take away the son that God had promised to give him? But Abraham didn't question God. He heard God's voice and he decided to obey.

## It's important to do what the Bible says.

Abraham must have been very sad as he and Isaac walked three days to the place God told them to go. When they got there, Abraham set up an altar and put Isaac on top of it. But an angel of the Lord called out, "Abraham! Abraham! Do not hurt your son! Now I know you truly fear the Lord."

Abraham didn't just hear God's word, he obeyed it. He listened to God's command and did exactly what God told him to do. And God blessed Abraham for his obedience.

Some of the things God asks us to do are hard. But He gives us the power to do whatever jobs He has for us. When we listen, He will help us to do. —T.M.

### FUN FACT

In the New International Reader's Version of the Bible, the word *listen* appears 582 times, and the word *obey* 614 times!

### READ MORE

Read Genesis 22:15–18 to see how God blessed Abraham because of his obedience.

# Choose Your Words

**Here's an old saying** you may have heard: "Sticks and stones may break my bones, but words will never hurt me." Even though people say that a lot, it isn't really true. Words have power and they can hurt.

Unkind words stick with a person long after they were said. Sometimes people say things that they later wish they hadn't said. But words can't be taken back. That's like trying to put toothpaste back into the tube after you've squeezed it out!

But our words can affect people in a good way, too. Kind words stick with people. Kind words encourage others and build them up. Kind words have the power to help others.

> Don't say anything that would hurt another person. Instead, speak only what is good so that you can give help wherever it is needed. That way, what you say will help those who hear you.
>
> **EPHESIANS 4:29 GW**

Timothy was a young man who studied under the apostle Paul. Timothy was often encouraged by the kind words Paul wrote in his letters. In one letter, Paul told Timothy, "I always remember you in my prayers, and I thank God for you. I want to see you so I can be filled with joy." In another letter Paul said, "Timothy, you are like a son to me. Be strong in the grace we have in Christ!" Can you imagine how happy and excited Timothy must have been to read those words?

## I can choose to speak kind words.

Your words can be helpful too. You can spread happiness to others by speaking the words God gives you. The book of Proverbs says that the right words spoken at the right time are as beautiful as gold apples in a silver bowl. Those words will never hurt anyone. —T.M.

### READ MORE
What does Proverbs 16:23–24 say about the words we speak?

### FUN FACT
Most seven-year-old children know between five thousand and ten thousand words. That gives kids a lot of chances to speak kindly!

> "Don't be afraid,"
> David told him.
> "You can be sure that
> I will be kind to you
> because of your father
> Jonathan. I'll give
> back to you all of
> the land that
> belonged to your
> grandfather Saul.
> And I'll always provide
> what you need."
>
> 2 SAMUEL 9:7 NIRV

# It's Contagious

**Have you ever caught** a cold from someone in your family? Did you ever have the flu and then your mom or dad got it too? People who have a cold or flu virus are often contagious. That means others can catch what they have. But sometimes being contagious is a good thing!

David and Jonathan were best friends. Jonathan had always been kind to David, so David promised that he would show kindness to anyone in Jonathan's family. After Jonathan died, David found out that Jonathan had a disabled son who was still alive. His name was Mephibosheth. (Aren't you glad you don't have to spell that name on your school papers?)

## I will show kindness to others.

David wanted to show God's kindness to Mephibosheth, so he sent for him. When Mephibosheth saw King David, he bowed down to David to show respect. But David said to him, "Don't be afraid. I will be kind to you because of your father, Jonathan." So Mephibosheth lived in the king's palace and ate at David's table. David treated him like a son.

Kindness can be contagious, just like a cold or a flu virus. When someone is kind to you, it makes you want to be kind to them. When you are kind to others, they will want to be kind to you. We are able to show kindness to others because God was kind to us first. He wants our kindness to be contagious! —C.B.

### FUN FACT

A cold virus spreads through the air when sick people sneeze, cough, or blow their nose. A person is most contagious for the first two or three days of the cold.

### READ MORE

What does James 2:1–8 say about showing kindness?

# It's Free!

**Can you imagine** what would happen if a grocery store started giving out free food? Not just free samples, but free meat and eggs and vegetables and ice cream! Mobs of people would hurry to the store to get free food, and they would take as much as they could. Then they would tell all their friends and neighbors about it, so they could get free food too. It's fun and exciting to get something for free—especially when the free gift is really great.

> For the wages of sin is death, but the free gift of God is eternal life through Christ Jesus our Lord.
>
> **ROMANS 6:23 NLT**

The Bible tells us about a free gift that is greater than anything we can imagine. That free gift is life in heaven that lasts forever and ever! The gift is free to everyone, but you have to receive it. The way to receive the free gift is by believing in Jesus as your

*The gift of eternal life is free.*

Savior. If you tell God you're sorry for the wrong things you've done, and if you believe that Jesus is the Son of God who died on the cross for your sins, you will receive the free gift of eternal life.

There is no greater gift on earth! If you haven't received this free gift yet, you can do that right now. Tell God you are sorry for your sins and ask Jesus to be your Savior. Then tell all your friends and neighbors how they can receive this amazing gift too! —C.B.

### FUN FACT

Many food companies give away free samples at grocery stores to get people to buy their products. It's less expensive than advertising, and shoppers love getting something for free!

### READ MORE

Read John 3:16 to find out why God gives us the free gift of eternal life.

> So Abram said to Lot, "Let there be no fighting between you and me or between the men who take care of our animals, for we are brothers."
>
> **GENESIS 13:8 NLV**

# Be a Peacemaker

**Abraham and his nephew,** Lot, were running out of room. God had blessed them so much there wasn't enough space for all of their stuff on the same piece of land. Before long, Abraham's shepherds and Lot's shepherds began to argue and disagree.

So Abraham decided to do something to bring peace back to the family. Instead of joining the argument, he gave Lot a good choice. Abraham took Lot to look at all the land around their campsite. He told Lot there was plenty of room for both of their families to live. Then Abraham gave Lot the chance to pick which side of the land he wanted to live on. Abraham told Lot that he would move his own family and things to the other side. When the two men went their different ways, the fighting stopped. God blessed the land where Abraham lived and gave it to his descendants, the family that came through his son Isaac.

## I can be a peacemaker.

Do you ever get into arguments with someone in your family? Maybe, like Lot and Abraham, you share space with someone and you have a hard time getting along. It's easy to fight and disagree. But the easy way isn't always the best way.

God wants His people to live in peace. When you have God's Spirit, He helps you to live in peace with others. The next time you feel like arguing, you can choose to be a peacemaker like Abraham. You can work to find answers to your problems that work for you and the other person. When you do that, you honor God, who is the God of peace. —T.M.

### FUN FACT

The Peace Corps began in 1961. Since then over 215,000 volunteers have served people in 139 countries.

### READ MORE

Read Matthew 5:9.
What are peacemakers also called?

# What Does a Church Look Like?

"But the Most High God does not live in houses made by human hands."

**ACTS 7:48 NIRV**

**What do you think** of when you hear the word church? Maybe you imagine a brick building with a steeple or a large auditorium with rows and rows of chairs. You might think of a Sunday school room or a preacher standing on a stage. These things are all part of what we call "church." But did you know God doesn't think of His church as a building or a place? God says His church is all of the people who love Him.

After Jesus went back to heaven, His disciples and many other followers received the Holy Spirit at Pentecost. The people who followed Jesus would meet in houses to learn more about Him. They would usually share a meal together. Then someone would teach about Jesus and the people would sing songs of praise. It didn't matter where the people were meeting, God was there because His followers had the Holy Spirit living in them.

*God's church is not a building.*

It's the same way today. The places where we meet are very different. Some people go to historic church buildings with tall, beautiful ceilings. Other people gather in school auditoriums or movie theaters. Maybe you know of a church that meets in someone's house, just like the first Christians did!

No matter where Christians go to church, God is there. It doesn't matter if there are three people or three thousand, when people meet together to worship God, they are His church. —T.M.

## READ MORE

Read Isaiah 66:1–2. What kind of people does God look for?

## FUN FACT

St. Peter's Basilica in Rome is one of the largest church buildings in the world. It took more than one hundred years to build!

# A Good Listener

> God, I call out to you because you will answer me. Listen to me. Hear my prayer.
>
> PSALM 17:6 NIRV

**God told Abraham** He was going to destroy the cities of Sodom and Gomorrah because of their wickedness. Abraham was concerned because his nephew, Lot, lived in Sodom with his family. Abraham wanted God to spare the good people who lived there. So he talked to God about it, and God listened. Abraham said, "What if there are fifty good people in the city? Will you save the city because of fifty people?"

The Lord said, "If I find fifty good people in the city of Sodom, I will save it. I will save the whole place because of them."

Abraham spoke again. "What if there are only forty-five good people in the city? Will you destroy it then?"

The Lord said, "If I find forty-five good people, I will not destroy it."

"What if only forty good people are found in the city?" asked Abraham.

"If there are forty, I will not destroy it," God said.

Abraham kept lowering the number as he talked with God until they finally got down to ten. The Lord told Abraham, "If I find ten good people I will not destroy the city."

## I can talk to God about my concerns.

Abraham spent a lot of time talking to God about his concerns because he knew God would listen. You can talk to God just like Abraham did. God has time to listen to your concerns and He hears every word you say. God never gets tired of hearing from you. He loves you and cares about you. Anytime you want to talk, God will listen!
—C.B.

**FUN FACT**

Tokyo, Japan, is the world's largest city with nearly 38 million people.

**READ MORE**

Read Genesis 19:23–29 to find out what happened to the cities of Sodom and Gomorrah.

# Quick or Slow

**If you were running** the 100-meter dash, you would run as fast as you could. If you were in a rowboat on a lake when it started to rain, you would quickly row to shore. If the wind blew your hat off, you would chase after it right away. It is good to do some things quickly.

> Understand this, my dear brothers and sisters: You must all be quick to listen, slow to speak, and slow to get angry.
>
> JAMES 1:19 NLT

But some things need to be done more slowly. If you eat ice cream too quickly, you could get a headache. If you rush through your homework, you might miss part of the assignment. When you first learn to read, you go slowly and pronounce each word carefully. Sometimes it's good to be quick, but sometimes it's better to be slow.

## I will be quick to listen to God.

Did you know the Bible says there are times to be quick and times to be slow? The book of James tells us to be quick to listen to God. That means we should pay attention to His Word and obey it immediately. But then James says we should be slow to speak and slow to anger. That means that when we're upset about something, it is important to think before we say words that might hurt someone else. We have to control our anger and our temper. Those are the times when it's good to be slow.

Next time you have a problem, remember to be quick and slow. Be quick to ask God for help, and be slow to get angry. —C.B.

## **READ MORE**

What does Proverbs 17:27–28 say about being slow to speak?

## **FUN FACT**

The three-toed sloth is the slowest mammal on the earth. The cheetah is the fastest land animal in the world.

> Then the Spirit led
> Jesus into the desert
> to be tempted
> by the devil.
>
> MATTHEW 4:1 ICB

# Temptation in the Desert

**After Jesus was baptized,** He went into the desert for forty days and nights. He didn't eat anything during that time, so He was very hungry. Then the devil came and tried to get Jesus to do something wrong. That's called "temptation."

The devil said, "If you are really the Son of God, turn these rocks into bread." Jesus could have done that and stopped His hunger. But He didn't want to do what the devil said. So Jesus answered him, "It is written in the Scriptures that a person does not live by eating bread alone, but by every word that comes from the mouth of God."

Next, the devil took Jesus to the top of the temple and told Him to jump off! The devil said that if God's words were true, angels would protect Jesus. But Jesus didn't do that either. He told the devil, "It says in the Scriptures, 'Do not test the Lord your God.'"

## When He was tempted, Jesus spoke the words of God.

Finally, the devil took Jesus up a high mountain and showed Him all the kingdoms in the world. The devil said Jesus could have everything He saw if He would bow down and worship the devil. Then Jesus said, "Get away from me Satan! It is written in the Scriptures, 'You must worship the Lord your God and serve only Him!'"

Satan had lost. He went away and God's angels surrounded Jesus.

We'll all be tempted to do wrong. Even Jesus was tempted! But He never sinned by doing anything bad. When temptation comes to us, we can follow Jesus' example. Speaking the Scriptures will help us remember God's strength and love—and He will help us to do right. —T.M.

## FUN FACT

Some people have gone without food for more than two months. But people can survive only three to five days without water.

## READ MORE

Read Hebrews 2:18.
Because Jesus was tempted, what is He able to do for us when we are tempted?

# Three Ways to Love God

> Israel, listen to me. The LORD is our God. The LORD is the one and only God. Love the LORD your God with all your heart and with all your soul. Love him with all your strength.
>
> **DEUTERONOMY 6:4–5 NIRV**

**After Moses received** the Ten Commandments from God, he gave them to the Israelites. When Moses had finished explaining these rules, he ended with one final command. Many years later, Jesus said this was the greatest commandment in the Bible. The rule said that God is the only true God, and we are supposed to love Him in three ways: with all of our heart, with all of our soul, and with all of our strength.

When we love God with all our heart, we choose to act in ways that show we are committed to Him. It doesn't mean we have a warm fuzzy feeling all the time. But it does mean we speak kind words and show respect to others. We spend time learning about God and praising Him.

When we love God with all our soul, we give our lives to Him. We honor God with our bodies and our minds. We try to respect God in everything that we do, and we stay committed to Him.

When we love God with all our strength, we use what we have for Him. We give our possessions and our abilities in ways that honor God by serving others.

*I will love God with my heart, soul, and strength.*

These verses are called a "command," which sounds like something we have to do. But when we really know God, we'll want to love Him with all our heart, soul, and strength. Loving God will be a joy to us—because He loved us with his heart, soul, and strength first! —T.M.

### READ MORE

Look up Matthew 22:35–40 in your Bible. When Jesus answered a question from a Pharisee, He said the Shema was the greatest commandment. What did Jesus say was the second greatest rule that God gave?

### FUN FACT

Jewish people call Deuteronomy 6:4 the Shema, the Hebrew word for "hear." Many write it on a piece of paper and hang it on their doorposts.

# Leave Home

The LORD said to
Abram, "Leave your
land, your relatives,
and your father's
home. Go to the land
that I will show you."

**GENESIS 12:1 GW**

**In Genesis, we learn** about a man named Abram whose name was later changed to Abraham. He lived in a land called Haran with his father's family. One day God told Abram to leave Haran. God didn't tell Abram where to go. God just told Abram to leave his home and his relatives. God said He would lead Abram to another place.

Abram didn't ask questions. He didn't argue with God or tell God he didn't want to go. Abram just packed up his stuff and obeyed. He took his wife, Sarai, and his nephew, Lot, and all of their servants. They traveled to a place called Shechem in the land of Canaan. While they were there, God promised Abram that He would someday give this land to Abram's descendants. So Abram built an altar to God and worshipped Him.

Have you ever had to move to another place? Sometimes families move across town, and sometimes they move to another country. Sometimes people change churches or schools. Most people have a reason to move. They might want to be closer to friends or relatives. They might want a new job or a different house. Moving to another place can be exciting, but it can also be scary. So if you ever have to move, remember the story of Abram. You might not understand just why you have to move. But God may have very good things for you in your new place. —T.M.

*I will go where God leads my family.*

### READ MORE

Read the promise God gave to Abram in Genesis 12:1–3. What did God say He would do for Abram?

# Keep Adding

**When children are** very young, they are taught how to count. Then, when they're a little older, they learn how to add numbers together. One plus one equals two. Two plus two equals four. Any time you add one number to another, the sum is larger than each of the numbers you started with. You can even add together things that are not numbers. If you add cocoa to milk, you get chocolate milk. If you add peanut butter, jelly, and bread, you get a yummy sandwich. When we add things together, we expect to get something bigger or better.

> You should try very hard to add goodness to your faith. To goodness, add knowledge.
>
> **2 PETER 1:5 NIRV**

The Bible talks about things we can add together. We start with our faith—believing that God loves us and that Jesus died on the cross for our sins. But the Bible says we can add other things to our faith, things like goodness and knowledge.

*I will keep adding to my faith.*

The early Christians were good examples of this. They met together in the temple every day and shared everything they had with each other. They wanted to learn more about God and be good to others. Because they added knowledge and goodness to their faith, more and more people were being saved.

The more we read the Bible and learn about God, the more knowledge we will have. When we are good to others, they will see the love of God in our actions. When we keep adding goodness and knowledge to our faith, others will see how great God is! —C.B.

## FUN FACT

The abacus is a very old counting tool. It was invented before our modern written number system. But it is still used by business people in some parts of Asia and Africa.

## READ MORE

Read Acts 2:41–47 to find out how the early Christians added to their faith.

> The man got up and took his mat. Then he walked away while everyone watched. All the people were amazed. They praised God and said, "We have never seen anything like this!"
>
> **MARK 2:12 NIRV**

# Four Good Friends

**When Jesus began** doing miracles, crowds of people followed Him wherever He went. One day He was teaching at a house in the town of Capernaum. The house was so crowded there was no more room for people to stand.

Four men came to the house carrying a disabled friend on a mat. The man could not walk. His four friends knew that Jesus could heal the man, but they couldn't even get near the door to the house. There were just too many people.

Then the four men had an idea. They went up to the roof of the house and made a hole in it! They carried their friend on his mat up to the roof. Then they lowered him down through the roof so he would be right in front of Jesus.

Jesus saw that the men had great faith. He told the one on the mat that his sins were forgiven. Then Jesus said, "Pick up your mat and go home." As the people watched, the man stood up, picked up his mat, and walked!

## I will help my friends to know Jesus.

Everyone was amazed and praised God. The people had never seen anything like that before.

Those four men brought their friend to Jesus because they knew Jesus could help him. They did whatever they could do to make sure their friend got to see Jesus.

Have you ever brought a friend into your home or church? You can't bring them to Jesus in person, since He is in heaven now! But you can take your friends to places where they can learn about Jesus. You can do whatever it takes to bring your friends to Jesus. —C.B.

## FUN FACT

The roof in this story was probably made of leaves, bark, and dirt on top of wooden beams.

## READ MORE

Matthew 8:5–13 tells the story of another man who had faith in Jesus. Read the story to find out how Jesus healed this man's servant.

# Ask, Seek, Knock

**Jesus used everyday examples** to help people understand more about God. One day He said to a crowd of people, "If a son asks his father for a fish, would the man give his boy a snake? Or if the boy asks his father for an egg, would he give him a scorpion?"

A loving father would never treat his son that way! Jesus said this to help the people understand that God would give them good things if they asked. Jesus was not talking about expensive clothing or fancy jewels. He was talking about good spiritual things like knowing more about God or having the Holy Spirit's wisdom.

We can ask God to help us understand the Bible when we read it. We can ask God to help us love others the way He wants us to. We can ask God for Christian friends and a good church to go to. When we ask for good things in prayer, it's like we're knocking on God's door. After we ask, we need to seek. To seek means to look for ways that you can learn more about God. Look for ways that you can help others. Look for friends and a good church to attend.

> "So I say to you: Ask and it will be given to you; seek and you will find; knock and the door will be opened to you."
>
> LUKE 11:9 NIV

## I will ask God for good things.

God never gets tired of us asking for good things. So keep asking. God will hear and answer you. Keep seeking and you will find God.

Like a father gives good gifts to his son, God gives good gifts to His children. —C.B.

### READ MORE
What does Jeremiah 29:12–13 tell us about seeking God?

### FUN FACT
Scorpions are poisonous creatures that are common in the area where Jesus lived. They are shaped like lobsters and are usually between two and three inches long (five to seven centimeters).

# Mustard Seeds

**Jesus and His disciples** once walked up to a crowd of people. A man in the crowd came to Jesus and said, "Lord, show kindness to my son." The man explained to Jesus that the boy had many health problems. The man told Jesus, "I brought my son to your disciples, and they could not heal him." Jesus told the man to bring the boy to Him. Then Jesus spoke healing words and the boy got better right away.

Later, the disciples asked Jesus questions in private. The disciples wanted to know why they couldn't heal the boy, even though they had tried. Jesus told His followers that they didn't believe in God as strongly as they should. He told them, "If you have faith like a grain of mustard seed, you will say to this mountain, 'Move from here to there,' and it will move. Nothing will be impossible for you."

**God can use a small amount of faith to do big things.**

Mustard seeds are tiny. They're less than one tenth of an inch around (one or two millimeters)! But when a mustard seed is planted and watered, it can grow into a large plant. Some mustard trees grow to be over eight feet tall (two meters).

Jesus used the mustard seed as an example to teach His disciples an important lesson. A mustard seed shows us that something great can come out of something very small.

We don't have to be a certain age or have special talents. If we have the faith of a mustard seed and place that faith in God, He can use us to do great things. —T.M.

## FUN FACT

Of all the countries in the world, Canada, Nepal, and the Ukraine produce the most mustard seeds.

## READ MORE

Read Nahum 1:4–5.
How does nature respond to God's voice?

# It Never Runs Out

**Have you ever run out** of something you needed? Maybe it was time to brush your teeth, but there was no toothpaste left. Or maybe you wanted to make a sandwich, but the bread was all gone. Many things we use every day run out. Then we either have to buy more at the store or find something else to use.

> The LORD's love never ends. His mercies never stop. They are new every morning. LORD, your loyalty is great.
>
> **LAMENTATIONS 3:22–23 ICB**

But two things that God gives us will never run out. One is His love. The other is His mercy.

After God brought the Israelites out of Egypt, they turned away from Him over and over again. Whether they were in the desert or the promised land, the people often followed false gods. They disobeyed the true God in many ways. But God never stopped loving the Israelites, because His love never runs out. When the people told God they were sorry, He showed them mercy. That means He didn't punish them the way they deserved. God's mercy never runs out either.

## God's love and mercy never run out.

The love and mercy God had for the Israelites is the same love and mercy He has for you. Like a river that just keeps flowing, God's love never ends. Like the sun that brings us a new morning, God's mercies are new every day. His love and mercy will go on and on forever and ever.

When you wake up in the morning, remember that God has a never-ending supply of love and mercy for you. Why not thank Him for His love and mercy each new day? —T.M.

## **FUN FACT**

Chocolate, bacon, and goat cheese are three foods that may someday run out—or at least be harder to find. Why? Lots of people want them, but they're becoming harder and more expensive to make.

## **READ MORE**

What does Psalm 36:5–10 tell us about God's love and how far it reaches?

# One Grateful Man

One of them, when
he saw that he was
healed, came back
to Jesus, shouting,
"Praise God!"

LUKE 17:15 NLT

**Jesus was on His way** to Jerusalem. He was traveling through a small village when ten men shouted to get His attention. The men had leprosy. That's a disease that causes bad sores on the skin. To keep the disease from spreading, people who had leprosy were not allowed to go near other people. But the ten lepers knew that Jesus could heal them, so they yelled out, "Jesus! Master! Show kindness to us!"

Jesus told the ten lepers to go and show themselves to the priest at the temple. If the priest saw that the men were healed, he would let them go back to their homes and live near other people again. While the ten men were walking away, their sores got better and their leprosy went away!

All ten men were healed of their disease. They were happy and excited as they went on their way to see the priest. But one of the men stopped and turned around. He ran back to Jesus and shouted, "Praise God!" Then he bowed at Jesus' feet and thanked Him.

Jesus asked, "Where are the other nine? Did only one come back to thank God?" Jesus told the man to stand up and go because his faith had made him well.

Like those ten men, we are loved and helped by Jesus. Every day He does good things for us. Let's remember to say thank you for all Jesus does for us. Like the one man who returned to Jesus, we can shout, "Praise God!" —C.B.

*I will remember to say thank you to Jesus.*

## FUN FACT

Jesus pointed out that the one healed leper who came back to thank Him was a Samaritan. The Jews and the Samaritans were related, but did not usually talk to each other.

## READ MORE

Read Matthew 8:1–4.
How did Jesus heal this man who had leprosy?

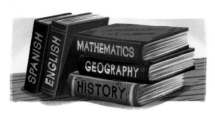

# Not Enough Room

Jesus also did many other things. If they were all written down, I suppose the whole world could not contain the books that would be written.

JOHN 21:25 NLT

**Have you ever** seen an encyclopedia? Before the Internet was invented, people got many questions answered from books like encyclopedias. An encyclopedia is a set of books, called "volumes." They are arranged in alphabetical order and contain articles and pictures to help people learn about many things. Encyclopedias are a collection of knowledge that can be handed down from parents to children, and from those children to their children.

The Bible is packed with knowledge too. The Old Testament tells how God created the world. It gives us the history of the first people on earth. It tells about the Israelites, who were God's chosen people, and their kings, judges, and prophets. The New Testament tells of the birth of Jesus and His teachings about God. It describes Jesus' followers and miracles. It tells how Jesus died on a cross and came back to life. It shows how the church began and how the message of Jesus spread throughout the world. It teaches that Jesus is coming back someday! The Bible is for people all over the world, and it can be handed down to children and to children's children.

*Jesus' life on earth can't be fully contained in books.*

John was one of Jesus' disciples. He spent three years following Jesus and saw almost everything He did. Then John wrote about Jesus' miracles and the lessons He taught. But John said he didn't write everything Jesus did because there wouldn't be enough room in the world for all the books!

We can't know everything there is to know about Jesus. But through the Bible, we can know everything God wants us to know about Him. —C.B.

## FUN FACT

The first encyclopedia, *Naturalis Historia,* was written by a man called Pliny the Elder in first century AD. The ten volumes of the encyclopedia covered topics like animals, plants, medicine, the weather, and the human body.

## READ MORE

In John 20:30–31, John tells us why he wrote down his story of Jesus' life. What was his reason?

# Good Days and Bad Days

The LORD was with Joseph, so he succeeded in everything he did as he served in the home of his Egyptian master.

**GENESIS 39:2 NLT**

**Do you remember Joseph,** whose brothers sold him as a slave? Joseph was taken to Egypt to work, and God gave Joseph success in everything he did. He was soon put in charge of the house of Potiphar, one of the king's important helpers. But just when everything was going well, Potiphar's wife lied about Joseph—and he was thrown into prison! Even in prison, though, God was with Joseph.

Two other prisoners had dreams they did not understand. But God helped Joseph understand the dreams. Joseph told the prisoners what was going to happen to them, and everything happened just the way Joseph said it would. Joseph hoped he would soon get out of prison, but he had to stay for two more years.

Then the king of Egypt, called Pharaoh, had some dreams that troubled him. Once again God helped Joseph explain the dreams. Joseph told Pharaoh that Egypt would have seven years of healthy crops, followed by seven years of famine.

## God is with me on good days and bad days.

Pharaoh was happy to know what his dreams meant, so he let Joseph out of prison and put him in charge of the whole country of Egypt!

Have you ever had a good day followed by a bad day, or a bad day followed by a good day? That's the way life is. Joseph had some good days and bad days. He went from being a slave to living in the king's palace. And whether he was in prison or in charge of Egypt, he trusted God.

God is with you just like He was with Joseph. On good days and bad days, you can trust Him to care for you.
—C.B.

**FUN FACT**

While he was a ruler in Egypt, Joseph had two sons. He named his first son Manasseh, which means, "God has made me forget all my troubles and the family of my father." He named his second son Ephraim, which means, "God has made me fruitful in this land of my suffering."

## ᴿREAD MORE

Read Genesis 37:5–11 to find out about dreams that Joseph had when he was a teenager.

# Remember God's Great Works

**Do you have any** special celebrations in your family? Maybe your family has a tradition for birthdays or anniversaries or holidays.

When God helped the Israelites escape from Egypt, He told them to eat a special meal. He wanted them to bake bread without yeast. Yeast makes bread fluffy, but that takes time. So God told the people to make dough without yeast so they could leave Egypt quickly.

After God rescued His people, He gave them instructions and rules He wanted them to follow. One of the things God told His people was to hold special festivals every year. God commanded the Israelites to celebrate their escape from Egypt with the "Feast of Unleavened Bread." During this feast, God told His people to eat bread without yeast for seven days. They

> "Celebrate the Feast of Unleavened Bread. For seven days you must eat bread without yeast as I commanded you. Do this during the month I have chosen, the month of Abib. This is because in that month you came out of Egypt."
>
> EXODUS 34:18 ICB

*I will celebrate God's great works.*

celebrated this feast every year during the month that God led them out of Egypt. God wanted the Israelites to stop and remember what He had done for them. He wanted them to be thankful for His protection and help. It was important that the Israelites didn't forget that God had saved them. As the years went by, their children and grandchildren would also learn about the great things God had done.

You could have a special celebration too, to thank God for all the great things He has done for you. You could do that every year, every week, or even every day! No matter when you do it, it's good to remember God's great works. —T.M.

## READ MORE

Read Mark 14:1–2.
What was happening during the Feast of Unleavened Bread while Jesus was in Bethany?

## FUN FACT

Bread made without yeast is called matzo.

> Later, when the boy was older, his mother brought him back to Pharaoh's daughter, who adopted him as her own son. The princess named him Moses, for she explained, "I lifted him out of the water."
>
> EXODUS 2:10 NLT

# A Baby in a Basket

**After Joseph ruled in Egypt,** the number of Israelites grew. But a new king took over. This new Pharaoh didn't know about Joseph. He was afraid of the Israelites. There were so many of them, Pharaoh thought they would take over his kingdom.

So Pharaoh made the Israelites his slaves. But the more Pharaoh tried to control them, the more the number of Israelites grew. Then Pharaoh came up with a terrible plan to keep the Israelites from growing even more. He said every baby boy should be thrown into the Nile River!

About this time, an Israelite man and woman had a baby boy. They hid him as long as they could. But when he was three months old, his mom put him in a basket made from papyrus reeds. Then she put the basket in the Nile River.

The baby's sister watched to see what would happen. Soon, Pharaoh's daughter came to the river. She saw the basket and found the baby boy crying inside. She felt sorry for him.

## God loves all of His adopted children.

So the baby's sister asked Pharaoh's daughter if she wanted a woman to take care of the baby. Pharaoh's daughter said yes, and the girl went to get her own mother— who was also the baby's mom!

When the baby was older, he was brought back to Pharaoh's daughter and she adopted him. She named him Moses. Many years later, God would use Moses to lead the Israelites out of their slavery in Egypt.

God used Moses' adoption for a special purpose. Whether your parents adopted you or not, you are adopted by God when you believe in His Son, Jesus. And God can use you for special things too. —T.M.

### FUN FACT

Papyrus is a thin material like paper. In ancient times, people wrote on it. Papyrus was also used to make baskets, mats, rope, and sandals.

### READ MORE

Read Exodus 8:1–6 to learn about something else Moses did at the Nile River.

# Too Great for Words

Let us give thanks to God for his gift. It is so great that no one can tell how wonderful it really is!

2 CORINTHIANS 9:15 NIRV

**What is the most** amazing thing you've ever seen?

Sometimes it can be hard to describe something wonderful or exciting that you have experienced. Have you ever seen a playful dolphin jump out of the ocean or a shooting star streak through the nighttime sky? Have you ever been close to a powerful waterfall splashing and roaring down the side of a mountain? Maybe you have seen a beautiful sunset with glowing shades of pink and orange and red. When you try to describe it to someone else, it's almost impossible to explain.

The gift of Jesus is too great for words to describe.

In the New Testament, the apostle Paul talks about the gift of God's Son, Jesus Christ. Jesus is the greatest gift anyone can receive, but Paul said it's hard to explain how great and wonderful and beautiful the gift of Jesus is. It's just too amazing! Jesus gives us hope and peace and love. Jesus gives us joy and comfort and friendship. But most of all, it is through Jesus that we receive forgiveness for all that we've done wrong.

Like something that is too wonderful for words, it is hard to describe the gift of Jesus. And if you can't find the right words to describe this wonderful gift, just tell God thank you. —C.B.

## READ MORE

Read Matthew 15:29–31 to learn about many people who were thankful to God for Jesus.

## FUN FACT

Angel Falls, in Venezuela, is an amazing thing. It's the world's tallest waterfall, dropping more than 3,200 feet (979 meters)!

> The power of the LORD came over me. The LORD brought me out by his Spirit and put me down in the middle of a valley. The valley was filled with bones.
>
> EZEKIEL 37:1 GW

# Dry Bones

**Ezekiel was a prophet** to the Israelites while they were forced to live in Babylon. One day he had a vision. In this vision, God took Ezekiel to a valley where he saw a bunch of dried-out bones of people. God said to Ezekiel, "Can these bones live?"

Ezekiel said, "Powerful Lord, only you know."

Then God told Ezekiel to speak to the bones. God told him to say, "Listen to the Word of the Lord! I will cause breath to enter you so you will live. I will put muscles on you. I will put flesh on you and cover you with skin. Then you will know that I am the Lord."

Ezekiel spoke, and the bones began to rattle and move and come together. Muscles and skin covered the bones, but they were not alive. So God told Ezekiel to call down breath on the bodies. Ezekiel spoke as God said, and the people came to life and stood on their feet.

## Jesus gives hope and life.

God told Ezekiel that the people of Israel were like those dry bones. Their hope had dried up. But God wanted Ezekiel to give them hope with these words: "The Almighty Lord will put my Spirit in you so you can live. I will bring you back to your own land."

People today are like those dry bones. Unless they follow Jesus, their hope is dried up. But the Holy Spirit can breathe life into them. God can give them a place to live forever, with Him. When you know Jesus, you always have hope. —C.B.

### FUN FACT

Adult humans have 206 bones. But babies are born with about three hundred bones. Some of them fuse together as a person gets older. More than half of people's bones are in their hands and feet.

### READ MORE

What promise does God give to the Israelites in Ezekiel 11:17–20?

# Roar like a Lion

**Have you ever been** to a zoo or an animal reserve and seen lions? If you have ever heard lions roar, you know how great and strong they sound. A lion's roar is powerful! It is so loud it can be heard up to five miles away (eight kilometers). It's hard to miss the big loud boom of a lion's roar. It almost sounds like thunder!

> "For someday the people will follow me. I, the LORD, will roar like a lion. And when I roar, my people will return trembling from the west."
>
> **HOSEA 11:10 NLT**

God is great and strong. Like a lion, He is very powerful. Did you know that God even said He would roar like a lion? After God brought the Israelites out of Egypt, they turned away from Him. They started worshipping false gods and weren't loyal to the one true God. Because of their disobedience, God had to punish His people. He told them they would be taken away from their land and live under the power of a tough and unkind king.

## God roars like a lion.

But that wasn't the end of God's plan for His people. God wouldn't stay angry and punish the Israelites forever. He is loving and kind. So God told His people He would call them back. He would roar like a lion and all the Israelites would come running toward the sound. But they would shake before God, because they would be afraid of His power.

God did what He said He would do. He brought the Israelites back to their home because He is both powerful and loving. God's power and love work for us too. The next time you see a lion, think of God's great strength. Remember that God's love is as big as His roar. —T.M.

## READ MORE
Read Joel 3:16–17.
What does God say He will do for His people?

## FUN FACT
A lion's roar is almost as loud as a jack hammer or jet airplane!

# Thirsty Souls

> "But those who drink the water that I will give them will never become thirsty again. In fact, the water I will give them will become in them a spring that gushes up to eternal life."
>
> JOHN 4:14 GW

**One time, when Jesus** was walking from one town to another, He met a woman at a well. Jesus asked the woman for a drink of water. She was surprised because she was a Samaritan. Jewish people didn't talk to Samaritans.

The woman asked Jesus why He was talking to her. Jesus said, "If you only knew what God's gift is and who is asking you for a drink, you would have asked Him for a drink. He would have given you living water."

The woman thought Jesus was talking about the water in the well. People called the water coming into the bottom of the well "living water." So she asked Jesus how He was going to reach the bottom of the deep well if He didn't have a rope and bucket to use.

## Jesus gives me living water.

Jesus explained that the water in the well wouldn't take care of her thirst forever. But if the woman drank the kind of water Jesus was talking about, she would never be thirsty again. So she said to Jesus, "Sir, give me this water! Then I won't have to come to the well anymore."

But Jesus wasn't talking about the water people drink when they're thirsty. He was using the example of water to explain how the Holy Spirit works. When we decide to follow Jesus, the Holy Spirit comes into us. Like water, the Holy Spirit cleans and refreshes us. Through the Holy Spirit, God satisfies our spiritual thirst forever. —T.M.

## FUN FACT

Depending on their age, kids should drink between five to seven glasses of water (one to one and a half liters) each day.

## READ MORE

Read John 7:37–39.
When we believe in Jesus, where does the "living water" come from?

# Road Signs

**Think of all the signs** you see along the road. Speed limit signs tell people how fast they can safely drive. Other signs tell people what road they are on or what direction they are traveling. When a sign says Do Not Pass, it tells drivers that it's not safe to pass the cars in front of them.

> When a wise person sees danger ahead, he avoids it. But a foolish person keeps going and gets into trouble.
>
> **PROVERBS 27:12 ICB**

Road signs help people understand where to go and what to do. People who are wise pay attention to road signs. The signs help people to stay safe and find their way. People who are foolish do not pay attention to the road signs. They may get lost and even put themselves and other people in danger.

The book of Proverbs is filled with words of advice and warning. The verses of Proverbs are like road signs for our lives. They were written to give us wisdom. The advice of Proverbs can point us in the right direction and keep us safe.

*The verses in Proverbs give me good direction.*

Some of the verses in Proverbs tell us what we should do. Proverbs 4:1 says, "My children, listen to your father's teaching. Pay attention so you will understand." Some of the verses in Proverbs give us a warning. Proverbs 1:10 says, "My child, sinners will try to lead you into sin. But do not follow them."

Wise people obey the words in Proverbs. Just like road signs, the Proverbs will help keep you safe. God put them in the Bible to help you. —T.M.

## FUN FACT

In 1861, the United Kingdom put up the first speed limit sign. It said 10 miles per hour (16 kilometers per hour)! Today, the highest speed limit in the world is 87 miles per hour (140 kilometers per hour), found on some roads in Poland and Bulgaria.

## READ MORE

Proverbs 1:1–7 explains the reasons why the book of Proverbs was written. How many reasons can you find?

# Look Up

> "And as Moses lifted up the bronze snake on a pole in the wilderness, so the Son of Man must be lifted up, so that everyone who believes in him will have eternal life."
>
> JOHN 3:14–15 NLT

**When the people of Israel** traveled through the wilderness, they needed to stay away from their enemies' lands. As they traveled from Mount Hor along the road to the Red Sea, they walked far out of their way so they wouldn't go through Edom. The people in Edom were related to the Israelites but were enemies.

The Israelites began to grumble. They were tired and hungry. They complained to Moses that they didn't have food or water. They said they were tired of the miracle food called manna that God gave them every morning!

God heard their complaints. He was angry that the people didn't trust Him to provide for them. So he sent poisonous snakes to punish them. Some of the people were bitten and died. The people quickly realized they had sinned against God. They asked Moses to pray that God would take the snakes away. So Moses prayed to God for the people.

God heard Moses' prayer. He told Moses, "Make a model of a snake and put it on a pole. Anyone bitten by the real snakes can look up at the model snake and live."

Moses made a snake from a metal called bronze. Everyone who had been bitten could look at the bronze snake and be healed.

When Jesus lived on earth, a man named Nicodemus asked Him how to be saved. Jesus explained that He was like the bronze snake in the wilderness.

## I will look to Jesus to be saved.

Jesus would be lifted up on a cross, and all who believed in Him would have eternal life.

God has made a way for His people to be saved. Look up to Jesus and live!
—C.B.

### FUN FACT

Bronze is a tough metal made of copper and tin. It was used so much between three thousand and five thousand years ago that those years are known as the "Bronze Age."

### READ MORE

Read 2 Kings 18:1–4 to learn more about the bronze snake. What happened to it?

Don't be proud at all. Be completely gentle. Be patient. Put up with one another in love. The Holy Spirit makes you one in every way. So try your best to remain as one. Let peace keep you together.

**EPHESIANS 4:2–3 NIRV**

# Peaceful People

**When the apostle Paul** wrote a letter to Christians in the city of Ephesus, he told them to treat each other with gentleness and live in peace. Paul wanted them to be patient with one another because they were all part of God's family. Paul also told them, "Never shout angrily or say things to hurt others. Be kind and loving to each other and forgive each other."

It doesn't feel good when we quarrel with our friends or fight with the people in our families. But sometimes it's hard to get along with others. Your friends might say mean things. Your brother or sister might use something of yours without asking. None of us is perfect. We are going to disagree sometimes and hurt each other's feelings. But there are things we can do to make our days more peaceful.

## It's good to live in peace with others.

Paul's letter to the Ephesians is also for Christians today. It tells us that we can choose to live in peace with those around us. We can say and do nice things on purpose. We can share what we have and be patient when things don't go our way. We can say we're sorry if we hurt someone. And when others hurt us, we can choose to forgive them.

The psalms say, "It is good and pleasant when God's people live together in peace." Peace makes us happy, and it pleases God too. —T.M.

**READ MORE**
Find 1 Peter 3:8.
What five things can you do to live at peace with others?

**FUN FACT**
There is a "peace bell" in New York City made from coins donated by children all over the world.

# Special Instructions

"But the blood on your houses will be a sign for your protection. When I see the blood, I will pass over you. Nothing will touch or destroy you when I strike Egypt."

**EXODUS 12:13 GW**

**The time had come** for the Israelites to leave Egypt. They had been slaves for many years but God was setting them free!

God had already sent nine terrible problems, called "plagues," on Egypt. The plagues showed God's power to the Egyptian king, called Pharaoh. But Pharaoh's heart was hard. He was stubborn and wouldn't let the Israelites go. So God gave special instructions to Moses and Aaron to protect the Israelites from the last plague He was going to send to Egypt.

Moses and Aaron told the people what God had said. The Israelites needed to make a special dinner. They had to make bread without yeast and roast a lamb with herbs. They needed to take some of the blood from the lamb and brush it on the doorframes of their houses. They had to eat their special meal with their sandals and clothes on, ready to leave at any moment. All of the people who obeyed God's orders would be saved.

## Jesus is the Lamb of God.

Night came and the Israelites waited in their homes. Then the plague started! All of the oldest Egyptian boys died that night. But God protected the Israelites because of the lamb's blood on their doorframes. The blood showed that the Israelites believed in God and trusted Him to save them. God "passed over" their homes. That night is known as Passover.

Jesus is called the "Lamb of God" because He died on the cross for our sins. When you believe in Jesus, you are like the Israelites at Passover. You are protected by God's love and power. You are saved by the Lamb of God! —T.M.

## FUN FACT

Jewish people still celebrate Passover every year. The special event lasts for seven or eight days.

## READ MORE

Find Mark 14:12–16 to read about the disciples' Passover with Jesus. Where did they meet?

# Tell Your Children

**Do your parents** or grandparents ever tell you stories about when they were kids? It's fun to hear about the things they did a long time ago. And if they learned a good lesson, it's good for them to tell you about that.

God did many amazing things for the Israelites. He helped them escape from Egypt and took care of them in the wilderness. Then, when He helped Joshua lead the Israelites across the Jordan River, God gave out a special assignment. God told Joshua to choose twelve men and have each one take a large rock from the middle of the river. The men were to put their stones in a pile at the place where the people would camp.

Do you know why God gave these instructions? He told Joshua, "In the future, when your children ask you what these rocks mean, you can tell them how the Lord caused the river to stop flowing. You can tell them that the river was dry until all the people had finished crossing. You can tell them that it was just like when God had helped the people cross the Red Sea. Tell them the Lord did this so all people know He has great power. Then they will always respect Him."

It's important for people to remember how great God is. When God answers your prayers or blesses you in a special way, you can write it in a notebook or journal to remember it. Then someday, when you have children or grandchildren, you can tell them stories about how great God is! —C.B.

> We will tell the next generation about the glorious deeds of the LORD, about his power and his mighty wonders.
>
> **PSALM 78:4 NLT**

## Remember the great things God does.

### FUN FACT

Before the invention of writing and paper, parents told stories to their children, and when they had children, they did the same. This is how important information was passed on, all by memory!

### READ MORE

Why does Psalm 78:1–8 say parents should tell stories about God to their children?

> "While he was still at a distance, his father saw him and felt sorry for him. He ran to his son, put his arms around him, and kissed him."
>
> LUKE 15:20 GW

# The Foolish Son

**One time when Jesus** was teaching, He told a story about two sons. The younger son wanted to leave home. So he went to his father and asked for money.

The boy was being selfish, but his father was kind. He gave his son the money he wanted. The boy took the money and went far away. Then he wasted his money on foolish things. When he had nothing left, the land ran out of food. The boy was in trouble! Finally, he got a job feeding pigs in a field. He was so hungry he wanted to eat the yucky food the pigs were eating.

Finally, the son realized that his father's servants had more than he had. The boy didn't think his father would want him back as a son. But he hoped his dad might let him become a servant. So he started walking home.

He was still far from home when his father saw him coming. And guess what? His dad ran to meet him! He gave his son a big hug and kiss. The boy said, "Father,

God always takes people back.

I've sinned against heaven and you. I don't deserve to be called your son anymore." But before he could even ask to be a servant, his father started planning a celebration! He was so happy to have his son back. The father held a party, gave his son his best clothes, and welcomed him back into the family.

This story shows that God takes people back even after they've sinned. He accepts anyone who wants to be part of His family. If you've done something wrong, you don't have to run away from God. You can turn back to Him and enjoy His welcome. —T.M.

## FUN FACT

Pigs are called "omnivores," meaning they eat many kinds of foods. In Jesus' story, the pigs were eating pods or husks—the parts of plants that are often thrown away.

## READ MORE

In this story, the father put his best clothes on his son. Read Zechariah 3:3–5 to learn about someone else who received new clothes.

# Gone Forever

**Have you ever** thrown a coin into the pool of a fountain? It's fun to toss the shiny metal into the water and watch it sink. If the pool is shallow, you might be able to see the coin after it lands on the bottom. If the pool is deep, you might not see the coin after you throw it in. You know you won't get the coin back because it's too far away from you. The coin is gone for good.

> Once again you will have compassion on us. You will trample our sins under your feet and throw them into the depths of the ocean!
>
> **MICAH 7:19 NLT**

The Bible tells us that we can think of our sins in the same way. When we give our lives to Jesus and tell Him we're sorry for our sins, He forgives those sins forever. God's Word says it's like He takes our sins and throws them into the deepest part of the ocean. Just like a coin drops to the bottom of a deep fountain pool, our sins sink to the bottom of the ocean. We can't get them back, and we will never see them again.

You can't really find a bunch of sins at the bottom of the ocean. But God wants us to think about our sins like that—so we realize how forgiving Jesus is. When we trust in Jesus and ask Him to forgive us, He takes away all of our sins. They are gone forever!
—T.M.

## Jesus takes away my sins.

### READ MORE

Read Psalm 103:12. How far does God remove our sins from us?

### FUN FACT

Every day, tourists in Rome throw coins into the Trevi Fountain. The total amount of money tossed in the fountain each day is about three thousand euros. That's more than four thousand American dollars!

> There is a time for everything. There's a time for everything that is done on earth.
>
> ECCLESIASTES 3:1 NIRV

# What Time Is It?

**When you get up** in the morning, it's time to get dressed and eat breakfast. When you're in school, it's time to learn. When you're on the playground, it's time to have fun! There are times when you can talk, and there are times when you need to be quiet. At night, it's time to sleep. Throughout the day, there are right times and wrong times for many things.

When Jesus was teaching His disciples, He told them a time was coming when the Jewish leaders would try to get rid of Him. He told the disciples that the time would soon come for Him to suffer and die. He also told them that three days after His death, He would rise from the dead. All of those things happened just like Jesus said.

After He came back from the dead, Jesus spent a little more time with His disciples. Then they watched as He went up to heaven. When He disappeared from sight, two angels said to the disciples, "Why are you looking into the sky? You saw Jesus taken up into heaven. He will come back in the same way you saw Him go."

## There is a time when Jesus will return.

No one knows the time when Jesus will return. Only God the Father knows when that time will be. But it's something we can look forward to. And until that time comes, Jesus can give you wisdom to use your time wisely.
—C.B.

### FUN FACT

A sundial is a device that tells time by the position of the sun. A pointer called a gnomon casts a shadow on the dial, which is like the face of a clock.

### READ MORE

Read Ecclesiastes 3:1–8 to learn about the right time for certain things.

> So the church fasted
> and prayed. They
> laid their hands on
> Barnabas and Saul
> and sent them out.
>
> ACTS 13:3 ERV

# The First Missionaries

**Do you know** anyone who is a missionary? A missionary is sent somewhere to tell people about Jesus and invite them to be a part of His church. Some missionaries travel to other countries. Other missionaries might go to a nearby city or tell people about Jesus in their own town. Missionaries are called by God to do His special work.

The first missionaries in the Bible were Saul, also known as Paul, and Barnabas. They were teachers in a city called Antioch. One of the first Christian churches was there. In the early days of the church, Jesus' disciples only told Jewish people about the good news of Jesus. They explained that He was the Messiah the Jews had been waiting for. But God told Saul and Barnabas to begin telling everyone about Jesus. It didn't matter if they were Jewish or not. Everyone was welcome to believe in Jesus and be forgiven for the wrong things they had done.

## I can encourage missionaries.

Saul and Barnabas knew the Holy Spirit had asked them to be missionaries. Their church prayed for them and sent them out to tell everyone about Jesus.

You can help missionaries by praying for them too. You can send them letters or e-mails to encourage them. Maybe God will call you to be a missionary someday! But even if you never travel far away, you can take the good news of Jesus to other people too. —T.M.

### READ MORE

Read Acts 13:44–48.
Who were the first people that Paul and Barnabas
shared the good news about Jesus with?

### FUN FACT

Barnabas and Saul's
first missionary journey
lasted about two years.
They preached about Jesus
in at least eight cities
along the way.

> Get all the advice and
> instruction you can,
> so you will be wise the
> rest of your life.
>
> PROVERBS 19:20 NLT

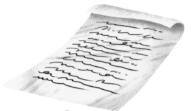

# As Much as You Can

**For many, many years,** God's people had done what was wrong. So God punished them by allowing a country called Babylon to take many of them away.

After seventy years in Babylon, the Israelites were free to go back to their own land. They rebuilt the altar of God and gave daily offerings to Him. Then they worked hard to rebuild the temple. They celebrated some of their feasts and tried to honor God. But they also kept doing things that were against the Law of God. They were living like people who did not belong to God. Some of the leaders were setting a poor example by doing things God had told them not to do.

A priest named Ezra knew it was time for the people to turn back to God. Ezra had worked hard to learn and obey the Law of God. Then he wanted to teach it to the Israelites. He prayed to God for the people, and told God about their sins.

One day, Ezra gathered the people together. He stood on a tall wooden platform so everyone could see and hear him. From morning until afternoon he read the Law of God out loud. Ezra praised the Lord, the great and mighty God of Israel. All the people held up their hands and said, "Amen!"

## I need God's Word.

Ezra knew the people needed the Law of God. In the same way, we need the Bible. It helps us know God and His wisdom. If you have a Bible, be sure to read it. God uses the Bible to make us better people. —C.B.

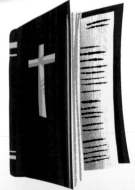

## FUN FACT

The first five books of the Bible are Genesis, Exodus, Leviticus, Numbers, and Deuteronomy. These books are known as the books of Moses, the Law, or the Torah.

## READ MORE

What does Psalm 119:97–104 tell us about God's Word?

# Sparkle in the Land

**Have you ever seen** a ring or necklace made of real jewels? Diamonds, rubies, sapphires, and emeralds are jewels known as precious stones. They are cut and polished to make beautiful jewelry. They're precious because they have great value.

> **They will sparkle in his land like jewels in a crown.**
> ZECHARIAH 9:16 NIV

Some jewelry is made from fake stones. They look similar to precious stones but do not have as much value as true, precious stones. God calls His people "jewels in a crown." A king's crown has real jewels of great value. It would not have cheap, fake stones!

When we are part of His family, God sees us as valuable, precious stones. We are precious to God and He wants us to sparkle for Him. That means He wants us to live in a way that lets others see we belong to Him. He wants us to be real and genuine Christians.

*I will sparkle like a precious jewel.*

Just like precious stones are polished to shine and sparkle, Jesus makes us shine and sparkle with His love and forgiveness and joy. People are attracted to precious stones for their value and beauty. And when we sparkle with Jesus in our lives, people will be attracted to us.

You are worth more than diamonds and rubies, or sapphires and emeralds. You have great value because Jesus makes you like a precious jewel—pure and shiny for His glory. —C.B.

## READ MORE

Revelation 21:10–21 describes a vision of heaven that John saw. What kinds of jewels are in the heavenly Jerusalem?

### FUN FACT

Colored diamonds are usually more expensive than clear or white diamonds. The most expensive diamonds are blue or red.

# God's Good Gifts

> She told the king, "What I heard in my country about your words and your wisdom is true! But I didn't believe the reports until I came and saw it with my own eyes."
>
> 1 KINGS 10:6–7 GW

**Have you ever noticed** that some people are really smart? Others are very funny and make people laugh. Some people are really good at sports. Others have plenty of money. Some people may not have a lot of things, but they know how to be happy. Any good gifts that we have come from God.

In the Bible, Solomon was rich. Not only did he have a lot of money, he was very wise. God made Solomon the king of Israel and gave him every good thing. News about Solomon spread to other kingdoms. One day the queen of Sheba came to visit Solomon to see if the stories she'd heard were true.

The queen tested Solomon. She asked him many hard questions to see if he was as wise as people said. The queen was amazed by everything she heard and saw. Solomon had built a magnificent house. He had many servants, who were dressed in beautiful clothes. She saw all of the delicious food he had and the sacrifices he gave to God. She told Solomon, "Everything that I heard was true. What I have seen is even greater than the stories I have heard!" Then she praised God and said, "Thank the Lord your God, who is pleased with you. He has put you on the throne of Israel."

## I can share my good gifts with others.

God blesses people in different ways. Whether you are smart or athletic or funny—or have any other gift the world needs—remember that God gave it to you. And be ready to share it with those who need it! —T.M.

### FUN FACT

Some people believe the queen of Sheba came from the part of the world that is now Ethiopia.

### READ MORE

Look up 1 Kings 10:14–20 to read more about the great wealth God gave Solomon.

# In God's Image

**When you look** in a mirror, you see a reflection of your image. You can see what you look like. Has anyone ever told you that you look like someone else? Kids often look like someone in their family.

When God created the world, He made everything—from the sun, moon, and stars to the trees, plants, and animals. Then He created a man and a woman. And God made people to be very special.

When God made people, He made them "in His own image." That doesn't mean we look exactly like God. It means we are similar to God in other very important ways. God made us so we can talk and think and have feelings. He created us so we can enjoy His wonderful world. He made us so that we can have friendship with Him.

Every person in the world is made in God's image. Every person in the world can believe in God and talk to Him. Every person in the world can love Him. But not every person chooses to do that. God doesn't make people love Him. He wants people to choose to love Him.

> So God created mankind in his own image, in the image of God he created them; male and female he created them.
>
> **GENESIS 1:27 NIV**

## I want to reflect God's image.

When we choose to love Jesus, we become more like God in the way we live and the things we say. If we truly love God, we reflect His image, just like a mirror reflects our image.

As your friendship with God grows, others will see a change in you. You will look like someone in God's family.
—C.B.

### READ MORE

Read John 14:8–12.
How did Jesus explain to Philip
that He was the same as God?

### FUN FACT

The first mirrors were made from polished volcanic glass thousands of years ago in the area we now call Turkey. Modern glass mirrors were first made in Germany almost two hundred years ago.

# Food from the Birds

Ravens brought Elijah food every morning and every evening, and he drank water from the stream.

1 KINGS 17:6 ERV

**King Ahab** was the most evil king who ruled over the Israelites. He didn't follow God's commandments. He worshipped a false god called Baal and even built temples and altars for false gods.

While King Ahab was in charge, Elijah was God's chosen prophet. Elijah loved God and obeyed His commandments. He did what was right in God's eyes. One day, Elijah went to talk to Ahab. He said, "I serve the Lord, the God of Israel. By His power, I promise that no dew or rain will fall for the next few years. The drought will end only when I command rain to fall!"

After this meeting, God told Elijah to leave Ahab's city and hide near a stream called Kerith. God promised to take care of Elijah in a special way during the drought. He told Elijah, "You can get your water from that stream, and I have commanded ravens to bring food to you there." Elijah listened to God. He went to live near Kerith. Every day big black birds brought Elijah meat to eat. And he drank water from the stream.

## God provides for those who obey Him.

God takes care of those who obey Him. He promises to provide for us. The way He helps us may be different from what we expect. God didn't send Elijah to a restaurant or give him a basket full of food. But when we trust Him, God will never let us down. It's exciting to see how He will meet our needs! —T.M.

### FUN FACT

Ravens are one of the smartest wild animals in the world. Their intelligence is almost as high as dolphins or chimpanzees.

### READ MORE

Find Psalm 147:7–11 to see how God provides. What does this passage say that God enjoys?

# Give Praise to God

**As Paul and Barnabas traveled** on their mission, they stopped in a place called Lystra. The people in Lystra were not from the family of the Israelites. They didn't know the history of Moses' law. And they didn't know about the one true God.

In Lystra, Paul and Barnabas met a man who had never been able to walk. In a loud voice, Paul told the man, "Stand up on your feet." The man jumped up and began to walk around!

All the people who saw this were amazed. They started shouting, "The gods have come down to us in human form!" They called Barnabas "Zeus" and Paul "Hermes." Those were the names of false gods the people of Lystra worshipped. Because they didn't realize the one true God was doing a miracle through His missionaries, the people wanted to worship Paul and Barnabas.

> "Why are you men doing this? We are only human, just like you. We are bringing you good news. Turn away from these worthless things. Turn to the living God. He is the one who made the heavens and the earth and the sea. He made everything in them."
>
> **ACTS 14:15 NIRV**

## God deserves the praise.

When Paul and Barnabas saw what was happening, they commanded the people to stop. Paul and Barnabas told the people they weren't gods. They were just humans who served the true living God. They explained that God had made the earth and the sea and everything in them. He was the one who deserved the people's praise.

Sometimes people may want to praise you for talents and blessings that came from God. It's okay for people to give you a compliment. But if they do, remind them where your gifts and talents come from. Like Paul and Barnabas, you can use your talents to tell others about God. When people praise you, you can give that praise back to God.
—T.M.

## READ MORE

Look up 1 Corinthians 3:5–7. When people are sharing the good news about Jesus, who should get the credit?

## FUN FACT

The Lystra in the Bible is now called Klistra. It is located in the country of Turkey.

# Extra Strength

> I can do
> everything
> through Christ,
> who gives me
> strength.
>
> **PHILIPPIANS 4:13 NLT**

**Before Jesus went back** to heaven, He told His followers that they would face many hard things. Some people would hate Jesus' friends just like they hated Jesus. Some people would be against them the same way they were against Jesus. But Jesus did not leave His followers without hope.

Jesus promised that He would send His Holy Spirit to give His followers strength. With the Holy Spirit's strength, Christians would be able to face hard situations. They could be bold when they told others about Jesus and what it meant to follow Him.

*The Holy Spirit gives me strength.*

The apostle Paul experienced many of the things Jesus had warned about. As Paul traveled and told people about Jesus, he was whipped and put in prison. He was in ships that were wrecked at sea. He went without food and sleep. He was in danger many times and sometimes even near death. But Paul said that he could do anything with the strength that Jesus gives. He understood that by following Jesus, he had the Holy Spirit to give him strength no matter what he had to do.

Do you want extra strength? We all need a little extra strength! If you know Jesus as your Savior, then you have His Holy Spirit inside you. He will give you the strength to tell your friends about Jesus. He will help you with any struggle that you face. —C.B.

### FUN FACT

The strongest bone in the human body is the femur. It's also known as the thigh bone. The femur is the heaviest and longest bone in the body, making up about one-fourth of your height.

## READ MORE

**What did Jesus say about the Holy Spirit in John 14:15–17?**

# Marching Ants

**Ants are amazing** little insects. Sometimes you hardly notice them because they are so tiny. But they are very strong. Ants can carry things that weigh ten or twenty times more than they do!

Ants are also very hardworking. They work well together. Ants divide themselves into groups of workers, soldiers, and queens. By splitting up their work, they are able to keep their nests—called "colonies"—going strong. Many kinds of ants store food in their nests. They go back and forth between the nest and the food source, building up a supply of food that will last them through cold weather.

> Ants have no ruler, no boss, and no leader. But in the summer, ants gather all of their food and save it. So when winter comes, there is plenty to eat.
>
> **PROVERBS 6:7–8 ERV**

When King Solomon wrote the verses in Proverbs 6, he told us to remember the ants. They have different groups of workers, but there's no one boss in charge of the colony. The ants do their work and take care of themselves without being told. They prepare for the future instead of being lazy. They stay busy and use their time wisely.

## I honor God when I work hard.

It's good for us to work hard too. We can figure out the things we're good at, and do them with all our might. We can work together with our families and friends, like ants do. When we work hard at everything we do, we make the most of the life God has given us.

God wants us to enjoy the life He's given us. You can show God you're grateful for your life by doing your very best. —T.M.

### READ MORE
Read John 6:27–29.
What is the most important work God wants us to do?

**FUN FACT**

Scientists guess that there are about twenty-two thousand different kinds of ants!

# Just a Touch

> She thought, "If I can just touch his clothes, that will be enough to heal me."
>
> MARK 5:28 ERV

**Jesus had just calmed** a stormy sea and amazed His disciples. When He stepped off the boat and onto dry ground, a large crowd gathered around. An important Jewish leader came through the crowd and fell at Jesus' feet. He asked Jesus to heal his daughter who was very sick at home. So Jesus went with the man.

The crowd followed Jesus. It continued to grow. It was so big, people were pressing in on Jesus. Suddenly, He stopped. "Who touched my clothes?" Jesus asked.

The disciples thought that was a strange question. They told Jesus, "There are lots of people pushing against you." But Jesus kept looking for the person who had touched him. Before long, a woman came forward. She was shaking in fear.

The woman had a disease, and had suffered for twelve years. She had tried everything to get well and had seen many doctors. But no one could help her. When she heard about Jesus and His power to make people well, she thought, "If I can just touch his clothes, that will be enough to heal me." She snuck up to Jesus in the crowd and touched His clothes. Immediately she was made well!

Jesus felt healing power go out from Him. That's why He turned around to look for the woman. When she told Jesus her story, He said, "Dear woman, you are healthy again because you believed. Go in peace. Your suffering is over."

## I can believe in Jesus' power.

Jesus' power is still at work today. Sometimes He heals people, like the woman who touched His clothes. But sometimes He shows His power by giving people strength through their sickness. One day, though, everyone who believes in Jesus will be perfectly healthy in heaven. —T.M.

### FUN FACT

Jesus probably wore something called a halug. It was like a poncho made from rectangular fabric, with a hole in the middle for His head.

### READ MORE

Read Mark 5:35–43.
What happened to the ruler's daughter?

# Awesome

**The word awesome** has been around for a long time. It dates back to the 1600s!

In the last several years, awesome has become a common word. When people use it today, they often mean they really like something. It's another way of saying, "Cool!"

But the word also has a bigger, better meaning. Something that "awes" us—something that is "awesome"—makes us feel amazed, full of worship, maybe even a little afraid. Many modern Bible versions use the word awesome to describe God.

God did a very awesome thing for the people of Israel when He helped them escape from Egypt. Egyptian soldiers chased the people to the edge of the Red Sea. What could the Israelites do? They were struck with fear. But God told Moses to hold his staff over the water. When Moses obeyed, God split the sea in half so all the people of Israel could cross over on dry ground. When they had finished

> "Who among the gods is like you, LORD? Who is like you—majestic in holiness, awesome in glory, working wonders?"
>
> **EXODUS 15:11 NIV**

## My God is awesome!

crossing, God told Moses to raise his hand over the sea. When Moses obeyed, the waters rushed back into place. All of the Egyptian soldiers were swallowed up by the crashing walls of water.

When the people of Israel saw the mighty work of the Lord, they sang a song of praise to Him. They honored Him for His greatness and strength and power. They called Him an "awesome" God.

He is still our awesome God today! He inspires awe and worship in His people. He is great and wonderful in every way. —C.B.

## READ MORE

Psalm 47 is another song of praise to God for being so great and awesome. What does this psalm say God is king of?

### FUN FACT

The Red Sea is connected to the Indian Ocean, which is between Africa, Asia, and Australia. The Red Sea is just over 190 miles (300 kilometers) across at its widest point, and about 1,200 miles (1,900 kilometers) in length.

God, who looks into our hearts, knows the mind of the Spirit. And the Spirit prays for God's people just as God wants him to pray.

ROMANS 8:27 NIRV

# All the Right Words

**When Jesus knew** His time on earth was almost over, He said a special prayer for His followers. It was a prayer for God to protect His people after Jesus returned to heaven.

Jesus prayed that God would be with His followers and protect them from evil. He prayed that all Christians would work together as one and have the joy of Jesus. He prayed that they would understand the truth of God's Word and be ready to serve. He prayed that the world would see that His followers belonged to Him and were filled with His love.

Because Jesus is the Son of God, His prayer was perfect. He knew just the right words to say and how to say them. Do you wonder if you have to say a perfect prayer

## The Holy Spirit helps me pray.

for God to hear you? Don't worry about that! You don't have to learn all the right words. You don't have to pray in any special way. All you need to do is talk to God from your heart. Just tell Him what you want to say. If you pray from your heart, your words will be just right.

You can pray to thank God for your food or ask Him to keep you safe during the night. You can pray for yourself and you can pray for other people. You can tell God anything you think is important. When you pray, the Holy Spirit is praying for you at the same time! —C.B.

## READ MORE

The "Lord's Prayer" is found in Matthew 6:9–13. According to verse 10, what are the two places God's will should be done?

### FUN FACT

More than five hundred years ago, children in England learned to read by using a hornbook. It was a wooden paddle with letters of the alphabet glued on top. The hornbook also included the Lord's Prayer.

> Hezekiah trusted in the LORD, the God of Israel. There was no one like Hezekiah among all the kings of Judah before him or after him.
>
> 2 KINGS 18:5 ERV

# The Good King

**Hezekiah was only** twenty-five years old when he became king of Judah. His father, Ahaz, had been king before him, and he was an evil man. So Hezekiah had a tough job ahead of him.

Since he was in charge of everyone and everything, Hezekiah could make any decision he wanted to. He could do whatever pleased him. But instead of being proud and evil, Hezekiah chose to follow God. He used his position as king to obey God and do what was right.

Hezekiah's first decision was to break down all the idols the people had worshipped. He smashed them into pieces. Hezekiah even demolished the bronze snake that Moses had made many years before, because people had started to worship it. Then Hezekiah stood up against the king of Assyria and refused to serve him. And he defeated Israel's enemies, the Philistines, to make his kingdom safe.

## I can choose to do the right thing.

Hezekiah ruled for twenty-nine years and did not stop following God. He kept all of God's commandments and was loyal to Him. God was with Hezekiah wherever he went. Everything the king did went well because he trusted God.

Hezekiah was a faithful man who was brave enough to do the right thing. The work he had to do wasn't easy, but God helped Hezekiah.

Do you ever feel like it's hard to do the right thing? Like Hezekiah, you can trust God to help you. You'll probably never be a king, but God still cares about the choices you make. —T.M.

### FUN FACT

Of all the kings of Judah, Manasseh reigned the longest. He was on the throne for fifty-five years!

### READ MORE

When Hezekiah faced challenges, he prayed.
Read 2 Kings 19:15–19 to learn how he talked to God.

# A Sweet Smell

**Jesus was at the home** of Mary and Martha and their brother Lazarus. He was a man Jesus had raised from the dead. The three siblings were giving a dinner to honor Jesus.

Martha was serving food while Lazarus was at the table with Jesus. Mary came toward Jesus with a small bottle of expensive perfume. She poured the perfume on Jesus' feet, then wiped His feet with her hair. The smell of sweet perfume filled the house.

One of Jesus' disciples was upset that Mary had wasted such expensive perfume. It was Judas, the disciple who would later turn Jesus over to His enemies. Judas was not an honest man. He said that if Mary had sold the perfume, she could have given the money to the poor. But since Judas was in charge of the money for Jesus' disciples, he really wanted to keep some of the money for himself. Jesus knew what was in Judas's heart, so He said to Judas, "Leave Mary alone."

> Lead a life of love, just as Christ did. He loved us. He gave himself up for us. He was a sweet-smelling offering and sacrifice to God.
> **EPHESIANS 5:2 NIRV**

## My life can be sweet for Jesus.

Jesus knew what was in Mary's heart too. She seemed to understand that Jesus would not be on earth much longer. Jesus was about to give His life for her. Mary loved Jesus and wanted to show her love while He was still with her. Nothing was too good or too expensive for Jesus.

Jesus showed His love for us when He died on the cross. His sacrifice was costly—like the expensive perfume that Mary poured on Jesus' feet. If you love Jesus and want to show it, live your life to please Him. You will be like a sweet perfume to those around you. The good smell will fill the room! —C.B.

## **READ MORE**

Read Matthew 26:6–12 to learn about another woman who wanted to show Jesus how much she loved Him.

### **FUN FACT**

The perfume Mary poured out was called nard, which is the oil from a flowering plant in faraway Asia. The Bible says Mary's perfume was very valuable—worth about as much as a person could earn in a year!

> "Scripture says,
> 'My house will be
> called a house of
> prayer for all nations,'
> but you have turned
> it into a gathering
> place for thieves."
>
> **MARK 11:17 GW**

# A House of Worship

**Jesus and His disciples** arrived in Jerusalem for the Passover celebration. They went to the temple, which the Jewish people were supposed to do during Passover.

But at the temple, Jesus saw something horrible. There were many business people in the temple. But they weren't there to worship. The business people wanted to make money from the other people who came to the temple during Passover. This made Jesus very angry!

The business people were greedy. Instead of honoring the holy day, they were thinking about money. But Jesus would not allow His Father's house to be disrespected. He pushed over the tables of the people making change. He turned over the benches of the men selling birds for sacrifices. Jesus threw out everyone who was selling and buying things in the temple. He shouted, "Scripture says, 'My house will be called a house of prayer for all nations,' but you have turned it into a gathering place for thieves."

## I will respect God.

Jesus was very upset by the greed He saw. He didn't want bad things to happen in the temple, because it was a special place God made for meeting with His people.

When we're in our own place of worship, the things we do and say can show honor to God. Today we can worship God in a church, in the outdoors, or even in our rooms by ourselves. Wherever you worship God, thank Him for His love and honor Him with respect. —T.M.

### FUN FACT

People could bring several different animals to the temple as a sacrifice. They included bulls, goats, lambs, doves, or pigeons.

### READ MORE

Read Isaiah 56:6–7.
Who does God say His "house" is for?

# Look at the Stars

**On a clear evening** it is delightful to look up at the night sky. You could even spread out a blanket on the ground and lie on your back to see what God has made.

> I look at the heavens you made with your hands. I see the moon and the stars you created. And I wonder, "Why are people so important to you? Why do you even think about them? Why do you care so much about humans? Why do you even notice them?"
>
> **PSALM 8:3–4 ERV**

If you're away from the lights of a city, you'll see a beautiful sight. Thousands and thousands of stars sprinkle the sky. It's like God scattered glitter above us! The stars twinkle quietly, making us feel small because they're so far away. When we spend just a few minutes gazing at the stars, we see God's greatness. Not only did He hang the sun, moon, and stars in their places, He also thought them up in the first place. He knew they would be beautiful and show us His power.

## We are important to God.

Many years ago, King David had the same feeling when he looked at the stars. He knew God was amazing—and it made him feel small. David wondered why God even pays attention to people, when He has the whole universe to think about. But David remembered that God loves people. He made humans different from the rest of creation. Of all the things God created, people are the most important, because we are made in His image. God put people in charge of everything He created.

We can look into the sky and see the greatness of God. But God looks down at us with love, because we are so important to Him. —T.M.

### READ MORE

Read Psalm 148:3–6. As you praise God, what are the sun, moon, and stars doing?

**FUN FACT**

Scientists guess that the Milky Way galaxy might have as many as four hundred billion stars in it. That's a four with eleven zeroes behind it! If you have really good eyes, you might be able to count about nine thousand of them.

> This is the day the LORD has made. We will rejoice and be glad in it.
>
> **PSALM 118:24 NLT**

# Be Glad

**Every new day** is a day that God creates. Every new day is a special gift from Him. God wants us to enjoy every day that He gives us. Some days are filled with fun and laughter. But other days don't turn out the way we want them to.

Job was a man who loved God. Job stayed away from evil. He had seven sons and three daughters, and he was the richest man in his area. But one day God allowed Satan to test Job. Satan said Job didn't really love God—Job just loved all the things God gave him. So the devil made bad things happen to Job until he lost everything. Job even lost his ten children! Then Job got bad sores on his skin. His friends turned against him. Job was completely miserable, but he never lost his faith and trust in God.

Job's bad days finally did come to an end. God gave Job twice as much as he had before. God blessed the last part of Job's life more than the first part of his life. God even gave Job ten more children.

## Every day is a day to be glad.

You may never have to suffer like Job did. But sometimes life is hard. Keep trusting God and He will bless you. When you think of how much God loves you and cares about you, you can be glad. On good days, and even on not-so-good days, God is worthy of our praise. Be glad for every day that God gives you. —C.B.

## FUN FACT

In a 24-hour day, there are 1,440 minutes, which equals 86,400 seconds. That is a lot of time for you to be glad!

## READ MORE

Read Psalm 96 to see a song of praise and gladness. What parts of creation are glad that the Lord will judge the earth?

# A Story of Forgiveness

**Peter had a question** about forgiving people. So Jesus told him a parable.

In Jesus' story, a king wanted to collect the money that his servants owed him. One servant owed him a huge amount of money. The servant had no way to pay it back. The king decided that the servant and his family and everything they owned should be sold. Then at least the king would get some of his money back. But the servant begged the king to be kind. He said, "Be patient with me. I will pay you everything I owe." The king felt sorry for the man and let him go free.

Later, though, the same servant found someone who owed him a tiny bit of money. He grabbed the man and said, "Pay me the money you owe me!" The man fell on his knees and said, "Be patient with me. I will pay you everything I owe." But the forgiven servant wouldn't forgive someone else. He told a judge to throw the man into prison.

> Peter came to Jesus. He asked, "Lord, how many times should I forgive my brother when he sins against me? Up to seven times?" Jesus answered, "I tell you, not seven times, but 77 times."
>
> MATTHEW 18:21–22 NIRV

## I can forgive others because God forgives me.

When the king heard about that, he was angry. He called his servant in and said, "You begged me to forgive your debt, and I said you didn't have to pay anything. You should have given that other man the same forgiveness I gave you!" Then the king put the servant in jail until he could pay his debt.

Jesus told this story to help us understand how important it is to forgive. The king is like God. When we ask God to forgive us, He does. It doesn't matter how big our sins are. We are like the king's servant. When people ask us to forgive them, we should. We should forgive like God forgives us. —T.M.

## READ MORE

Read Luke 17:3–4.
How many times should we forgive someone in a day?

### FUN FACT

The English word *forgive* comes from two Greek words that mean "grace" and "to send away." Because of God's grace, He sends our sins away!

# Jacob Gets Married

When Laban heard the news about his sister's son Jacob, Laban ran to meet him. Laban hugged him and kissed him and brought him to his house.

GENESIS 29:13 ICB

**Has somebody ever** played a trick on you? Some tricks are funny. Others are mean.

Jacob and Esau were twin sons of Isaac and Rebekah. When Jacob tricked his brother and their father, Rebekah told him to go away for a while. Isaac told Jacob to go see his uncle Laban and marry one of his daughters.

One day, Jacob went to a well and met a young woman named Rachel. She was a daughter of his uncle Laban. Laban was happy when he heard about Jacob. He brought Jacob home and gave him a job. Jacob worked for Laban for one month for free. Then Laban said, "It's not right for you to work without pay."

Jacob was in love with Rachel. He said, "Let me marry Rachel, and I'll work for seven years." So Laban agreed.

So Jacob worked for seven years. But because he loved Rachel so much, the time seemed like only a few days. Then Laban threw a big wedding party.

Jacob was excited to marry Rachel. But somehow, Laban tricked Jacob. In the morning Jacob found out he had married Rachel's sister, Leah! "Why did you trick me?" asked Jacob.

## Consequences follow bad decisions.

"In our country the older daughter must get married first," Laban said. "After one week, you can marry Rachel too, but you must work another seven years."

Jacob had tricked his father and brother, and now he had been tricked by Laban. Jacob learned that there are consequences when we do things we shouldn't. But Jacob would also learn that if he trusted in God, God would be with him and bless him. —C.B.

### FUN FACT

The wedding of Britain's Prince William and Catherine "Kate" Middleton got a lot of attention! They were married on April 29, 2011, in London. About two billion people watched it on TV, while one million people lined the streets in London.

### READ MORE

Read Genesis 28:10–15.
What did God tell Jacob in a dream?

# Sowing and Reaping

**When farmers plant** seeds, they hope to get a large crop. Farming is a hard job, because many things can hurt a farmer's crop. The crop won't be good if there is too much rain, too much sun, too many bugs, or too many weeds. The farmer plants seeds and hopes for the best. But one thing is sure. Farmers will only get back what they planted. If they plant corn seeds, they'll get corn. If they plant wheat seeds, they'll get wheat. If they plant watermelon seeds, they'll get watermelons!

> "So plant the seeds of doing what is right. Then you will harvest the fruit of your faithful love. It is time to turn to me. When you do, I will come and shower my blessings on you."
>
> **HOSEA 10:12 NIRV**

Planting is also called "sowing." When the crops are ready to be picked, the farmer "reaps." Have you ever heard the saying, "You reap what you sow"? It comes from the Bible. The saying means that the things you do and the choices you make have certain results. If you're mean to your friends, they'll probably be mean to you. If you want others to be kind to you, you'll need to sow seeds of kindness.

*I will sow the right kind of seeds.*

In the Old Testament, God sent the prophet Hosea to the Israelites. The people had turned away from God, and Hosea told them they would pay for their sin. Hosea told the people their hearts were like hard ground that needed to be plowed. They needed to change their ways. So Hosea reminded the people that if they sowed seeds of love and obedience, God would be pleased.

If we plant seeds of doing what is right, we will reap God's blessings. God's blessings don't always come to us in ways we expect. They don't always look like blessings right away. But the words of Hosea are still true today. Sow good seeds! —C.B.

## READ MORE
Hosea 14 tells how the people of Israel could turn back to the Lord. What are some of the good things they would reap?

## FUN FACT
Even very old seeds can sprout into new plants. Some seeds can last fifty years before growing. A few years ago, scientists say they grew a tree from a two thousand-year-old seed!

Then Jesus asked,
"Who do you say
I am?" Peter answered,
"You are the Christ."

**MARK 8:29 ICB**

# Peter's Important Words

**The disciples had** been following Jesus for almost three years. They saw Jesus perform many miracles. They saw Him feed five thousand men—besides their wives and children—with just the lunch of a young boy. They saw Him walk on the water during a storm. The disciples also heard Jesus teach many important lessons. He explained the meaning of parables to them and taught them to live in peace. He helped them understand the rewards that will be given in heaven. Jesus' followers saw Him do things no one else had ever done. They knew He taught with wisdom no one else had.

Everyone who saw or heard Jesus wondered who He might be. They knew there was something special about Him. So they talked together about who He really was. One time, as Jesus and His disciples were walking, He asked them, "Who do people say I am?"

They answered, "Well, some say John the Baptist. Some say Elijah. And others say you are one of the other prophets."

Then Jesus asked, "But who do you say I am?"

Peter answered, "You are the Christ."

## Jesus is the Christ.

God had promised the Israelites that He would send someone to save them. They waited for this person, called the Christ or the Messiah, for a long time. But not everyone believed Jesus was the Christ God had promised. Peter was the first disciple to clearly say that Jesus was the promised Savior. God helped Peter see the truth of who Jesus is.

At some point, all people will have to decide if they believe Jesus is the Christ. But right now, like Peter, we can have faith to say with confidence that Jesus is the Savior of the world. —T.M.

### FUN FACT

The word *Christ* comes from the Greek language. In the Hebrew language, the word is *Messiah*. Both mean "the anointed one," or the one specially chosen by God.

### READ MORE

Read Philippians 2:9–11.
In the future, how many people will admit that Jesus is Lord?

# Eight Bags of Money

**A rich man** was going on a trip. Before he left, he asked his servants to watch over his things. He gave three of his servants some money to use.

The first servant got five bags of money. The second servant got two bags of money. The third servant got one bag. While the rich man was gone, the servants handled the money in different ways. The first servant used his five bags to earn five more bags. The second servant used his two bags to earn two more bags. But the third servant took his one bag and buried it in the ground.

When the rich man returned, he asked his servants what they had done with his money. The first and second servants told him they had earned more money. They each had twice as much as he had given them.

"After a long time the master came home. He asked the servants what they did with his money. The servant who got five bags brought that amount and five more bags of money to the master. The servant said, 'Master, you trusted me to care for five bags of money. So I used them to earn five more.'"

MATTHEW 25:19–20 ERV

## *God gives me gifts and talents to use for Him.*

So the master said, "You did right. You are good servants who can be trusted." But when he learned that the third servant had buried his money, the rich man said, "You are a bad and lazy servant!" Then he threw that servant out of his house.

Jesus told this story to help His followers understand that God gives each of us gifts to use for Him. He doesn't want us to hide our gifts and talents, like that servant who buried his money bag in the ground. It doesn't matter how big or small your talents may seem. Each one is important to God. He wants you to use your gifts, to help others and to honor Him. —T.M.

### **READ MORE**

Read Romans 12:6–8.
What does it say about using your own special abilities?

**FUN FACT**

Some Bible versions call the bags of money *talents*. A talent was a lot of money. During the time Jesus was on earth, it was the amount a worker would earn in about twenty years!

# God Calls Jeremiah

**When Josiah was king** of Judah, God spoke to a man named Jeremiah. He told Jeremiah that he would be a prophet to the nations.

"My Lord and King," Jeremiah said, "I don't know how to speak. I'm too young."

"Do not say you are too young," God said. "Do not be afraid of people. I am with you and will protect you."

Then the Lord reached out His hand and touched Jeremiah's mouth. He said, "I have put my words in your mouth. I want you to speak to the nations and kingdoms."

God told Jeremiah what was going to happen to His people because they had turned away from Him. God wanted Jeremiah to carry His messages to the people.

It was a tough job for Jeremiah. But God said, "Stand up and get ready! Tell the people everything I command you to say. Do not be afraid. I have made you like a city with a high wall around it. I have made you like an iron pillar and a bronze wall. They will fight against you, but they will not overcome you. I am with you and will save you."

Jeremiah served God for forty years. God was always with him because when God asks people to do something, He gives them the strength for the job.

## God will help me to do what He asks me to do.

If God asks you to serve Him, He will give you the strength you need. He will give you the right words to say. You can stand up and get ready to serve God, just like Jeremiah did. —C.B.

### FUN FACT

Jeremiah is known as the "weeping prophet." He was sad because he knew what was going to happen to the people but they wouldn't listen to him.

### READ MORE

Read Jeremiah 13:1–11. What did God use to help Jeremiah understand how God felt about His people?

# God Humbles a King

**King Nebuchadnezzar** had a strange dream. He saw a large, strong tree that the animals were using for food and shelter. The leaves were beautiful and people enjoyed eating the good fruit. But then an angel came from heaven and said in a loud voice, "Cut down the tree and its branches. Strip off its leaves. Scatter its fruit around. But let the stump and roots stay in the ground." King Nebuchadnezzar called his wise men to explain the dream, but they couldn't. Only Daniel knew what the dream meant because God explained it to him.

Daniel told Nebuchadnezzar, "King, you are that tree! This is the meaning of the dream. You will be forced to live among the wild animals. You will learn that God is the ruler over human kingdoms and He gives them to whoever He wants."

A year later, the king was walking on the roof of his palace. He said, "Look at Babylon! I built this great place by my power to show how great I am!" Because Nebuchadnezzar was proud, he thought he was more important

> "King Nebuchadnezzar, you will be forced to go away from people. You will live among the wild animals. You will eat grass like cattle, and you will become wet with dew. Seven seasons will pass, and then you will learn this lesson. You will learn God Most High rules over human kingdoms and gives them to whoever he wants."
>
> DANIEL 4:25 ERV

## God will humble the proud.

than God. But as soon as the king said that, God spoke from heaven and repeated what Daniel had told the king. Then all those bad things happened to Nebuchadnezzar.

After seven years of being confused and living like an animal, Nebuchadnezzar's mind finally became clear again. He praised God and gave Him honor for being the One who rules forever. Then God gave Nebuchadnezzar his kingdom back.

No one is greater than God. Even kings and rulers are under His authority. God does not like it when people are proud. Even when He allows us to do great things, God is the one who deserves the praise. —T.M.

## READ MORE

Find Daniel 4:34–35 to read the prayer Nebuchadnezzar prayed to God after his punishment.

## FUN FACT

Nebuchadnezzar's kingdom was called Babylon. Babylon was located in the part of the world that is now Iraq.

# Perfect Rules

> The Lord's teachings are perfect. They give new strength. The Lord's rules can be trusted. They make plain people wise.
>
> **PSALM 19:7 ICB**

**God put Adam and Eve** in a beautiful garden with lots of plants and trees. Then God gave them one rule. He said Adam and Eve could eat the fruit from almost any tree in the garden, except for one.

God gave Adam and Eve that rule, and He explained what would happen if they disobeyed. Adam and Eve ate from the tree they shouldn't have. They brought sin and all of its problems into God's perfect world.

God loves us like a father loves his children. God knows what is best for us. His rules are perfect because He is perfect. People who follow God's rules and teachings are wise and happy.

*I will learn and follow God's perfect rules.*

When Noah did what God told him to do, he and his family were kept safe in the ark. When Abraham obeyed God, he became the father of a great nation. When Moses followed God's instructions, God helped him become a great leader of the Israelites. When Daniel obeyed God instead of the king's rule, God protected him from the lions.

Following God's rules can keep us safe and protect us from harm. But to follow God's rules we need to know what they are. God's rules and teachings are in the Bible. The more we read the Bible, the more we will learn how God wants us to live. God loves us and wants us to enjoy our lives. That is why He gives us perfect rules! —C.B.

### FUN FACT

In Matthew 7:12, Jesus gave us a special rule: "Do to others what you would want them to do to you" (NIRV). Around the 1700s, people started calling this the "Golden Rule."

### READ MORE

Read Psalm 19:8–11.
**What are some good reasons to obey God's rules?**

# Eat Your Vegetables

**When they were only teenagers,** Daniel and his friends were captured and taken to Babylon. Because they were smart and strong and hardworking, they were chosen to live in the king's palace.

Daniel and his friends were in a strange new place. They read new books and learned a new language. The king wanted them to eat his fancy food and drink his wine. But Daniel didn't want to do that. The Israelites had special instructions about what they were supposed to eat. The food from the king's palace was not made in the right way. Daniel knew if he ate the king's food he would be disobeying God.

So Daniel came up with a plan. He asked the king's guard to give him and his friends only fruits and vegetables. The king's guard was afraid at first. He thought Daniel and his friends would become sick and weak if they didn't eat the king's fancy foods. If that happened, the guard thought he would be in trouble!

But Daniel said, "Please give us this test for ten days. After ten days, compare us with the other young men who eat the king's food. See for yourself who looks healthier, and then decide how you want to treat us."

> He said, "Please give us this test for ten days: Don't give us anything but vegetables to eat and water to drink. Then after ten days, compare us with the other young men who eat the king's food. See for yourself who looks healthier, and then decide how you want to treat us, your servants."
>
> **DANIEL 1:12-13 ERV**

## I can trust God.

The guard agreed. At the end of ten days, Daniel and his friends looked healthier than all the young men in the kingdom who had eaten the fancy food. Daniel and his friends kept eating the fruits and vegetables. And they became smarter and wiser than all the other servants in the kingdom.

God loved Daniel and his friends. God took care of them, even while they were in a land far from home. God will do the same for you. No matter where you are, He loves you—and you can trust Him. —T.M.

## READ MORE

Read Leviticus 11:1–8.
What are some of the animals
God told the Israelites not to eat?

### FUN FACT

Fruits and vegetables provide many vitamins and minerals that growing kids need. You should eat at least five servings of fruits and veggies each day!

> Joyful is the person who finds wisdom, the one who gains understanding.
>
> **PROVERBS 3:13 NLT**

# Understand It!

**There are three men** in the Bible named Philip. One of them is called "the evangelist" because he told people the good news about Jesus.

One day an angel told Philip to go into the desert, on a road that goes from Jerusalem to Gaza. He saw a man sitting in a chariot and reading the book of the prophet Isaiah. The man was an important official for the queen of Ethiopia. Philip asked the official, "Do you understand what you are reading?"

The man said he needed help, and asked Philip to explain the Scripture he was reading. The verses were about Jesus, but the man didn't understand them. So Philip told him all about Jesus and how to be saved. When the Ethiopian saw some water, he asked Philip to baptize him. Philip said, "If you believe with all your heart, you may be baptized." The man answered, "I believe that Jesus Christ is the Son of God."

Philip was happy to baptize the man. The Ethiopian traveled home full of joy because he understood the words of Isaiah. And even better, now he knew Jesus!

Until they know Jesus as their Savior, people don't understand the things of God. They might hear others say how happy they are to be Christians. They might read the Bible themselves. But without God's Spirit inside them, they can't really understand.

## I can understand the Bible when I believe in Jesus.

But when we believe in Jesus as our Savior, the Holy Spirit helps us understand the words in the Bible. He fills our hearts with joy! —C.B.

### FUN FACT

The queen of Ethiopia was called "Candace." It was a title (like "Pharaoh") rather than a name. But about five hundred years ago, people began naming their daughters Candace.

### READ MORE

Read the words that the man from Ethiopia was reading in Isaiah 53:7–8. How did Philip know these verses were about Jesus?

# Grace Is Enough

**The apostle Paul** faced a lot of challenges while he preached the gospel. He was shipwrecked three times and beaten three times. He spent many days in jail. And he faced another struggle. In one of his letters Paul said he had a problem that was like a thorn stuck in his side.

Three different times I begged the Lord to take it away. Each time he said, "My grace is all you need. My power works best in weakness."

**2 CORINTHIANS 12:8–9 NLT**

We don't know exactly what Paul's problem was, but it might have been some pain or problem in his body. Paul prayed three times for God to take it away. But God chose to leave Paul's "thorn." Instead, God told Paul something very important. God said His grace was the strength Paul needed to face the pain. And Paul learned that God's power is most real when people feel weakest.

*God is strong when I feel weak.*

We can pray for God to heal us from sickness or injuries or disabilities. He is able to fix any problem we face. But sometimes He doesn't heal us the way we want Him to. He still loves us and hears our prayers. It's just that sometimes God allows people to go through hard times. We don't always understand why, but we have to trust that God has a purpose in everything He does.

If God doesn't answer our prayers for healing, we can remember the words He told Paul. God is strongest in our lives when we feel the weakest. His grace gives us and the people we love strength to face the pain. —T.M.

## **FUN FACT**

Scientists have done studies to measure the power of prayer in healing people. One study found that patients who were prayed for needed less medicine and had fewer problems with their recovery!

## **READ MORE**

Continue reading 2 Corinthians 12:9–10. How did Paul feel when he learned that his weakness allowed God's strength to flow?

## JUNE
# 18

"He must become greater; I must become less."

JOHN 3:30 NIV

# Greater or Less

**When you study** math you learn about ideas like "greater than" and "less than." Five is greater than four. Six is less than seven. Numbers can be greater than or less than other numbers, but when it comes to people, God sees us all the same. No one person is greater than another person—except for Jesus. He is greater than all of us because He is the Son of God.

John the Baptist was Jesus' cousin. John was born shortly before Jesus, and he had a special purpose in life. John was supposed to get people ready for Jesus. Even though he preached in the wilderness, lots of people came out to see and hear him. Maybe some liked to see his funny clothes—he wore a coat made of camel's hair. Maybe some liked to watch him eat bugs called locusts! But when they came, John told them to turn from their sins and be baptized.

Some of the religious leaders didn't trust John. They wanted to know just who he was. So they asked him if he was a special

## Jesus is greater than all.

prophet or God's chosen Savior, the Messiah. John said, "I am not. I am the voice of one crying in the desert, 'Make things ready for the Lord.'"

John told everyone that his job was to lead people to Jesus. Many people came to John to admit that they had done wrong. They asked John to baptize them. One day, John even baptized Jesus! But John made it clear that Jesus was greater than he was.

We can be like John when we point people to Jesus. We become less, and Jesus becomes greater! —C.B.

## FUN FACT

God said some kinds of bugs were good food for His people to eat. They included locusts, katydids, crickets, and grasshoppers!

## READ MORE

John 3:31–36.
What do these verses tell us about Jesus?

# Words on the Wall

**Belshazzar was the king** of Babylon after its greatest king, Nebuchadnezzar. One night, Belshazzar had a big party for a thousand people in his palace. King Belshazzar commanded his servants to bring special gold and silver cups for everyone to use. Many years before, Nebuchadnezzar had stolen these cups from God's temple when he attacked Jerusalem. They were supposed to be used only in worshipping the one true God. But while he used the cups, King Belshazzar praised his false gods.

Suddenly, the king saw something strange! What looked like a human hand was writing a message on the palace wall. As he watched, the king's face turned white. Because he couldn't read the message, he called for the wise men of Babylon to explain it. Belshazzar said he would reward the person who could read the message with special clothes and an important job.

The wise men came, but none of them could read the words. Then the queen remembered Daniel. He had explained dreams to King Nebuchadnezzar many years earlier. When Nebuchadnezzar died, most people forgot about Daniel. But the queen knew Daniel would be able to read the message.

He said to these wise men of Babylon, "Whoever can read this writing and tell me what it means will be dressed in purple robes of royal honor and will have a gold chain placed around his neck. He will become the third highest ruler in the kingdom!"

DANIEL 5:7 NLT

## I can stay true to God no matter where I am.

So Daniel came to speak to the king. He didn't want a reward, but he did tell Belshazzar what the words meant. Daniel said that God would bring the king's rule to an end, and he was going to be defeated by his enemies.

Like many people today, Daniel lived in a country where people did not love and respect God. But Daniel stayed true to God and God was always with him. No matter where you are, you can be like Daniel and stay true to God. You can help others know that God is always in control. —T.M.

### FUN FACT

"The writing is on the wall" is a common saying. It means that something bad is going to happen and it can't be changed. The saying comes from today's story in Daniel.

### READ MORE

Read Ezra 5:13–15.
What happened to some of the gold and silver cups that Nebuchadnezzar stole from the temple?

# God Sends Gideon

"You have the strength to save the people of Israel. Go and save them from the Midianites. I am the one who is sending you."

**JUDGES 6:14 ICB**

**The Israelites were** being bullied. For seven years the Midianites had been smashing their crops and stealing their animals. The Israelites had to hide in the mountains for safety. They cried out to God for help, so God chose Gideon to fight the Midianites.

God sent an angel to tell Gideon the news. "The Lord is with you mighty warrior!" the angel said. When Gideon turned to see who was speaking to him, he saw the angel sitting under an oak tree. "You have the strength to save your people," the angel said. "Go and defeat the Midianites."

But Gideon was afraid. He said to the angel, "My family is weak and I am the least important member in my family."

The Lord answered him, "I will be with you."

Gideon asked God to prove that He would help. Gideon laid a piece of wool outside that night. Then he asked God to cover the wool with dew but to leave the ground around it dry. God did what Gideon asked. The next night Gideon asked God to keep the wool dry but to make the ground around it wet. Again, God did what Gideon asked. So Gideon knew that God would be with him.

Gideon called together a huge army, but God said he needed only three hundred men. God wanted the people to realize their victory would come from Him and not a lot of soldiers.

## God uses the weak because He is strong.

It was a strange battle. Gideon gave each man a torch, a clay jar, and a trumpet. In the dark of night, when Gideon gave the order, the men broke their jars and blew their trumpets. They shouted, "For the Lord and Gideon!" The Midianites were so scared they started fighting each other instead of the Israelites!

Gideon thought he was weak, but God used him to defeat the Midianites. When we forget about our own weakness and depend on God, He can use us too! —C.B.

### FUN FACT

The Israelites and the Midianites were related. The Midianites were from the family of Midian, who was a half brother to Isaac. Isaac's mom was Sarah. When she died, Isaac's dad, Abraham, married a woman named Keturah. Midian was one of their sons.

### READ MORE

Read Judges 6:11–12.
What was Gideon doing when the angel came to visit him?

# Two Kings in a Cave

**David was only** a young shepherd when God chose him to be the next leader of Israel. It was a special job and David was eager to do it. But he had to wait.

King Saul was still ruling over the Israelites. It wasn't David's turn yet. David was famous and becoming more popular. Many men had started to follow him. They wanted David to be king and thought he had a right to take over Saul's kingdom. Saul was scared of David and wanted to get rid of him.

One day, Saul was out looking for David to hurt him. Saul decided to rest in a cave. He thought he was alone, but David and his men were hiding in the back of the cave! David's men whispered to him that this was his chance to become king. If he killed Saul, he would take over the kingdom. But David knew that wasn't God's way for him to become king. He trusted God to keep His promise at the right time. David didn't hurt Saul, because he knew it was best to do things God's way.

> "This very day you have seen with your own eyes how the LORD handed you over to me in the cave. Some of my men begged me to kill you. But I spared you. I said, 'I will never lift my hand to strike my master down. He is the LORD's anointed king.'"
>
> **1 SAMUEL 24:10 NIRV**

## I can use self-control to obey God.

David showed self-control. He could have done something bad to make himself more important, but that would have gone against God's law. David chose to be patient and let God work out His plan. One day, God did make David king, just as He said He would.

We can learn from David and practice self-control too. Someday, someone might tell you to do something to make yourself more important. But if it's something that goes against God's plan, remember David. God blessed him because of his obedience. —T.M.

### FUN FACT

There are more than a thousand caves in Israel. One of these caves is named Malcham. It is the largest cave in Israel and the largest salt cave in the world.

### READ MORE

Read 2 Samuel 5:1–5.
How did God keep his promise to David?

# A Holy God

> "There is no one holy like the LORD. There is no one but you, O LORD. There is no Rock like our God."
>
> 1 SAMUEL 2:2 GW

**The words in today's** Bible verse are part of a prayer by a woman named Hannah. She loved God and worshipped Him. But Hannah was very sad because she was unable to have a baby.

So Hannah prayed that God would give her a child. She asked God with a humble heart. Hannah promised to give her child back to God if He would answer her prayer.

After a while, God did answer Hannah's prayer. She became pregnant and had a baby boy named Samuel. And when Samuel was old enough, she gave him back to God. Hannah sent Samuel to live in God's temple. He would serve as a priest for his whole life.

*My God is holy.*

Before Hannah left the temple, she praised God for His greatness. She understood that God is holy. That means God is perfect in His goodness. There is no one else like Him. God deserves our attention and love. He should be respected for who He is.

Hannah knew God was the only one who could answer her prayers. She gave up Samuel as a way of showing she believed in God's holiness. She wanted to honor God. She praised Him for being the only God in the universe.

No person is holy like God. He is completely perfect! That's why we sing songs of praise to Him. When we sing, we join the angels of heaven who say, "Holy, holy, holy, is the Lord God Almighty." —T.M.

### FUN FACT

Another word for "holy" is *righteous*. It means honorable, respectable, and good.

### READ MORE

What does Psalm 89:5–9 say about God's holiness?

# Two Brothers Make Peace

**Jacob was afraid.** He was about to see his brother, Esau, for the first time in many years. Jacob and Esau were twins. Esau had been born first, so he was the one who would receive the family blessing. Esau should have become the head of the family when his father, Isaac, passed away.

> When Esau saw Jacob, he ran to meet him. He put his arms around Jacob, hugged his neck, and kissed him. Then they both cried.
>
> **GENESIS 33:4 ERV**

But Jacob wanted that blessing. He wanted to be the most important son. So one day when Esau was very hungry, Jacob tricked him into trading his blessing for a bowl of stew. Then Jacob went to Isaac, who was old and blind. Jacob tricked his father, too, and took the blessing that was supposed to go to Esau. When Esau found out, he was so angry that Jacob had to run away and live with his uncle.

Jacob didn't know what Esau would do when they met each other again. So Jacob sent Esau many animals as presents to make things right. He went ahead of his family to talk to Esau. When he saw Esau coming, Jacob showed respect to Esau by bowing down to the ground seven times. Then Esau ran toward Jacob—and hugged him! The brothers both cried. Esau asked, "What are all these animals for?"

Jacob answered, "These are my gifts to you so that you might accept me."

## I can forgive others because God forgives me.

But Esau said, "You don't have to give me gifts, brother. I have enough for myself."

Jacob knew he had hurt his brother. But when he had the chance to make things right, he did. Esau forgave Jacob and accepted his brother's apology. When one person apologizes and the other person forgives, it brings peace. —T.M.

### READ MORE
Find Matthew 5:23–24.
What does God want us to do before we give gifts to Him?

### FUN FACT
When Jacob was born, he was holding onto his twin brother Esau's heel. The name Jacob means "heel grabber."

# David Seeks Revenge

**David was not** yet king. He was hiding from King Saul, and living in a desert. A rich man named Nabal lived near there. Nabal had many shepherds and sheep.

It was the time of year when sheep have their wool clipped off. David and his soldiers had always treated Nabal's shepherds and sheep with respect. Now David wanted to ask Nabal for a favor.

David's men greeted Nabal with kindness. They said, "May everything go well with you and your family. We have treated your shepherds well. Please be kind to us and share some of your food and drink."

But Nabal was rude. He said, "Who is David? I have bread, water, and meat for my men. Why should I give food to people I don't know?"

When David's men reported what Nabal said, David was angry. He told four hundred of his men to pick up their swords. He wanted to kill Nabal!

Someone warned Nabal's wife, Abigail, who was a wise woman. She quickly loaded her donkeys with lots of bread, meat, and drinks. She took grain and fig cakes too and went to find David.

## I will not seek revenge.

When she saw David, Abigail bowed down in respect. She begged David for forgiveness. She told him to ignore Nabal because he was foolish. She gave David her gifts and reminded him to fight only the Lord's battles.

Abigail's words calmed David. They kept him from killing Nabal and his men. David realized it was up to God to deal with Nabal. It wasn't David's job to get revenge.

We should not seek revenge either. When we're upset with others, we need to leave them in God's hands.
—C.B.

## FUN FACT

Sheep are usually clipped (or "sheared") in early spring. This helps them stay cool through the warmer months. And it gives them time to grow a nice heavy coat of wool for winter.

## READ MORE

Read 1 Samuel 25:39–42.
What happened to Abigail after Nabal died?

# The Snake Bite

> But Paul shook the snake off into the fire and was not hurt. The people thought he would swell up or fall down dead. They waited and watched him for a long time, but nothing bad happened to him.
>
> ACTS 28:5–6 ERV

**Paul and his group** of missionaries traveled to an island called Malta. When they arrived, the people who lived there were very kind to them. It was raining and cold, so the people of Malta built a fire to help Paul and his friends warm up.

Paul helped gather some sticks for the fire. As he reached over the flames, a snake hiding in the sticks sprung out when it felt the heat. The snake sunk its teeth into Paul's hand and held on tight. When the people of Malta saw the snake attack Paul, they were afraid. They thought the snake bite meant that Paul was a bad person.

But Paul wasn't afraid. He didn't run around screaming. Paul just shook the snake into the fire. He wasn't hurt at all! The people kept watching Paul, thinking he would swell up or fall over dead. After a long time, they saw that nothing bad happened. They were amazed and knew that a miracle had happened.

## I can trust God no matter what happens.

When the snake bit him, Paul had a choice. He could have been scared or angry. But Paul knew God had a plan for him. God was in control of whatever happened. So Paul didn't let trouble keep him from doing the job God gave him to do.

Sometimes, like Paul, we'll face some hard things. Hopefully we never get bitten by a snake! But no matter what happens, we can know God is with us. God might use unusual things in our lives to help us tell others about Jesus. —T.M.

### READ MORE
Continue reading Acts 28:7–10. What other things happened on the island while Paul was there?

### FUN FACT
Malta is a small island southwest of Italy. It is only 122 square miles (316 square kilometers), making it one of the smallest countries in the world.

# Stand Up

> All the people were happy for the wonderful things Jesus was doing.
>
> LUKE 13:17 ICB

**Jesus was teaching** on the Sabbath, the day of rest for Jewish people. He saw a woman who was bent over. She couldn't stand up straight. She had been that way for eighteen years.

So Jesus asked the woman to come to Him. He said, "Woman, your sickness is gone. You will no longer be disabled." Then He put His hands on her. The woman stood up straight and began praising God!

The Jewish leaders saw what Jesus did, and they were upset. They complained that Jesus had done work on the Sabbath by healing the woman. "There are six days for work," one of leaders told everyone. "Do not come for healing on the Sabbath!"

Jesus was not happy with the leaders. He said, "You are hypocrites! You don't do what you say. You pretend not to work on the Sabbath, even though you really do. Don't you untie your donkeys on the Sabbath and lead them to water so they can drink? This woman is one of your own people. She has been disabled for eighteen years. Shouldn't she be set free from her sickness on the Sabbath?"

The leaders who criticized Jesus were ashamed. But the other people who saw what Jesus did were happy. They praised God for all the wonderful things Jesus was doing.

## I will stand up and praise God.

The reason for the Sabbath day was so people would rest. But Jesus said it was fine to do good things on the Sabbath. Helping other people is a good thing. Praising God is a good thing. And we can help others and praise God any day of the week. —C.B.

## FUN FACT

Some Jewish people today still try to avoid work on the Sabbath. In some cities, they don't even press buttons on elevators. The elevators are set to run by themselves and stop at every floor.

## READ MORE

Read Luke 4:14–21.
What other important thing did Jesus do on the Sabbath?

> By wisdom a house
> is built. Through
> understanding it
> is made secure.
> Through knowledge
> its rooms are filled
> with priceless and
> beautiful things.
>
> PROVERBS 24:3–4 NIRV

# Building Houses

**When construction workers** build a house, they need the right supplies and materials. First they lay a foundation with concrete. Next they frame the walls with wood. Then they put bricks, stones, or siding on the outside. A roof covered with shingles or tiles protects the house below.

When a family moves into their new house, they fill the rooms with their favorite things. They add beautiful decorations to make the rooms pretty. Some of the decorations—like family pictures—have special meaning. They are considered priceless.

Building our lives is a lot like building a house. The supplies and materials we need are understanding, wisdom, and knowledge. We can get all of these supplies from the Bible, by reading it and learning what it says.

## I can build my life like a beautiful house.

When you understand what God wants you to do and how He wants you to live, you can be strong and secure. That's your foundation. When you use the Bible's wisdom to make good choices, you are safe. That's like having a good roof over your head. When you know how much God loves you and cares about you, you have joy and peace inside. You are one of His priceless possessions.

As you read the Bible, ask God to give you lots of wisdom, understanding, and knowledge. When you build your life with these supplies, it will be more beautiful than the fanciest house in the neighborhood! —T.M.

### FUN FACT

Many houses in Japan have more than just walls and windows and roofs. They also have shock absorbers to keep from falling down during an earthquake!

### READ MORE

Read John 14:2–4.
Why is Jesus building a house right now?

# Jesus Blesses the Children

> But Jesus said, "Let the children come to me. Don't stop them! For the Kingdom of Heaven belongs to those who are like these children."
>
> MATTHEW 19:14 NLT

**Jesus had many** followers of all ages. Older people, younger people, and little children were almost always in the crowds as Jesus taught and healed.

One day some parents brought their children to Jesus so He could place his hands on their heads and pray for them. But Jesus' disciples tried to make the parents and children stay away. They thought the children would bother Jesus. They were very wrong!

Jesus said to His disciples, "Let the children come to me and don't stop them! The Kingdom of Heaven belongs to them, and those who are like them." So the disciples allowed the children to come to Jesus. When grown-ups brought their kids to Jesus, He placed His hands on them and blessed them. He loved the children as much as He loved His grown-up followers.

Children are excited to know Jesus. They love to listen to stories about Jesus and learn more about Him. They are ready to believe what Jesus tells them. They come to Him humbly, without pride. That's how Jesus wants everyone to come to Him.

## Jesus wants me to come to Him.

Parents and grandparents can take children to church and Sunday school. They can read Bible stories and teach kids how to sing praises to Jesus. No one is too young (or too old) to come to Jesus. We are all His children and He loves us all the same. —C.B.

### FUN FACT

Many churches have baby dedication ceremonies. That's when parents make a promise to the Lord to raise their children in the ways of God, to pray for them, and to be a godly example.

### READ MORE

Read Genesis 48:8–16.
Who blessed Joseph's two sons?

# The Trail of Food

When you are gathering crops in your field, you might leave some grain behind by mistake. Don't go back to get it. Leave it for outsiders and widows. Leave it for children whose fathers have died. Then the LORD your God will bless you in everything you do.

DEUTERONOMY 24:19 NIRV

**God gave Moses** laws for the Israelites to follow after they left Egypt. Moses read the laws to the people and explained them one by one. Many of the laws were about food. One special law told farmers how to take care of their fields.

As the growing season turned into harvest time, farmers would collect their crops. It took a lot of work to pick all of the grains or fruits, so they would usually miss some along the way. God knew the farmers would leave some behind by mistake, and He had a plan for those leftovers. Moses told the people what God wanted them to do. He said, "Don't go back and get what you missed. Leave it for the outsiders and the widows. Leave it for children whose fathers have died." God said the same thing to people who grew olive trees.

## I can be generous and give to others.

God reminded His people that they had been slaves in Egypt. He wanted them to remember how hard it was to be treated unfairly. And He wanted His people to be generous and to give some of what they had to those who needed it.

You might not have a field of crops or rows of olive trees to share. But you can give some of what you have to others who need help. When you share with others, you please God! —T.M.

### READ MORE

Read Deuteronomy 15:7–8.
What does it say about helping the poor?

### FUN FACT

Some of the fruits and vegetables that grow in Israel today include oranges, kiwi, guava, avocado, mangos, and grapes. Wheat and corn also grow there.

# Three Ingredients

> The LORD has told you what is good, and this is what he requires of you: to do what is right, to love mercy, and to walk humbly with your God.
>
> MICAH 6:8 NLT

**Do you ever help** make breakfast or dinner for your family? Do you follow a recipe when you cook? Most people who cook use a recipe. It tells you which ingredients to mix together so the dish turns out right.

In Old Testament times, before Jesus came to earth, God gave a "recipe" for how He wanted His people to live. The recipe is simple. It contains only three ingredients!

The first ingredient is this: do what is right. When God shows you the difference between right and wrong, choose to do the right thing. Choose to be honest instead of telling a lie. Choose to be a friend to someone who is lonely.

The second ingredient is this: love mercy. Love other people the same way God loves you. Even when people mess up or say hurtful things, forgive them and continue to be kind.

The third ingredient is this: walk humbly with God. Put God's way ahead of your own way because He is God. When your mom asks for help with the dishes, you might not want to join in. But you do it anyway because God wants you to serve others whenever you can.

These three ingredients are easy to remember. You can never have too much of them. It doesn't matter what order you mix them together. When God pours them into your life, you'll be amazed at what He can make! —T.M.

## Do what is right. Love mercy. Walk humbly.

### FUN FACT

Som tam, a famous salad from Thailand, includes ingredients like tomatoes, string beans, peanuts, dried shrimp, lime juice, and sugar cane paste.

### READ MORE

When God gave the Israelites His law, He mentioned a similar "recipe" for pleasing Him. Find Deuteronomy 10:12–13 in your Bible to read about it.

> "Honor your father
> and your mother,
> so that you may live
> long in the land the
> LORD your God is
> giving you."
>
> EXODUS 20:12 NIV

# Honor Your Parents

**In Bible times,** some people lived for hundreds of years. Adam lived 930 years. Noah was 950 years old when he died. Abraham lived to be 175. Today people don't live that long, but a few reach the age of 100.

"Honor your father and your mother" is the fifth of the Ten Commandments that God gave to Moses. To honor your parents means to obey, respect, and trust them. It's a commandment that comes with a promise. God told His people to honor their fathers and mothers so that they would live long in the land He was giving them.

God knows that honor and respect for others begins in the home. Good parents know what is best for their children, and that is why God wants children to obey their parents. It is respectful to obey your parents, and it can protect you from harm.

## I will honor God and my parents.

Some children live with their grandparents or other adults who love them and take care of them just like parents would. God wants children to honor those adults too. In the Bible, Queen Esther did not have a mom or dad. They had died when she was young, so her cousin Mordecai adopted her and took care of her. Esther honored and obeyed Mordecai. Because she obeyed him, God used her to save her people.

God can help you to honor your father and mother. He wants all of us to honor our parents the same way He wants us to honor Him. When we show honor—to our parents on earth and our Father in heaven—we will have God's blessing on our lives. —C.B.

## READ MORE

What does Ephesians 6:1–4
say about children and parents?

### FUN FACT

Methuselah was the oldest man who ever lived. He lived to be 969 years old!

# Judge Deborah

Then Deborah said to Barak, "Get ready! This is the day the LORD will give you victory over Sisera, for the LORD is marching ahead of you."
So Barak led his 10,000 warriors down the slopes of Mount Tabor into battle.

JUDGES 4:14 NLT

**Deborah is an unusual woman** in the Bible. She was a prophet and judge over Israel in a time when most of Israel's leaders were men.

In Deborah's time, the Israelites' enemies were the Canaanites. Their army leader, Sisera, was mean to the people of Israel, so they cried out to God for help.

One day Deborah asked a man named Barak to talk with her under a palm tree. Deborah told Barak, "The Lord God of Israel commands you: 'Go and gather 10,000 men for a fight. I will help you defeat Sisera.'"

Barak was afraid. He didn't have the courage to face Sisera alone. So he said, "I will do this if you will go with me, Deborah. But if you won't go with me, I won't go either."

"I will go with you," Deborah replied, "but because of your attitude, you will not be honored when Sisera is beaten. The Lord will allow a woman to defeat Sisera."

## God will help me when I do what He asks.

Everything happened exactly as Deborah said. Barak defeated Sisera's army but Sisera escaped. Sisera went to the tent of a woman named Jael and she defeated him all by herself.

For a woman of her time, Deborah was given an unusual job. But God helped her with everything He asked her to do. When God gives you a job to do, He will help you too. You can depend on God's strength! It doesn't matter how prepared you feel. It doesn't matter what anyone else might say. When you are ready to obey God, He will help you. —T.M.

## FUN FACT

Some of the first women leaders in history were queens of Egypt. Hatshepsut ruled about fifteen hundred years before Jesus was born. Nefertiti ruled about one hundred years after Hatshepsut.

## READ MORE

Find Judges 5:1–12 to read some of the songs the Israelites sang after they defeated Sisera.

# How Big Is It?

**Have you ever** thought about how big the earth is? Even though the earth is gigantic, people have been able to measure it.

We usually think of the earth as a ball, but it is not completely round. It's a little wider in the middle where the equator is. When you measure the widest part of the earth at the equator, it's about 7,926 miles (12,756 kilometers). But if you measure the tallest part of the earth, from the North Pole to the South Pole, it's about 7,900 miles (12,720 kilometers). If you measure all the way around the earth at the equator, the distance is about 24,902 miles (40,075 kilometers). But if you measure all around the earth from pole to pole, you get about 24,860 miles (40,008 kilometers). It's hard to believe anyone can measure something so big. But scientists have done it!

> May you have power with all God's people to understand Christ's love. May you know how wide and long and high and deep it is.
>
> **EPHESIANS 3:18 NIRV**

*God loves me more than I can imagine.*

In the Bible, the apostle Paul talks about something else that's very big. We can try to measure it, but we'll never be able to. Paul is talking about God's love.

God's love is wide and long and deep and high. It's bigger than the earth, bigger than the solar system, and bigger than the whole universe! The more we read the Bible and pray, the more we learn about God—and the more we will understand the greatness of His love.

God loves us so much that He sent His Son to die on the cross to pay for our sins. He loves us so much that He wants us to live with Him forever. God's love is bigger than anything we can imagine. —C.B.

## READ MORE

Read Psalm 136:1–9.
How long does God's love last?

### FUN FACT

The "diameter" of a circle is the length of a straight line passing through the center of the circle. The circle's "circumference" is the distance around its outer edge.

# Soul Medicine

Jesus answered them, "Healthy people don't need a doctor; those who are sick do. I've come to call sinners to change the way they think and act, not to call people who think they have God's approval."

**LUKE 5:31–32 GW**

**One day Jesus** saw a tax collector named Levi. Jesus walked up to Levi and said, "Follow me!"

Levi left everything he had and went with Jesus. Then Levi held a big feast at his house for Jesus. Levi invited some other tax collectors to come too.

Most people didn't like tax collectors because they were dishonest. They took a lot of money from other people for taxes, but they kept some of the money for themselves. People thought tax collectors were like thieves. So when some of the Jewish leaders saw Jesus eating with tax collectors, they looked down on Him.

"Why do you eat with tax collectors and sinners?" they asked. Jesus had a good answer. "Healthy people don't need a doctor," He said. "Those who are sick do."

The Jewish leaders thought they were perfect. They believed they had earned God's approval and didn't think they needed Jesus. They felt just like a healthy person who doesn't need a doctor. The Jewish leaders thought the tax collectors were bad and were not accepted by God.

But Jesus' words explain how God sees people. He wants to help those people who need Him most. There were many who thought they were not good enough for God. But Jesus loved them and wanted to save them.

## Jesus wants to help those who need Him.

Everyone sins. No one is perfect. Levi was an unpopular tax collector, but Jesus called him to be one of the twelve disciples. His name was later changed to Matthew. He is proof that Jesus takes away sins. —T.M.

## FUN FACT

Penicillin is a medicine that doctors give to sick people. A Scottish scientist named Alexander Fleming discovered penicillin by accident in 1928.

## READ MORE

Read Isaiah 61:1–3.
What kind of people did Jesus come to help?

# Happy Songs

**Listening to music** can make you feel happy. When you want to hear music, you can turn on a radio or play a CD. But in Bible times it wasn't like that. People didn't have recorded music. If people wanted to hear a song, they would have to find someone who could sing or play an instrument.

One day, King Saul was in a bad mood. He had turned away from God and was very troubled. Saul's servants said, "We will look for someone who can play the harp for you when you're upset." Saul thought that was a good idea.

One of Saul's servants said, "Jesse of Bethlehem has a son named David who can play the harp. He is a brave man and the Lord is with him!"

> Speak to each other with psalms, hymns, and spiritual songs. Sing and make music in your hearts to the Lord.
>
> **EPHESIANS 5:19 ICB**

*Singing to God can make me feel happy.*

So Saul sent messengers to Jesse's house. They brought Jesse a message which said, "Send me your son David." Then Jesse loaded a donkey with gifts for the king and sent them with David. When Saul met David, he liked the young man very much. Whenever David would play music on his harp, Saul would feel much better. Saul liked David so much that he invited David to live with him for a while.

David wrote over half the psalms in the Bible, and many of them are songs of praise to God! When you're feeling down, David's songs might help you to feel better. Or maybe you could create a song of praise that's all your own. Music that honors God can put a smile on your face! —C.B.

**FUN FACT**

The United States government says there are about forty-four thousand radio stations in the world!

## READ MORE
Why does Psalm 145 say we should praise God?

Simon Peter answered him, "Lord, where would we go? You have the words that give eternal life. We believe in you. We know that you are the Holy One from God."

JOHN 6:68–69 ERV

# Keep Following

**Jesus had twelve disciples,** but Peter was one of the three who were the closest to Jesus. Peter loved Jesus very much. He saw Jesus perform many miracles and was even a part of some of those miracles.

Peter knew Jesus was the Son of God. Peter wanted to be faithful to Jesus, and that made him a good disciple. He didn't want to leave Jesus' side or be untrue to Him.

One day Jesus was teaching His followers in His hometown of Capernaum. Jesus explained to the people that He was going to die so their sins could be forgiven. Jesus said He was the only way people could be made right with God. He taught this lesson using an example that people thought sounded strange. They were confused by what He said.

After this, many of Jesus' followers stopped following Him. They thought His teaching was too hard. So Jesus asked His twelve disciples, "Do you want to leave too?"

## I will continue to follow Jesus.

Peter answered, "Lord, where would we go? You have the words that give eternal life. We believe in you. We know that you are the Holy One from God."

Even when Peter found it hard to understand Jesus' teachings, he didn't give up. He was committed to following Jesus. There may be times when we don't understand everything about following Jesus. There may be times when following Him is hard. But like Peter we can keep going. That's because we know Jesus is God's Son, and only He can make us right with God. —T.M.

### FUN FACT

The ruins of ancient Capernaum were found in 1838. Edward Robinson, an American explorer, discovered what was left of the old city where Jesus lived.

### READ MORE

Find John 6:47–51. What was the strange lesson Jesus tried to teach His followers?

# Friends of Jesus

**If you were going** away on a trip, you would tell a friend. If you were going to have a new brother or sister, you would tell a friend. If your tooth came out on the playground, you would tell that to a friend too! Friends tell each other things that are important.

Jesus is our Lord and Savior. He is our Creator and King. He is the one we worship and praise. He is very, very important! But did you know that Jesus also wants to be your friend? Many of Jesus' followers became His friends, and He wants you as His friend too.

> "I no longer call you servants, because servants don't know what their master is doing. But now I call you friends, because I have told you everything that my Father told me."
>
> **JOHN 15:15 ERV**

When Jesus spent time with His followers, He told them many important things. He told about the love, forgiveness, peace, and joy He wanted to give them. He told them about God's kingdom and what was going to happen in the future. He told them He was

*I can be a friend of Jesus.*

going to die, but that He would come back to life again. He told them how they could be with Him in heaven forever. Jesus wanted His friends to know all the things that God had told Him.

Jesus is the best friend anyone could ever have. Sometimes friends move away. Sometimes friends let us down or hurt our feelings. But Jesus is a friend who never lets us down. He could never hurt your feelings. He will never leave you or move away. Jesus loves you more than anyone else loves you. He is a true friend! —C.B.

## READ MORE

Read John 15:14.
How can we be friends with Jesus?

## FUN FACT

The letters BFF stand for "best friends forever." The phrase has been used since the 1980s, but has become very popular in recent years.

# Two Pillars

By day the LORD went ahead of them in a pillar of cloud. It guided them on their way. At night he led them with a pillar of fire. It gave them light. So they could travel by day or at night.

EXODUS 13:21 NIRV

**The Israelites were** slaves in Egypt for many years. After God sent ten plagues on Egypt, Pharaoh agreed to let the Israelites leave.

God gave His people clear orders to leave Egypt in a hurry. But God did not lead the people on the shortest route to their promised land. God didn't want them to go into the land of the Philistines and get into a fight with them. So He took them on a route through the wilderness—a big, empty desert area—toward the Red Sea. To help them find their way, God led the people with two amazing sights. A pillar of cloud gave them direction during the day, and a pillar of fire gave them light at night.

God was helping His people to escape their hard life in Egypt. He was leading them to a new land He had promised to Abraham many years before. Exodus 13:22 (NIV) says, "Neither the pillar of cloud by day nor the pillar of fire by night left its place in front of the people." The pillar of cloud and the pillar of fire showed the people that God was always with them.

## God is with me day and night.

And do you know what? God still leads His people today. But you don't have to look for a pillar of cloud or a pillar of fire. Today God uses the Bible to lead us, and He leads us by His Holy Spirit inside us.

Just like God was with the Israelites day and night, He is always with us too. —C.B.

### FUN FACT

The Israelites wandered in an area called Sinai. It's the only part of Egypt located in Asia instead of Africa.

### READ MORE

Read Exodus 40:34–38.
How did the Israelites know when God wanted them to travel to another place?

# The Holy Tent

**While the Israelites** were in the wilderness, God told Moses He wanted the people to make a big, important tent. It would be a place where the people could worship and offer sacrifices. It would be a place where God would meet with His people.

Moses said to the Israelites, "Those who want to can bring an offering to the Lord. Bring your gold, silver, and bronze. Bring blue, purple, and bright red yarn and fine cloth. Bring wood, ram skins, olive oil, and spices. Bring precious stones and jewels."

> Moses called Bezalel, Oholiab, and all the other skilled people to whom the Lord had given skills. And they came because they wanted to help with the work.
>
> EXODUS 36:2 ICB

The people all wanted to help, so they brought many, many offerings. God told Moses to choose two men named Bezalel and Oholiab to work with others to make the holy tent. Before long, Bezalel and Oholiab told Moses, "The people brought more than we need!"

Many people worked hard to make the holy tent. Women spun yarn with their hands. They made curtains for the tent and special clothing for the priests. Men carved designs in wood and made special tables and altars. Everyone wanted to be a part of making the holy tent. They gave what they could give and helped however they could.

## I can meet with God wherever I am.

The holy tent was also called the "meeting tent" or the "tabernacle." It helped the people know that God was with them in the wilderness.

Today, many people go to church to meet with God. But if you ask Jesus for forgiveness, God's Holy Spirit lives inside you. You don't need to go to a holy tent or any other special place to be near God. You can pray to Him anywhere, at any time. He will be with you wherever you are. —C.B.

### READ MORE
Read Exodus 39:32 and 43.
How did the people make the tabernacle?

### FUN FACT
In some Bible versions, Exodus 25:5 says that the Israelites used the skin of the "sea cow" in making the tabernacle. Other versions use the word porpoise.

# The Story of the Twelve Spies

"So don't turn against the LORD! Don't be afraid of the people in that land. We can defeat them. They have no protection, nothing to keep them safe. But we have the LORD with us, so don't be afraid!"

**NUMBERS 14:9 ERV**

**God had promised** to give the land of Canaan to the Israelites. But while the people were still in the wilderness, God told Moses to send twelve spies into Canaan. The spies went in to learn everything they could. After forty days they returned to their people to give a report.

The land was filled with lots of fruit, the spies said. The bunches of grapes were so big that two men had to carry the grapes on a pole between them! But even though the land was rich with food, ten of the spies were afraid. "The people living there are very powerful," they said. "We can't fight those people! They are much stronger than we are."

This report scared the Israelites. They wanted to leave Moses and go back to Egypt—the place where they had been slaves. Then the two other spies spoke up. "The land is very good," Joshua and Caleb said. "If the Lord is pleased with us, He will lead us into the land and give it to us."

## I can trust in God because He is strong.

But the people didn't listen to Caleb and Joshua, so God punished them. He made them live in the desert for the next forty years. Joshua and Caleb would get to move into the promised land, but none of the other adult Israelites would. Only their children were allowed to go into Canaan.

God was ready to fight for His people, but they didn't trust His promise. Only Joshua and Caleb trusted God. Have you ever wondered if you can trust God? Instead of thinking like the ten scared spies, you can be like Joshua and Caleb. You can trust in your great God! —T.M.

## FUN FACT

Joshua would later send spies into the city of Jericho in Canaan. Jericho is known as an oasis because it is a desert city with many water springs.

## READ MORE

Read Joshua 6:1–20.
How did God help the Israelites defeat Jericho?

# "Here I Am"

**Samuel grew up** in God's temple. He was raised by a priest named Eli. Eli had sons of his own, but they were very bad men.

One night when young Samuel was in bed, he heard someone calling his name. Samuel went to Eli and said, "Here I am. You called me."

"I didn't call you," Eli said. "Go back to bed."

Again Samuel heard someone calling his name. He went to Eli again. And again Eli said, "Go back to bed."

Samuel went back to bed and heard the voice a third time. When he went to Eli one more time, Eli realized it was God who was calling Samuel. So Eli said, "Go back to bed. If someone calls you again, say, 'Speak, Lord. I am your servant. I am listening.'"

Samuel went back to bed. Soon, he heard a voice saying, "Samuel! Samuel!"

Samuel answered, "Speak, Lord. I am your servant. I am listening."

> Samuel said,
> "Speak, Lord.
> I am your servant,
> and I am listening."
> **1 SAMUEL 3:10 ICB**

## I will listen to God.

The Lord told Samuel that Eli's sons were evil. God said He was going to punish Eli's family. In the morning, Samuel was afraid to tell Eli what God had told him. But Eli wanted to know, so Samuel gave Eli God's message.

"He is the Lord," said Eli. "Let Him do what He thinks is best."

Samuel became a great prophet. He continued to listen to God. Someday when you read the Bible or spend time in prayer, you might feel like God is telling you something. Like Samuel, you can say, "Here I am, Lord. I am listening." —C.B.

## READ MORE

Read 1 Samuel 7:12.
What did Samuel do to help the Israelites remember God's help?

## FUN FACT

Samuel was the last judge of Israel. He was the person who anointed Saul to be Israel's first king. Samuel's name means "God has heard."

# The Christians

For a whole year Barnabas and Saul met with the church. They taught large numbers of people. At Antioch the believers were called Christians for the first time.

**ACTS 11:26 NIRV**

**After Jesus went** back to heaven, His disciples traveled around to tell everyone about Him. The news about Jesus spread to many different cities.

At first the disciples only told Jewish people the good news about Jesus. But when some of Jesus' followers went to a town called Antioch, they started teaching people who weren't Jews. God worked in the hearts of the people from Antioch. A large number of them decided to follow Jesus.

Leaders in the church in Jerusalem wanted to know more about what was happening in Antioch. So they sent Barnabas to find out. When he saw that people who weren't Jewish were believing in Jesus, he was glad. "Always be faithful to the Lord," Barnabas told them. "Serve him with all your heart."

As more and more people became part of God's family, Barnabas went to find Saul so he could help teach the people. Saul, who was later called Paul, stayed in Antioch with Barnabas for a whole year. They met with the followers of Jesus and taught many people. And while they were in Antioch, people started calling Jesus' followers "Christians."

Today, the word Christian can mean different things to different people. But in Barnabas and Paul's time, it meant "Christ-follower." In Antioch, the word they used for follower was so strong, the name Christian meant "belonging to Christ."

## Being a Christian means I belong to Jesus.

When we call ourselves Christians, we tell others that we belong to Jesus. It's a way of saying the most important thing in our lives is following Him. Just like the Christians at Antioch, we can be known by our love for Jesus.
—T.M.

## FUN FACT

The English word *Christians* came from the Greek language. In Greek the word is *Christianos*.

## READ MORE

Read John 13:34–35.
How will people know that we are followers of Jesus?

# Carry the Cross

**As Jesus walked** along the road, He was weary. The road led to Golgotha where He would die on a cross.

Jesus had been through a lot since the night before. He had been arrested even though He'd done nothing wrong. Jewish leaders had judged Jesus, then sent Him to the Roman governor for his final judgment. The governor knew Jesus hadn't done anything wrong. But he gave Jesus over to the people who wanted Him to die.

Jesus was beaten by Roman soldiers. But He didn't fight against the people hurting Him or try to get out of His punishment. After hours of being hurt and made fun of, Jesus was weak. When the soldiers placed a big, heavy wooden cross on Jesus' shoulders, He could hardly stand up. As Jesus walked toward Golgotha, the soldiers pulled a man named Simon out of the crowd. They made him carry the cross for Jesus.

> As the soldiers led Jesus away, they grabbed a man named Simon, who was from the city of Cyrene. Simon was coming into Jerusalem. They laid the cross on him and made him carry it behind Jesus.
>
> **LUKE 23:26 GW**

*I can carry a cross for Jesus.*

Simon had to change his own plans to walk with Jesus. He saw the pain Jesus went through as He walked toward His death. And Simon felt some pain like Jesus did as he carried the large, heavy cross down the road.

Simon is a good example for us. He walked with Jesus just as we can. Simon did something hard for Jesus. When we face hard things as we follow Jesus, we begin to understand some of the hard things Jesus went through for us. That's what it means to carry His cross. —T.M.

## READ MORE

Read Matthew 16:24–25.
What does Jesus say you will find when you pick up a cross and follow Him?

### FUN FACT

No one knows for sure what Jesus' cross was made from. Some people guess it might have been olive, cedar, or cypress wood.

> I may speak in
> different languages
> of men or even angels.
> But if I do not have
> love, then I am only a
> noisy bell or a ringing
> cymbal.
>
> 1 CORINTHIANS 13:1 ICB

# A Missing Ingredient

**If you want** to bake a cake, it's important to follow the recipe. If you skip one of the ingredients, the cake could flop! No one would enjoy eating it, and you might have to throw it away. The right ingredients are very important.

Did you know the most important ingredient in your life is love? We can do many great things, but if we do them without love, they won't be quite right.

Cain and Abel were sons of Adam and Eve. They were the first two children in the Bible. Cain was a farmer and Abel was a shepherd. One day they each brought an offering to the Lord. Cain brought some of his crops and Abel brought a lamb. The Lord accepted Abel's offering but He did not accept Cain's.

## Love is the best ingredient.

Cain was missing an important ingredient. He did not love God the way that Abel did. If Cain had loved God with all his heart, his offering would have been accepted. Sadly, Cain didn't love Abel the way God wanted him to either. Cain became so angry that he killed his brother. So God punished Cain by sending him away from his home.

God wants us to love Him. He wants us to love the people in our family. He wants us to love our friends and neighbors, and He will even help us to do that. Love is the one ingredient of life that should never be missing. Whatever you do, remember to include love! —C.B.

### FUN FACT

Ancient Egyptians were good at baking. They made sweet breads with things like honey and dried fruits. Soft, fluffy cakes weren't invented until hundreds of years later.

### READ MORE

Read Genesis 4:13–15.
How did God still show love to Cain,
even after Cain killed his brother?

# Jealous Sisters

**Because Laban was** sneaky, his nephew Jacob ended up with two wives! Jacob really liked his wife Rachel. But he didn't like his wife Leah as much. There were many problems in their home.

> When Rachel saw that she had not given birth to any children for Jacob, she became jealous of her sister.
>
> **GENESIS 30:1 NLV**

Rachel had a lot of good things. She was beautiful and Jacob loved her very much. By marrying Jacob, Rachel became part of Abraham's family. That meant that she would be included in the promise God made to Abraham about blessing his family and making them into a great nation.

But Rachel was unhappy. She couldn't have children while her sister, Leah, had several sons. So Rachel became jealous. She demanded that Jacob do something. Jacob knew it was God's decision if Rachel would become a mother or not.

"I am not God," Jacob said. "He's the one who has caused you not to have children."

In her jealousy, Rachel tried to fix things her own way. But that only made the fight between her and Leah worse. Finally, God answered Rachel's prayers and gave her a son. She named him Joseph.

## I can be thankful instead of jealous.

It's easy to compare ourselves to others when we see that they have something we want. When we focus on things we don't have, we often forget all the good things God has already given us. Comparing ourselves to others can lead to jealousy, just like Rachel was jealous of Leah.

God doesn't want us to be jealous. He wants us to be thankful! When you feel jealous, try to remember that God is in control. He will take care of your needs, but in His own way and His own time. Whatever happens in our lives, we can always be thankful that God will do what is best. —T.M.

## READ MORE

Read James 3:16–18.
What happens when we live by jealousy?
What happens when we live by wisdom?

## FUN FACT

Jacob had a total of twelve sons. The families of those sons became the "twelve tribes of Israel."

"Don't be afraid or discouraged because of this large army. The battle is not your battle. It is God's battle."

2 CHRONICLES 20:15 ICB

# "I Don't Know What to Do"

**Jehoshaphat was the** king of Judah. Some men told him that a large army was coming to attack his country. The king was afraid so he asked God what to do. Then Jehoshaphat told the people to stop eating and to pray instead. The people met in front of God's temple. Jehoshaphat stood before them and prayed.

"Lord, you are the God of our people and the God who is in heaven," the king said. "You rule over all of the kingdoms and nations. No one can fight against you and win. We don't have the power to face this huge army that's attacking us. We don't know what to do. But we're looking to you to help us."

One of God's prophets was named Jahaziel. He said to King Jehoshaphat, "Do not lose hope because of the huge army coming against you. You will not have to fight. The battle belongs to the Lord." So Jehoshaphat and all the people bowed down and worshipped God.

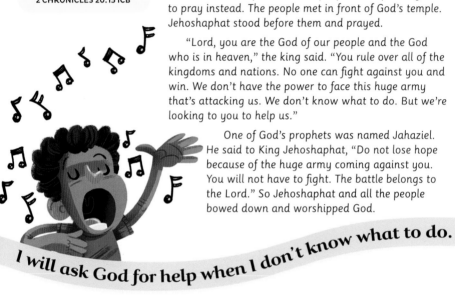

*I will ask God for help when I don't know what to do.*

The next morning, Jehoshaphat's army started out. But the king asked some men to march in front of the army and sing praises to the Lord. "Give thanks to the Lord," the men shouted. "His faithful love continues forever!"

When the singers and soldiers of Judah reached the enemy army, they saw that the enemies had attacked each other! Not one was left alive. God's people won the battle without even having to fight because they turned to God for help.

When you face a big problem, you can pray like Jehoshaphat did. Say, "Lord, I don't know what to do, but I'm looking to you for help." —C.B.

### FUN FACT

Four days after this victory, Jehoshaphat and the people gathered in the Valley of Beracah to praise God. *Beracah* means "blessings."

### READ MORE

Read 2 Chronicles 20:27–30.
What happened after God helped His people win this battle?

# Day by Day

**If you march** around outside on a hot day you'll get very thirsty! After a while, you'll want to go inside for a glass of cold water. That's exactly how the Israelites felt after crossing the Red Sea.

God had saved the Israelites from the Egyptians when He helped His people cross the sea on dry ground. When they got to the other side, the Israelites walked through a desert for three days. They couldn't find any water. Finally they came to place called Marah that had a spring. But the water in the spring was too bitter so the Israelites couldn't drink it. The people started complaining. They shouted at Moses, "What are we going to drink?"

> So Moses cried out to the LORD for help, and the LORD showed him a piece of wood. Moses threw it into the water, and this made the water good to drink.
>
> **EXODUS 15:25 NLT**

Moses cried out to God for help, and God showed him a special piece of wood. When Moses threw the wood into the spring, the water suddenly changed. Now the people could drink the water!

*God takes care of me day by day.*

The Israelites were feeling better. They left Marah and kept walking. Before long they found an oasis called Elim, with twelve springs of water and seventy palm trees. The people set up camp and stayed there.

God took care of the Israelites' needs day by day. He helped them by making bitter water good to drink. Then He gave them more water and some shade so they could rest. God can do the same thing for you. He will provide for you day by day and help you with what you need. —T.M.

## READ MORE

Read Philippians 4:18–19.
What did God do for Paul?
What does Paul say God will do for you?

## FUN FACT

The word *marah* means "bitter" in Hebrew. The Hebrew word for "sweet" is *mathoq*.

# Too Much Quail

Now the LORD sent a wind that brought quail from the sea and let them fall all around the camp. For miles in every direction there were quail flying about three feet above the ground.

**NUMBERS 11:31 NLT**

**Eating the same thing** every day can get boring! That's how the Israelites felt while they were in the wilderness. Every day God sent them a kind of bread called manna. At first the Israelites were thankful, but after a while they started to complain. "Oh, to eat meat!" they cried. "We remember the fish we used to eat when we were slaves in Egypt. But now we're not hungry. All we ever see is this manna!"

Moses was angry about the Israelites' whining. God heard the people complaining too. He told Moses to give them a message. So Moses told the people, "Tomorrow you will have meat to eat, and it won't be for just a day or two. You will eat it for a whole month until you are sick of it and gag. This is because you have rejected the Lord."

Moses wondered how God was going to send a month's worth of meat for hundreds of thousands of people. But the next day tons of birds appeared everywhere! These birds were called quail and there were so many that everyone gathered at least fifty big baskets full! The people ate so much quail they made themselves sick. As always, God's word was true!

## If I feel like complaining, I can thank God instead.

The Israelites had complained instead of thanking God. And when He gave them what they asked for, they still weren't happy. We can learn from their bad example.

It's good to thank God for what He gives us, even if it's not what we would have chosen for ourselves. Grumbling about the things we don't have only makes us more unhappy. Instead, we can praise God for the good things He has given us, and for the good things He will give us in the future. —T.M.

## FUN FACT

There are two different families of birds people call quail—"Old World" and "New World." The Israelites ate Old World quail in the wilderness.

## READ MORE

Read Psalm 105:37–45.
What are some of the things David thanked God for?

# Important Followers

The Twelve were with him. There were also some women in their company who had been healed. . . . Joanna, wife of Chuza, Herod's manager—along with many others who used their considerable means to provide for the company.

LUKE 8:1–3 MSG

**It's easy to think** of Jesus' disciples as only the twelve men He picked to help Him with His ministry. These men were very important to the work Jesus did, and they started the Christian church after Jesus rose from the dead. But many other people followed Jesus, and they were important too. One of these other people was a woman named Joanna.

Joanna was the wife of a man named Chuza. He was in charge of King Herod's house. Jesus had healed Joanna of a problem that made her very sick. After Jesus made Joanna better, she traveled with Him and His other followers. She helped Jesus with her own money, and she was faithful to Him even when others deserted Him.

After Jesus died, Joanna went to Jesus' tomb with some other women. They wanted to put spices on Jesus' body to honor Him. But when the women got to the tomb, they

## God can use me to tell the story of Jesus.

saw the stone covering the opening had been rolled away. The tomb was empty! Two angels inside the tomb told the women, "Jesus is not here. He has risen!"

Then Joanna and the other women remembered what Jesus had said earlier. They remembered how He said He would die and rise from the dead on the third day. Joanna was one of the women who first told the disciples the great news that Jesus was alive.

No matter how old you are, you can be an important follower of Jesus. It doesn't matter where you come from, or whether you're a boy or a girl. When you follow Jesus, you can tell others about Him just like Joanna did. —T.M.

## READ MORE
Look up Acts 18:24–28.
Whom did God use to tell others about Jesus?

**FUN FACT**
The name Joanna means "God has been gracious."

"Take your shepherd's staff with you, and use it to perform the miraculous signs I have shown you."

EXODUS 4:17 NLT

# Three Signs

**When God chose** Moses to lead the Israelites out of Egypt, Moses didn't think he was the right man for the job. He said to God, "What if the people don't believe me or listen to me? What if they say, 'The Lord did not appear to you'?"

So God told Moses to throw his shepherd's staff on the ground. When the staff hit the ground, it became a snake! God told Moses to pick up the snake by its tail. When Moses picked up the snake, it became a staff again.

Then God said to Moses, "Put your hand inside your coat." Moses obeyed. When he took his hand back out, it was white with leprosy. Moses put his hand back inside his coat and took it out again, and his skin was healthy.

## God can use anything to show His power.

"If the people don't believe you after these two miracles," God said to Moses, "take some water from the Nile River and pour it on the ground. The water will become blood when it touches the ground."

But Moses was still afraid to go back to Egypt. So God said Moses could take his brother, Aaron, with him. God would tell them what to say, and together Moses and Aaron would speak to the Israelites.

Many things can frighten us. Even grown-ups are afraid sometimes! But God gives us everything we need to be bold. God might use our friends and family to give us courage. And God himself will always be with us. We never need to be afraid. —C.B.

### FUN FACT

The Bible mentions at least ten different times Moses used his staff to show God's power.

### READ MORE

Read Exodus 7:14–21.
How did Moses and Aaron use their staffs this time?

# The Party Invitation

> "God's kingdom is like a king who prepared a wedding feast for his son. He invited some people to the feast. When it was ready, the king sent his servants to tell the people to come. But they refused to come to the king's feast."
>
> MATTHEW 22:2–3 ERV

**If you were** invited to an important party, you would want to say yes right away. If a president or a king was giving the party, you would want to be there. Even if you had other plans, you would change them so you could attend the party.

Jesus said that God's kingdom is like an important party. He told the story of a king who planned a great feast for his son's wedding. The king sent his servants to invite the people he wanted to attend. But none of them would come. They wanted to do ordinary things instead. Some of the people were even mean to the king's servants who were inviting them.

When the king heard this, he was angry. He decided to invite the whole town. His party was now open to everyone! Many people accepted the invitation and attended the feast. The room was filled with happy guests.

## Everyone is invited to be a part of God's kingdom.

Just like the king who threw a party, Jesus invites everyone to be part of His kingdom. We all have the choice to accept His invitation. Some people say they're too busy to care about Jesus' invitation. Some people make fun of those who invite them to join God's family. Some people might think they can get to heaven without Jesus. But all of us who say yes to Jesus will be with Him in heaven someday. It will be the best party ever! —T.M.

## READ MORE

Read Revelation 19:6–9 to learn about a wedding celebration in heaven. Whose celebration is this?

## FUN FACT

Weddings in ancient Israel took place at the groom's house. They usually lasted for seven days! The bride and groom wore special clothes and were treated like a king and queen.

# All the Same

> Then Peter began to speak. "I now realize how true it is that God treats everyone the same," he said. "He accepts people from every nation. He accepts all who have respect for him and do what is right."
>
> ACTS 10:34-35 NIRV

**A man named Cornelius** was a Roman army officer. He and his family loved God and prayed to Him. They often gave money to help the poor. One afternoon an angel came to Cornelius and called his name. Cornelius was afraid and said, "What do you want, Sir?"

The angel said, "God has heard your prayers. He has seen how you give to the poor. Send some men to the town of Joppa to bring back a man named Peter."

Cornelius obeyed the angel. While his men were on their way to find Peter, Peter was having a dream. He saw a big sheet filled with animals come down to earth from heaven. Some of the animals in the sheet were "clean." That means the Israelites were allowed to eat them. Some of the animals were "unclean." That means God's people were not allowed to eat them. But then Peter heard a voice saying, "God has made all these things clean."

## God loves all people the same.

Peter didn't understand what his dream meant. While he was thinking about it, the men Cornelius sent came to his house. The next day Peter went with them to see Cornelius.

In the home of Cornelius, Peter met many people who were not Jewish. And then Peter, who was Jewish, understood his dream! He realized that God doesn't look at what country a person comes from or what family a person was born into. God sees everyone the same way. He loves those who respect Him and believe in Him. Everyone has the chance to be part of God's family. —C.B.

### FUN FACT

Some Jewish people today still follow the food rules God gave in Leviticus 11. They avoid "unclean" animals such as pigs, and eat only "clean" animals. The foods the Jews are allowed to eat are called "kosher."

### READ MORE

Read Acts 10:44-48.
What happened to the non-Jewish people who believed Peter's message about Jesus?

# Strong Tower

**"Tag" is a popular** game kids like to play. If you have played tag, you know the rules. One person is "it" and chases the others around until someone is tagged. When the person who is it tags someone else, that person becomes it next. The game keeps going this way. Everyone runs around trying not to get caught—usually laughing the whole time!

> The name of the LORD is like a strong tower. Godly people run to it and are safe.
>
> **PROVERBS 18:10 NIRV**

Players may be tagged anywhere unless they are standing on a safety spot known as "home base." Home base is chosen before the game begins. Anyone who runs to home base is safe. That means any player standing on home base cannot be tagged by the person who is it. All the players in the safe area are protected.

The Bible's book of Proverbs says we can think of God like home base. He is a safety zone we can run to when we need help. God is like a strong tower that surrounds us with protection. He puts up a shield to keep us from danger. God is like a mighty castle with heavy walls.

The next time you feel afraid, you can run to God. You can run to God by praying to Him. You can run to God by reading His words in your Bible. You can run to God by calling out His name. When you need help, He is your strong tower and safety zone. God will always be the safest place you can go. —T.M.

## I can go to God for safety.

### READ MORE

Read Psalm 18:1–3.
What are some ways David described
God and His protection?

### FUN FACT

There is another game like tag where players run from one safety zone to another safety zone. This game is called "Wall-to-Wall" in Great Britain.

> My God will use his wonderful riches in Christ Jesus to give you everything you need.
>
> **PHILIPPIANS 4:19 ICB**

# All You Need

**The apostle Paul** was thankful for the way other followers of Jesus helped him. They were kind to him and gave him what he needed. Sometimes Paul had very little, so what the people shared was very important. But Paul said he could be happy whether he had a little or a lot, because God would always provide whatever he needed.

Paul told his friends in Philippi that God would supply everything they needed too—because of all the riches God has. Paul didn't mean that God would give them everything they wanted. But as they loved and served God, He would give them just what they needed. God would help them to grow in their love for each other. He would help them when they had problems. And He would never stop loving them.

Did you know that God will give you everything you need too? He sends the sunshine and rain so you will have food to eat. He has put grown-ups in your life to love you and take care of you. He has given you a mind so you can learn about many things—especially about Jesus. And when you believe in Jesus, God gives you the Holy Spirit to help you love and obey Him.

## God gives me everything I need.

There may be times when you have more than you need. That's when you can share what you have with others, just like Christian people shared with Paul. When you share with others, you show the love of God, the one who has given everything to us. —C.B.

## FUN FACT

The city of Philippi was started about 350 years before Jesus was born, by a king named Philip II. He built the city because there were gold mines nearby!

## READ MORE

Read Philippians 4:14–18.
Why did Paul say it was good for people to help him?

# Name Change

**Names are important.** People who lived during the time of the Bible had names with special meanings. Their names told others what they did or where they came from. Sometimes angels even visited parents to tell them what to name their child!

At times, God would change a person's name. He changed Abram's name to Abraham, and Sarai's name to Sarah. God also changed Jacob's name.

> "Your name is Jacob, but I will change that name. You will no longer be called Jacob. Your new name will be Israel." So God named him Israel.
>
> **GENESIS 35:10 ERV**

When he was a young man, Jacob tricked his dad into giving him the blessing that was supposed to go his brother, Esau. That made Esau really mad, so Jacob ran away. But God was still with Jacob.

One day God told Jacob, "Your name is Jacob, but I will change your name. You will no longer be called Jacob. Your new name will be Israel." God also said, "I give you this blessing: Have many children and grow into a great nation. Other nations and other kings will come out of you."

Jacob listened to God and had many sons. They became the twelve tribes of Israel. From then on, God's people were called "the children of Israel" or "Israelites," and their nation was called "Israel."

## God tells me who I am.

God changed Jacob's name and his whole life. Jacob had done many bad things, but when he realized that he needed God, God used Jacob to do great things. God can change our lives and make us useful too. —T.M.

## READ MORE

Read Genesis 32:22–32.
What happened to Jacob as he wrestled with God?

### FUN FACT

Bible experts think the name Israel might mean "he fights with God." That's because Jacob wrestled with God at the Jabbok River.

Cleanse me with hyssop, and I will be clean; wash me, and I will be whiter than snow.

PSALM 51:7 NIV

# Time for a Bath

**If you spend** a day playing outside, you might need a bath or shower when you get home. Being on the playground, playing a sport, or just running around can make you feel sweaty and dirty. Washing your body with soap and water will get you clean again. And it feels so good to be clean!

Did you know you can be clean on the inside too? When we disobey God and sin, it's like we get dirty on the inside. But we don't need to stay that way.

In Old Testament times, people had to make sacrifices for their sins. They would tell God they were sorry for their sins and give Him the gift of an animal. Then God would forgive them. But because people do many wrong things, they had to keep making their sacrifices over and over again.

## Jesus makes me clean.

When Jesus died on the cross, He became the sacrifice for our sins. His sacrifice was everything God wanted, and it only needed to be done one time. When we believe in Jesus as our Savior and tell God we are sorry for our sins, God forgives our sins and washes them away. It's like taking a bath on the inside.

Since Jesus died and rose again, we don't have to make sacrifices for our sins anymore. But we still need to admit to God when we sin. When we do things we know are wrong, we can tell God we're sorry and ask Him to forgive us. He will wash away our sins, over and over again. And it feels so good to be clean! —C.B.

## FUN FACT

Hyssop is a plant that is related to mint. In Bible times, people used it as a symbol of purity.

## READ MORE

Read Psalm 32:1–5.
What happens when we confess our sins?

# Ten Signs of God's Power

> **"But I will make Pharaoh stubborn so that he will not do what you tell him. Then I will do many miracles in Egypt to prove who I am."**
> **EXODUS 7:3 ERV**

**God sent ten plagues** to Egypt because Pharaoh would not let the Israelites leave. First, God turned the Nile River into blood. The river became smelly across the land and all the fish in the river died. Pharaoh still wouldn't let the Israelites go, so God sent a swarm of frogs. They were in the Egyptians' houses and beds and everywhere else. Pharaoh told Moses that if God would take away the frogs, he would let the Israelites go. Moses prayed and God answered, but then Pharaoh changed his mind.

The next two plagues were gnats and flies. They were everywhere! Pharaoh's heart was still hard. Then God caused all of the Egyptians' cattle to die. Next God put sores all over the Egyptians and their animals. After that, God sent hail. It pounded everything in sight. Pharaoh told Moses he would let the people go if God stopped the hail. Moses prayed and the hail stopped. But Pharaoh changed his mind again, so God sent locusts and then darkness over the land.

Finally, God brought death over all Egypt. The oldest son of every Egyptian family died. When Pharaoh's son died, he finally told Moses and the Israelites to leave.

## No one can stop God's power.

Pharaoh had many chances to believe God, but he didn't use them. Today, God gives us many chances to know Him too. He may use a parent, a teacher, a pastor, or a friend to help us learn who He is and how much He loves us. God might even use the words of this book to show us His greatness! Whichever way God calls us, He is showing another sign of His power. —T.M.

### READ MORE

Read Exodus 15:1–18 to see what the people said to God after He saved them from Pharaoh.

### FUN FACT

Gnats live for a very short time. Some don't even live for twenty-four hours! At the longest, a gnat can live for a few months.

# Keep Growing

Grow in the grace of our Lord and Savior Jesus Christ. Get to know him better.

2 PETER 3:18 NIRV

**Have you ever heard** the saying, "They're growing like weeds"? Parents sometimes say that about their children. It's a common saying because weeds grow quickly. And so do kids!

Good food and exercise help kids to grow. Most kids keep growing until they are around sixteen or eighteen years old. But some parts of our bodies keep growing even after we become adults. Fingernails and toenails keep growing. So does hair. Growth is a sign of a healthy body.

Did you know we can also grow spiritually? The more we learn about God, the more we grow spiritually. The more we pray and see God answer our prayers, the more we will grow in our faith. The more we understand how much God loves us, the more we will grow in our love for Him.

And there's still another kind of growth. Just like our bodies grow, the body of Christ can grow too. What is the body of Christ? It's all the people who love and follow Jesus. As we grow spiritually in our own lives, we will look for ways to share our joy with other people. We will enjoy telling others the good news of Jesus and what He does in our lives. And as they believe in Jesus too, the body of Christ will grow!

## I can keep growing in Jesus.

Jesus Christ is the head of the body of believers. The whole body needs to grow together and build itself up in love. When Christians keep growing together, it's a sign of a healthy body. —C.B.

### FUN FACT

Kids have times when they grow faster. During these "growth spurts," they can grow as much as four inches in a year.

### READ MORE

What does Ephesians 4:4–16 tell us about the body of Christ?

# Solomon Builds God's House

**After Solomon** had been king for a few years, he started a big building project. God gave him the special job of building the first temple in Jerusalem. Solomon worked with the friendly king of Tyre to collect all the materials needed for the building. When everything was prepared, the construction of the temple began.

The temple was so big and fancy it took seven years to build. The workers were careful to build the temple exactly as they were told. It was ninety feet long (twenty-seven meters), thirty feet wide (nine meters), and forty-five feet high (fourteen meters). A wide porch ran along the front of the temple. There were narrow windows high in the temple walls. A row of rooms three stories tall was built around the main part of the temple. And walls were built outside the temple to create a courtyard.

Only the finest materials were used to build God's house. All of the stones were cut to the right size before they were brought to the building site. That way there weren't any noisy construction sounds at the temple. Cedar and olive wood were used inside the building. The most important room was covered in pure gold.

> Solomon began to build the temple of the LORD. It was 480 years after the people of Israel had come out of Egypt. It was in the fourth year of Solomon's rule over Israel. He started in the second month. That was the month of Ziv.
>
> **1 KINGS 6:1 NIRV**

## The temple was built to give glory to God.

God's temple was a beautiful masterpiece. Solomon built it with the most expensive things he could find because he knew that's what God deserved.

God deserves our best too. Whether we're with our family or in school or playing a sport, we should serve God with all our strength. When we do our best, we honor Him. —T.M.

### READ MORE
Read 1 Kings 6:11–13.
What promise did God make to Solomon as he built the temple?

### FUN FACT
The first temple was built about 950 years before Jesus was born, to replace the "meeting tent" the Israelites had used before. The temple lasted about four hundred years, until it was destroyed by the Babylonian army.

# Let It Rise

Then Jesus told them another story: "God's kingdom is like yeast that a woman mixes into a big bowl of flour to make bread. The yeast makes all the dough rise."

**MATTHEW 13:33 ERV**

**You need many** ingredients to make bread from scratch. Depending on the recipe, a baker will mix flour with other ingredients like eggs, salt, honey, and milk. But the most important ingredient in making bread is yeast.

Yeast doesn't make the dough look any different. It's even hard to see it after you've mixed it in. But without yeast, that dough will not rise. If the dough doesn't rise, the mixture will not become that fluffy, yummy bread you like for toast or sandwiches. Yeast makes the dough grow from a clump of ingredients into a food you want to eat.

Jesus once said that telling others about Him is like adding yeast to dough.

Here's what Jesus meant: Christianity began with just a small group of believers. But the number of believers got bigger and bigger as the news about Jesus spread from neighbor to neighbor and friend to friend. Christians would care for sick people and help the poor. They would pray to God and tell others how He answered their prayers. When Christians did good and kind things, other people became Christians too. It was just like yeast, making bread dough rise.

## God can use me to spread the news of Jesus.

Today, the number of Christians is still rising! You can help spread the news about Jesus by telling your friends and neighbors. You can help sick people and poor people. When you tell others about Jesus, the people you tell can then tell other people! The words you say to one person can spread to many other people. It's just like a batch of dough that keeps rising! —T.M.

### FUN FACT

The bread-slicing machine was invented by an American named Otto Rohwedder. By the 1930s, sliced bread was being sold in stores and "the best thing since sliced bread" became a common phrase.

### READ MORE

Read Mark 4:26–29.
What other example did Jesus use to show how His message keeps spreading?

> Rehoboam replied,
> "Give me three days
> to think this over.
> Then come back
> for my answer."
> **1 KINGS 12:5 NLT**

# Two Pieces of Advice

**Rehoboam was the son** of King Solomon. When Solomon died, Rehoboam became king.

A man named Jeroboam and the people of Israel went to see the new king. They said, "Your father, Solomon, made us work very hard. Don't make us work so hard. Then we will serve you."

Rehoboam told the people to talk to him again in three days. During that time Rehoboam spoke to the older leaders of Israel to get their advice. They said, "Be kind to the people. Then they will serve you."

Rehoboam also talked to some younger men who were his friends. They said, "Tell the people that you will force them to work even harder than your father did."

Rehoboam decided to listen to his foolish friends rather than the wise older men. When Rehoboam told the people he would force them to work harder, they broke away from Israel and started their own country.

## I will listen to good advice.

King Rehoboam only ruled over the Israelites who lived in the towns of Judah. His nation was called "Judah." The rest of the people made Jeroboam their king and kept calling their nation "Israel." King Rehoboam wanted to fight against Israel, but God spoke to him through a prophet. "Do not fight against Israel," the Lord said. "They are your relatives."

King Rehoboam lost much of his kingdom because he listened to the wrong advice. When you have an important decision to make, be sure to get advice from someone you can trust. Always ask God to help you make the right decision. —C.B.

### FUN FACT

The northern kingdom of Israel lasted about two hundred years before it was defeated by the Assyrians. The southern kingdom of Judah lasted over three hundred years before it was defeated by the Babylonians.

## READ MORE

**Read Ezekiel 37:15–23. What did the prophet Ezekiel say would happen to Israel and Judah someday?**

# The Temple Curtain

Suddenly, the curtain in the temple was split in two from top to bottom. The earth shook, and the rocks were split open.

MATTHEW 27:51 GW

**Do you have** a place that's very special to you? Maybe you have a secret hideout in the woods. Or maybe you just like to hang out in your bedroom.

The temple in Jerusalem had a very special room that was different from any other place in the building. It was called the "holy of holies" and it was filled with God's presence. A heavy curtain separated the rest of the temple from the holy of holies. The curtain was made from the finest fabric with blue, purple, and red yarn.

This curtain was made to protect the priests in the temple from God's holiness. The priests knew that God was perfect. Their sins kept them apart from God. His presence was so powerful that the priests could die if they didn't make up for their sins the right way. Even though there were many priests, only one—called the "high priest"—was allowed to enter the holy of holies. The high priest was only allowed to go there once a year.

## We can go to God anytime because of Jesus.

On the day Jesus died on the cross, something amazing happened in the temple. The curtain tore in half from top to bottom! The holy of holies was open for everyone in the temple to see. God was the only one who could have ripped the curtain. It was too high and too strong for any person to do that.

Jesus' death on the cross made a way for people to be cleansed from their sins. When we have been made clean through Jesus, we can go directly to Him. We don't need a high priest to go to God for us. We can be in God's presence anytime. —T.M.

### READ MORE
Read Hebrews 10:19–23.
Why does the apostle Paul say we can go boldly into God's holy place?

### FUN FACT
God gave Moses the directions to make the curtain for the holy of holies. God wanted creative people to sew a picture of an angel onto the curtain!

# Bless the Lord

Therefore David blessed the LORD before all the assembly.

1 CHRONICLES 29:10 NKJV

**When King David** grew old, he knew that his son Solomon would soon be the next king. David knew that God had chosen Solomon to build the temple for the Lord in Jerusalem. David wanted God's people to help.

As an example, David gave gold, silver, bronze, iron, and wood for the temple. He also gave valuable stones and jewels. Now he asked the people to do the same. He said to them, "Who is ready to give to the service of the Lord today?"

The Israelite leaders responded to David's request. They followed David's example and gave gold, silver, bronze, and iron. The people who had valuable gems gave them for the temple. David was very happy when he saw everyone giving so much for the work.

Then David "blessed the Lord" in front of the people. In some Bible versions it says David "praised the Lord." To bless the Lord means to give Him honor and to praise Him for His greatness.

## I can bless God for blessing me.

Christians often talk about God's blessings. They say things like, "God has blessed our family with children," or "God has blessed us with a beautiful day." When we say that God blesses us, it means that He gives us good things. It means that He makes our lives better with His kindness.

But we can also bless God! Everything we have comes from Him. You can bless God today by telling Him how great He is. You can bless Him every day! —C.B.

## FUN FACT

King David's people gave about 190 tons of gold (more than 172,000 kilograms) for the temple. That's the weight of about 95 minivans!

## READ MORE

Turn to 1 Chronicles 29:10–14 in your Bible to read the prayer that David said as he blessed God in front of the people.

# The Potter's Wheel

He was making a pot from clay. But something went wrong with it. So the potter used that clay to make another pot. He used his hands to shape the pot the way that he wanted it to be.

JEREMIAH 18:4 ICB

**God told Jeremiah** to go see a man who made clay pots. So Jeremiah went to the man's house and saw him working at the potter's wheel. On top of the wheel was a lump of clay. As the wheel went around and around, the potter used his hands to mold the clay and shape it the way he wanted it to be. He was shaping the clay into a pot.

But the pot wasn't turning out the way the potter wanted. So he started over again. He used the same lump of clay to make another pot.

God told Jeremiah that the Israelites were like that clay. God was like the potter. He decides how to mold and shape the clay. If He is not pleased with the way His clay is turning out, He will start over again and make another pot.

## God will make my life what He wants it to be.

All of God's people are like clay in His hands. He can shape us whatever way He wants to. The clay does not decide what kind of pot it's going to be or what it will be used for. The potter decides.

Life is like the potter's wheel that goes around and around. Sometimes good things happen to us and sometimes bad things happen. But as we trust God during the good times and the bad times, He will shape our lives into something beautiful. Our lives will be something that He can use for good. —C.B.

### READ MORE
Read Isaiah 45:9–13.
What do these verses say about
the works of God's hands?

### FUN FACT
Pottery is a common craft in Mexico. Mexican potters often dig up the clay by themselves or pay someone to bring the clay by donkey or truck.

# A Ride in a Basket

One night some followers of Saul helped him leave the city. They lowered him in a basket through an opening in the city wall.

ACTS 9:25 ICB

**Before Paul became** a missionary, his name was Saul. For a long time Saul hated Christians and tried to get rid of them. But everything changed one day as Saul was going to Damascus. A bright light shined on Saul and Jesus spoke to him. After that, Saul believed that Jesus was the Son of God.

Saul stayed with followers of Jesus for a few days in Damascus. It wasn't long before Saul started preaching in the Jews' meeting places, called synagogues. Saul said, "Jesus is the Son of God!" The people who heard him were amazed. They knew about Saul's past and couldn't believe he had changed. He went from hurting Christians to becoming one of them!

The Jews in Damascus were upset with Saul. They couldn't argue with his teaching. They knew his preaching was strong. They were afraid more people would begin to

## God will help me finish the job He's started.

believe in Jesus. So after many days, the Jews made plans to kill Saul! They kept their eyes on the city gate day and night so they could attack him when he left.

But Saul learned about their plans and asked his new friends for help. One night some of Saul's friends helped him sneak away. They put him in a big basket, tied it to a rope, and lowered Saul over the wall of the city. He escaped from Damascus and went to Jerusalem.

Saul learned quickly that being a Christian isn't easy. Many times, Christians will face trials. But God is always there to help us through our trials. God will protect us so we can finish the job He wants us to do. —T.M.

**FUN FACT**

Basket weaving is one of the oldest crafts in the world. Weavers use grasses, reeds, twigs, and leaves to make baskets. Weavers also make mats, bags, and sandals.

**READ MORE**

Read 1 Samuel 19:11–12.
Who escaped in this story? How did he get away from the person that was trying to hurt him?

# Honor God's Name

**Do you know** the "Lord's Prayer?" That's a prayer that Jesus used to teach His disciples how to pray. It begins with the words, "Our Father in heaven, hallowed be your name."

> I will honor you, my God the King. I will praise your name for ever and ever.
>
> **PSALM 145:1 NIRV**

The word hallowed means "holy" or "special." When something is hallowed, it is set apart from everything else. Jesus said that God's name is holy. It is not like any other name! Many years before Jesus lived on earth, God had told the Israelites that His name is holy. In the third of the Ten Commandments, God said, "Do not misuse the name of the Lord your God. The Lord will find guilty anyone who misuses his name."

Other verses in the Bible also tell us how special God's name is. Psalm 52:9 says, "I hope in your name, God, for your name is good." And Jeremiah 10:6 says, "LORD, you are great. Your name is mighty in power." And Psalm 8:9 says, "Our LORD, your name is majestic in the whole earth!" God's name is "majestic." That means it is fit for a king!

Do you like it when someone shouts your name in an angry way? Of course not! You want people to use your name in a kind and loving way. Did you know God feels the same way about His name? God's name is not only holy, it is also good, powerful, and majestic. That is why it's important for us to honor His name. If you love God, you can show it by the way you use His name. —C.B.

## I will honor and respect the name of God.

## READ MORE

Read Psalm 135:1–3.
Why should we praise God's name?

### FUN FACT

In 1551 the Scottish government made it against the law to swear or misuse the name of God in public. People who broke the law could get a fine or jail time!

# Super Strength

Suddenly a young lion came roaring toward Samson! The Spirit of the Lord entered Samson with great power. Samson tore the lion apart with his bare hands.

JUDGES 14:5–6 ICB

**Before Israel** had a king, people called "judges" were leaders in Israel. One time, a group of people called the Philistines began to rule over the Israelites. This was because Israel had disobeyed God. The Philistines were bullies. It was hard for the Israelites to live under their power. But God did not forget His people.

God planned for a special judge to fight the Philistines. He gave a special son to a man named Manoah and his wife. An angel told them to treat their son in a special way because God would use him to save Israel from the Philistines. Manoah and his wife obeyed. They named their son Samson and the Spirit of the Lord began to work in him.

One day when Samson was grown up, he was walking down a road. Suddenly, a lion roared loudly and jumped toward Samson! Samson just grabbed the lion with his hands and tore it to pieces. He didn't need a weapon or help from anyone else. God gave Samson super strength to defeat the lion.

## God makes me strong.

God gave Samson more super strength to fight the Philistines. Samson didn't always obey God, but God still used Samson to help the people of Israel. Just before Samson died, God gave him super strength one more time to defeat all the Philistine kings.

God used Samson to show that people can do great things with God's strength. God gives all of us strength. We probably won't fight a lion, but we don't have to be afraid when we face challenges. God will help His children to be strong, just like He helped Samson. —T.M.

## FUN FACT

Samson's parents set him apart for God and followed special rules. He was not allowed to eat grapes or cut his hair. Because of this, Samson was called a "Nazirite."

## READ MORE

The Israelites were afraid the Philistines would bully them more because of Samson. Read Judges 15:13–15 to see what happened when they tied up Samson.

# Lost Donkeys

**When Saul was** a young man he lived with his father, Kish. One day their donkeys got away from them. So Kish told Saul to take a servant with him and look for the donkeys.

> "The LORD has anointed you to be the leader of his people."
> 1 SAMUEL 10:1 NIRV

Saul and the servant searched everywhere, but they couldn't find the missing animals. It was getting late, and Saul wanted to go back home so his father wouldn't worry about him. But the servant said, "There is a man of God in the town of Ramah. Everything he says comes true. Let's find him. Maybe he will tell us which way to go."

When Saul and his servant got to the town, they met the prophet Samuel. Saul didn't know it, but God had already told Samuel that Saul was coming!

## God will work out His plans in our lives.

"You and your servant will eat with me today," Samuel said to Saul. "Don't worry about the donkeys you lost three days ago. They have already been found."

But then Samuel gave Saul a special message from God. "Who do all the people of Israel want?" Samuel asked. "It's you and your father's family!" The next day, Samuel anointed Saul's head with oil and told him he would become the king of Israel.

God will work out His plans in our lives. Sometimes, though, we don't understand God's plans right away. Saul never imagined that when he went looking for donkeys, he would become the king of Israel! God sometimes works in ways that surprise us. —C.B.

### READ MORE

Read 1 Samuel 10:17–25.
How did Samuel tell the people
that Saul would be their king?

### FUN FACT

Donkeys are smart animals with good memories. Their large ears help them hear well and also keep them cool on hot days.

## AUGUST
# 8

> When Jesus saw the crowds, he went up a mountain and sat down. His disciples came to him, and he began to teach them.
>
> MATTHEW 5:1-2 GW

# Blessed People

**One day many people** followed Jesus to a mountainside. He sat down and began to teach them about blessings in the kingdom of God.

"The people who know they have great spiritual needs will be blessed," Jesus said. "The kingdom of heaven belongs to them.

"The people who are sad will be blessed and comforted. The people who are humble will be blessed because the earth belongs to them. The people who want to do what is right will be blessed because God will satisfy them.

"The people who show mercy to others will have mercy shown to them. The people who have pure hearts will be blessed because they will see God. The people who are peacemakers will be blessed and be called the children of God. Those who suffer for doing what is right will be blessed. The kingdom of heaven belongs to them."

## I can be blessed when I follow Jesus.

Jesus told the people to be glad even when others made fun of them. If they followed Jesus they would have a great reward in heaven.

The words Jesus spoke on the mountain are known as the "Beatitudes." The word beatitude means "blessed" or "happy." To be blessed means to have God's kindness and help. Can you think of a time when you have enjoyed God's favor?

Jesus never promised that following Him would be easy. But He did promise that those who follow Him would be blessed. —C.B.

## FUN FACT

In the 1930s, a church was built near the place where Jesus preached on the mountainside. The building has eight sides, standing for the eight beatitudes of Jesus.

## READ MORE

Read Matthew 5:43–48.
What did Jesus say about loving others?

# Family Ties

**Moses had a big job** to do while the Israelites were living in the wilderness. God told Moses to count all the people and write down their names. This project was called a "census." It's kind of like when a teacher takes attendance at school—except Moses had more than six hundred thousand men to count!

When the census was finished, God told Moses and his brother, Aaron, to help the people set up a camp. God wanted Moses and Aaron to organize the people by their families and tribes. The tribes were groups of families that were related to the twelve sons of Jacob. Moses said, "The Israelites will put up their tents with each family under the flag that stands for its tribe. They will set up their tents to face the 'meeting tent.'"

Each tribe was given a special place to set up camp. God told the tribe of Judah to camp on the east. Next to Judah, God placed the tribes of Issachar and Zebulun. On the south side God put the tribes of Reuben, Simeon, and Gad. The tribes set up on the west side were Manasseh, Benjamin, and Ephraim. The tribes of Dan, Asher, and Naphtali camped on the north, while the family of Levi was set up in the middle. The Israelites did everything just like God told them.

> The LORD said to Moses and Aaron: "The Israelites should make their camps around the Meeting Tent. Each division will have its own special flag, and everyone will camp near their group's flag."
>
> **NUMBERS 2:1–2 ERV**

## I will be a good relative and neighbor.

Our families and our communities are important. God puts us in a certain family to live in a certain place. He gives us relatives and neighbors to learn from and to serve. God created us to live with others. He is pleased when we work together and live in love. —T.M.

## READ MORE

Read Ephesians 2:18–19.
What family can you belong to besides the one you are a part of now?

### FUN FACT

"Coat of arms" designs were put on knights' shields starting almost a thousand years ago. The designs stood for the knights' families.

> "My sheep listen
> to my voice;
> I know them,
> and they follow me."
>
> JOHN 10:27 NLT

# A Story about Sheep

**Many people followed** Jesus to hear Him teach. One day He told them a story about sheep.

"The person who enters through the gate is the shepherd of the sheep," Jesus said. "The sheep listen to his voice and he calls them by name. The sheep follow him because they know his voice. The sheep will not follow a stranger, but will run away from that man."

The people didn't understand what Jesus meant, so He said more. "What I am telling you is true," Jesus said. "I am like a gate for the sheep. Anyone who enters through me will be saved. I am the Good Shepherd and I give my life for my sheep. I know my sheep and they know me, just like I know my Father and He knows me. My sheep know my voice and they follow me. I give them eternal life. No one can snatch them away from the Father because the Father and I are one."

## Jesus is the Good Shepherd.

When Jesus said "sheep" He was talking about the people who trust Him to be their Savior. He is the Shepherd who gave His life for all who follow Him. Jesus knows His followers and they know Him. He will protect His people because He loves them like a shepherd loves his sheep.

Some of the people who heard Jesus' story were upset because He said that He and the Father were one. But other people believed in Jesus that day. They knew His story was true and became His sheep. Have you become one of Jesus' sheep? —C.B.

### FUN FACT

The female sheep is called a "ewe." The male sheep is called a "ram" or "buck." A baby sheep is called a "lamb" until it is a year old.

### READ MORE

Read Matthew 9:35–38.
Why did Jesus feel sorry for the people?

# You Can't Buy It

**Have you ever seen** magicians do tricks? Some of their tricks are amazing, but they are only tricks. Magicians can't really pull a coin out of your ear or make a person float in the air!

In the Bible, magicians did tricks to fool people. They wanted people to believe they had special powers like God. A magician named Simon, who lived in Samaria, amazed people with his tricks. Simon was proud and called himself a great man. Many people said, "This man has the power of God." But he wasn't working by God's power. People didn't know that Simon's power was fake.

When some of Jesus' disciples went to Samaria to preach about Jesus, the Samaritans listened and believed. Because these people trusted in Jesus, the disciples asked God to give them the Holy Spirit—and God did! When Simon saw that the disciples could help people receive the Holy Spirit, he wanted the power of God too. But it wasn't for the right reason. Simon just wanted to impress people and make himself more important.

> Peter said to him, "You and your money should both be destroyed! You thought you could buy God's gift with money."
>
> **ACTS 8:20 ICB**

## God's gifts are free.

Simon brought money to the disciples and asked them to give him God's power. But Peter was angry. "You cannot share with us in this work," Peter said. "Your heart is not right before God. Turn away from these evil thoughts and pray to the Lord."

Peter knew that our place in God's family is a free gift. When we believe in Jesus as God's Son, God gives us the Holy Spirit because He loves us. No one can buy the Holy Spirit. No one can pay to get into heaven. God is happy to give His good gifts to anyone who wants them for the right reasons. —T.M.

## FUN FACT

"The best things in life are free" is an old saying in the English language. It means we don't have to pay for the most valuable things in life—like love and friendship.

## READ MORE

Read Ephesians 2:8–10.
Who is allowed to brag about being part of God's family?

# The Widow's Son

Everyone was struck with fear and praised God. They said, "A great prophet has appeared among us," and "God has taken care of his people."

**LUKE 7:16 GW**

**During Bible times,** if a woman's husband died her children would take care of her. But if she didn't have children, she would be very poor.

One day Jesus and His disciples were traveling to a place called Nain. As Jesus came near the town He saw a funeral going on. Many people were walking with a widow whose only son had died. The woman was very sad. Her husband had died earlier and now her boy was gone too.

When Jesus saw the widow, He felt sorry for her. Then He said to the widow, "Don't cry." Jesus walked up to the men who were carrying the body and said, "Young man, get up!" The young man sat up and began to talk! Then Jesus gave the young man back to his mother.

Everyone who saw what happened was filled with wonder. It was a miracle! The people began praising God and calling Jesus a great prophet. They believed God was taking care of His people through Jesus.

But Jesus was more than a great prophet. He performed this miracle because He is the Son of God. He has the power to raise dead people back to life! But Jesus was also a man. He had feelings just like we do. He felt sorry for the widow because He knew what a hard life she would have without her son. So he helped her.

## Jesus cares for His people.

God still helps His people through his Son, Jesus. Like the people who saw Jesus' miracle at Nain, we can praise God too! —C.B.

### FUN FACT

Nain was a town in the area called Galilee. It is only mentioned once in the Bible. The miracle at Nain was the first time Jesus raised someone from the dead.

### READ MORE

Read 2 Kings 4:32–37.
How did Elisha help a woman from Shunem?

# Nehemiah and the King

**Nehemiah was an Israelite,** but he was an important helper to the Persian king Artaxerxes. Persia was the world's strongest country after it defeated Babylon. Babylon was the country that had attacked Jerusalem and taken many of its people away.

One day some Jewish men came to Persia from their homeland of Judah. Nehemiah asked the men how things were going in Jerusalem. "The Jews who weren't taken away are in trouble," the men said. "They are having many problems because the wall of Jerusalem is broken down and its gates were burned."

Nehemiah was so sad to hear the news that he sat down and cried. It was hard for him to do his job because he was so worried about his people and his homeland.

The king noticed that something was bothering Nehemiah. "Why do you look sad?" Artaxerxes asked. "I think your heart is full of sadness."

Nehemiah was afraid when the king spoke to him. He knew the king was powerful. He knew that the king had stopped the work in Jerusalem once before. So before Nehemiah answered the king, he prayed. Then Nehemiah said, "If it would make the king happy, and if I've been good to you, please send me to Jerusalem. I want to go and rebuild the city."

> Then I answered the king, "Are you pleased with me, King Artaxerxes? If it pleases you, send me to Judah. Let me go to the city of Jerusalem. That's where my people are buried. I want to rebuild it."
>
> NEHEMIAH 2:5 NIRV

## I can ask for the things that honor God.

King Artaxerxes agreed to let Nehemiah go! Nehemiah was brave enough to ask the king for the things he needed. And God used Nehemiah to help change the king's mind about rebuilding Jerusalem.

If we are doing work that honors God, He is happy to listen to our prayers and give us what we need. We can ask for what we need like Nehemiah did! —T.M.

### READ MORE
Read Nehemiah 2:11–18.
What did Nehemiah do when he got to Jerusalem?

### FUN FACT
When enemies tried to scare Nehemiah into stopping his work, he gave weapons to the people rebuilding the walls. Some people carried supplies for the wall in one hand, and a weapon in the other hand!

# He Is One of Them

Peter said to Jesus,
"Lord, I am ready to
go to prison with you.
I will even die
with you!"

**LUKE 22:33 ICB**

**Jesus knew** He was soon going to be arrested like a criminal. He said to Peter, "I have prayed that you will not lose your faith. Help your brothers to be strong."

Peter said, "Lord, I will go to prison for you. I will even die with you!"

"Peter," Jesus answered, "before the rooster crows you will say three times that you don't know me."

Later that night, Jesus was arrested and taken away. Peter followed Jesus, but stayed far away. One time, Peter joined some people who were sitting around a fire. A servant girl looked at Peter and said, "He is one of Jesus' followers."

"I don't even know him," Peter said.

Later, another person said, "You are one of them!"

"No, I'm not!" said Peter.

About an hour later, another man said, "This man is one of Jesus' disciples. He is from Galilee."

Peter said, "I don't know what you're talking about!"

## I know Jesus.

Just then a rooster crowed. Jesus turned and looked at Peter, and he remembered what Jesus had said. So Peter ran away from the people and cried.

It must have been a scary night for all of Jesus' disciples. Peter was probably afraid that the soldiers would arrest him just like they had arrested Jesus. In his fear, he said he didn't even know Jesus. But when Peter saw Jesus' face, he was deeply sorry for what he had done.

When people ask if you know Jesus, don't be afraid. He will help you to say yes. Then maybe other people will learn to know Jesus too. —C.B.

### FUN FACT

Scientists have learned that roosters don't need daylight to tell when it's dawn. They have a good sense of time and just know when to crow.

### READ MORE

Read Acts 4:13–20.
How do these verses show that Peter was no longer afraid to be a follower of Jesus?

# Never Too Late

**Three men** hung on crosses at a place called "The Skull." Jesus was in the middle. There were criminals on each side of Him.

> Then Jesus said to him, "I promise you, today you will be with me in paradise."
>
> **LUKE 23:43 ERV**

As the three suffered, one of the criminals yelled at Jesus. "Aren't you the Messiah?" he said. "Then save yourself, and save us too!"

But the other criminal stood up for Jesus. "You should fear God," he said. "All of us will die soon. You and I are guilty. We deserve to die because we did wrong. But this man has done nothing wrong." This criminal believed that Jesus was who He said He was. He looked at Jesus and said, "Remember me when you begin ruling as king!"

Jesus felt love for the dying man. "I promise you," Jesus said, "today you will be with me in paradise."

*It's never too late for Jesus to forgive us.*

One man on a cross believed in Jesus just a few moments before he died. And Jesus accepted that man into God's kingdom! Jesus promised the man that he would see Him again in heaven. It wasn't too late to believe in Jesus!

Some people think it's too late for God to accept them. Others believe they have messed up so much that God won't forgive them. But this story shows us it's never too late for someone to become a part of God's family. Nothing we do is too big for Jesus to forgive.

If you ever meet someone who thinks God can't forgive the bad things they've done, you have a good answer. You can tell that person about the criminal on the cross. —T.M.

## **FUN FACT**

The cross was seen as a shameful punishment in the Roman Empire. It was saved for the worst kinds of criminals—like enemies of the government, pirates, and slaves who had committed crimes.

## **READ MORE**

Read Colossians 1:13–14. Where does God bring us?

> Joshua had told the people not to give a war cry. He said, "Don't shout. Don't say a word until the day I tell you. Then you will shout."
>
> JOSHUA 6:10 ERV

# Seven Days of Marching

**The people of Jericho** were really scared when the Israelites crossed the Jordan River. The Israelites set up camp just outside the city. The people in Jericho hoped the city's walls and gates would protect them.

Joshua was leading the Israelites into the land that God had promised them. God told Joshua that He had already given Jericho, its king, and its army to the Israelites. All God's people had to do was march around the city for seven days. For each of the first six days the people would march around the city one time as the priests blew their trumpets. The priests would lead the way.

So Joshua and the people did what God told them. They marched around the city one time while the priests blew the trumpets. Then they went back to camp. They did that for six days.

## God's ways show His power.

But on the seventh day, as God told them, the Israelites marched around the city seven times. After the last lap, the priests blew a long blast on their trumpets. The people gave a loud shout. And the big strong walls of Jericho crumbled to the ground!

Marching around a city is not how armies beat their enemies. Armies fight with weapons! But God wanted to do things His way. God's way of capturing Jericho showed the Israelites that they needed to depend on Him for their victory. It showed the people of Jericho that God was much greater than their big, thick city walls.

If you want to be successful in what God asks you to do, trust Him. No matter what anyone else does, do everything God's way. Do everything in God's power!
—C.B.

### FUN FACT

Jericho is believed to be one of the oldest cities in the world. Today about twenty thousand people live in Jericho.

### READ MORE

Read Deuteronomy 26:16.
How were the Israelites supposed to obey God?

# The Lord's Treasury

**When people go** to church, they often put money in an offering plate. This money can be used to take care of the church building and pay the people who work at the church. It can be used to help missionaries who work in faraway places. It can also be used to help people nearby who need food or clothes. When we bring our gifts of money to church, we are giving to the Lord.

> "All the things made from silver, gold, bronze, and iron belong to the LORD. They must be put in the LORD's treasury."
> **JOSHUA 6:19 ERV**

When God helped the Israelites take over the city of Jericho, He gave them some very clear orders. God said that everything made of gold, silver, bronze, and iron had to be given to His work. Everything else had to be burned. Anyone who disobeyed would bring trouble to the Israelites' camp.

A man named Achan did not follow God's orders. He took some of the silver and gold things that were supposed to be put into the Lord's treasury. Israel's leader, Joshua, didn't know what Achan had done. When Joshua led the army out to fight, the Israelites were defeated.

Joshua was so upset that he tore his clothes and cried out to God. Then God told Joshua that someone in the camp had disobeyed. Joshua found out that Achan was the one who took what belonged to God. Achan's choice brought trouble to the camp and caused him to lose his life.

## I can give what God asks me to give.

When we obey God by giving back part of what He has given us, He is pleased. Being selfish, like Achan, will bring us trouble. Being willing to give to God brings happiness. —C.B.

### READ MORE
Read Malachi 3:6–12.
What did God promise the ancient Israelites?

## FUN FACT

Many churches use offering plates made from wood or metal. Some churches take up offerings in a velvet bag. Sometimes churches use different containers—like sand buckets or hub caps from cars—to tie into the day's sermon!

# A Second Chance for Israel

They gave a loud shout and praised the LORD because the foundation of the LORD's Temple had been laid. But many of the older priests, Levites, and family leaders, who could remember seeing the first Temple, began to cry aloud.

**EZRA 3:11–12 ERV**

**The Israelites were** slaves in Babylon for seventy years. The Babylonians had attacked Jerusalem, destroyed the temple, and taken many Israelites away from their homes. But many years later King Cyrus of Persia defeated the Babylonians. After this victory, King Cyrus said: "The Lord has called me to build a temple for Him in Jerusalem. All of you who are God's people may go to Jerusalem. May the God of Israel be with you. Those who stay behind should support anyone else who wants to go. Give them silver and gold, supplies and cattle. Give them special gifts for the temple of God."

So people collected gold and silver, supplies, and special gifts for the temple. They gave these things to the others who were going back to Jerusalem. Once they arrived in Jerusalem they laid a foundation—the very bottom part of the temple. Then the priests played their trumpets and cymbals in celebration. Many people praised the Lord, singing, "He is good; His love for Israel goes on forever." They shouted with joy. But many of the older men cried. They remembered the first temple and were sad because of all the bad things that happened.

## God gives second chances.

The Israelites had lost their temple and their country because they had done many wrong things. But God was giving Israel a second chance. He brought the people home and let them start over. That's the kind of God He is!

Even when we don't do what's right, God lets us start over. We might feel sad about the wrong things we have done. But when we admit our sins, God is ready to forgive. Then we can shout for joy too. —T.M.

## FUN FACT

The Israelites lived in Babylon for seventy years. Those seventy years made up for the "Sabbath rests" the people had not kept. God had commanded a Sabbath rest every seven years, when the people were not supposed to farm their land.

## READ MORE
Read Micah 7:18–19.
What does God enjoy doing?

# The Author

**Do you like** to write? Maybe someday you'll be an author. An author is someone who writes books.

Do you know who wrote the Bible? Because the Bible is a collection of books, it has many authors. Moses wrote the first five books of the Bible. People called "prophets" wrote many other books in the Old Testament. King David wrote more than half of the psalms, and King Solomon wrote many of the proverbs. Some of Jesus' twelve disciples wrote books in the New Testament. So did the apostle Paul.

Even though many different people wrote books of the Bible, God is the real author. God's Holy Spirit guided all the writers as they wrote. God used people to write the words, but He told each one what to say.

> All Scripture is given by God. And all Scripture is useful for teaching and for showing people what is wrong in their lives. It is useful for correcting faults and teaching the right way to live.
>
> **2 TIMOTHY 3:16 ERV**

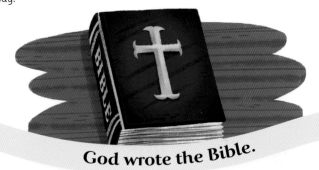

## God wrote the Bible.

The Bible is God's message to everyone who reads it. God's words in the Bible help us to know, love, and obey Him. The stories in the Bible help us understand God. They help us to see how He blesses us when we do what is right, and what happens when we disobey Him.

The Bible teaches us about God's love and forgiveness. It helps us to know God's grace and mercy. And the Bible shows us how to treat other people too.

We can trust everything that is written in the Bible because God's words are true. Since God is the author of the Bible, it is the greatest book anyone can read! —C.B.

## READ MORE
Read 2 Timothy 3:14–15.
What advice does Paul give to Timothy?

**FUN FACT**

The Bible is the world's most popular book. It is estimated that more than five billion copies have been printed in the last two hundred years.

# The Vineyard Owner's Son

> "The man had only one person left to send to the farmers. It was his son. He loved his son, but he decided to send him. He said, 'The farmers will respect my son.'"
>
> **MARK 12:6 ERV**

**Jesus told a parable** about a man who planted a vineyard. The man got everything ready for his grapes to grow. Then he let some other farmers use the vineyard while he went away.

When it was time to pick the grapes, the vineyard owner sent a servant to get his share of the grapes. But when the farmers saw the servant, they beat him up. He went back to the owner with nothing. So the vineyard owner sent another servant. The farmers treated that servant badly too. The vineyard owner kept sending servants to the farmers, but the farmers hurt each one.

Finally, the owner of the vineyard had only one person left to send. It was his son. The man loved his son very much, and hoped the farmers wouldn't hurt him. "The farmers will respect my son," he said.

But when the farmers saw the son coming, they made a very bad plan. "This is the owner's son—the vineyard will be his," they said to each other. "If we kill him, it will be ours!" So the farmers killed the owner's son.

## Everyone has a choice to accept God's Son.

Jesus' parable was really about the story of God sending prophets to the Israelites. The prophets told the Israelites how to please God. But a lot of times the people didn't listen to God's prophets. The people hurt and killed them. Finally, God sent His own Son, Jesus, to save the people. But the Jewish leaders didn't accept Jesus. They killed Him instead.

The Bible tells us just who Jesus is. Everyone has the choice to accept Him or not. When people do believe in Jesus, it changes the sad parable of the vineyard owner into a story with a happy ending. —T.M.

## FUN FACT

The law of Moses allowed the ancient Israelites to eat a few grapes from their neighbors' vineyard. But they were not allowed to carry grapes away in a basket!

## READ MORE

Read Isaiah 27:2–5.
How are God's people like a vineyard?

# "What Should We Do?"

**Jesus' disciples knew** He was going back to heaven soon. They were probably sad because they wouldn't see Jesus again on earth. But before He went up to heaven, Jesus told His disciples that He would send them the gift of the Holy Spirit. The Holy Spirit is the third person of the "Trinity"—God the Father, Jesus the Son, and the Holy Spirit. The Holy Spirit is God, who comes to live inside the people who follow Jesus!

> "You will receive the gift of the Holy Spirit. The promise is for you. It is also for your children and for all who are far away. It is for everyone the Lord our God calls to himself."
>
> ACTS 2:38–39 ICB

On a special holiday called Pentecost, the Holy Spirit came to earth. He sounded like a strong wind! The Holy Spirit filled the disciples with power from God. The disciples began doing miracles like Jesus had done. They began teaching and preaching in different languages.

Some people who were from other countries were amazed to hear the disciples speaking in their languages. But others who didn't understand what was happening began to make fun of the disciples.

## I receive the gift of the Holy Spirit by believing in Jesus.

Peter was bold! He stood up to tell the people about Jesus and His promise. Peter told how the Old Testament prophets said that Jesus would die on a cross and come back to life. Peter told the people that the Holy Spirit was coming to everyone who believed in Jesus.

"What should we do?" many people asked.

"Change your hearts and be baptized in the name of Jesus," Peter said. He told them that God would forgive their sins and they would receive the gift of the Holy Spirit.

This promise is for everyone who believes in Jesus—including you! —C.B.

## READ MORE
When Peter was talking to the people he quoted Psalm 16:8–11. Read the verses to see what he said.

## FUN FACT
When the disciples received the Holy Spirit, small flames of fire appeared and settled on each of them.

# Fast Food

Elisha said, "Listen to the message from the LORD! The LORD says, 'About this time tomorrow, there will be plenty of food, and it will be cheap again. A person will be able to buy a basket of fine flour or two baskets of barley for only one shekel in the marketplace by the city gates of Samaria.'"

2 KINGS 7:1 ERV

**The Samaritans** were neighbors of the Israelites. They were in big trouble! An evil king had sent his soldiers to surround the city of Samaria. They wouldn't let anyone bring food into the city.

The people in Samaria got so hungry they paid a lot of money for things they would not usually eat—like a donkey's head! One day the king of Israel was walking on top of the big wall around Samaria. A woman shouted to him, "My lord and king, please help me!" She told the king that the people were dying from hunger.

The king was upset when he heard that news. He blamed the prophet Elisha. But Elisha sent a message to the king. "Listen to the message from the Lord!" Elisha said. "About this time tomorrow, there will be plenty of food, and it will be cheap again."

## God always comes through.

There were four men with leprosy living outside the city walls. They were so hungry they decided to see if the enemy soldiers would help them. But when they got to the soldiers' camp, it was empty! During the night, the soldiers thought they had heard the Israelite army coming for them. God had sent that sound to scare the enemy soldiers. So they ran away and left all of their food and supplies behind! When the men with leprosy sent a message back to the city, the Samaritans ran to the soldiers' camp and took all the food they needed.

God provided food for Samaria just like Elisha said He would. God always comes through the way He says He will. We just need to trust Him. —T.M.

**FUN FACT**

In some parts of the world, people eat something called "a-ping." It is fried tarantulas!

## READ MORE

Read Genesis 22:12–14.
What did God provide for Abraham and Isaac? What did Abraham name the place where this happened?

# A New Disciple

**After Jesus went** back to heaven, the disciples went into the city of Jerusalem. They got together in the upstairs room of a building along with Jesus' brothers, Jesus' mother, and some other women.

> "Lord, you know the minds of everyone. Show us which one of these two you have chosen to do this work."
>
> **ACTS 1:24 ICB**

Peter stood up and told the group it was time to choose another disciple. They needed to replace Judas Iscariot, who had turned Jesus over to be arrested. "The disciple will have to be a man who was with us the whole time the Lord Jesus lived among us," Peter said. "That time began when John was baptizing and ended when Jesus was taken back to heaven. The one we choose must be able to say that he knows Jesus rose from the dead."

The disciples put the names of two men before the group. One man was called Joseph Barsabbas. The other was named Matthias. The believers all prayed to God and said, "Lord you know the minds of everyone. Show us which one of these two you have chosen to do this work."

### God knows what people are like on the inside.

God answered their prayer. He showed them that Matthias should be the twelfth disciple instead of Judas.

We don't know what's in another person's heart or mind, but God does. Just like the disciples asked God to help them choose the right man to be the twelfth disciple, you can ask God to help you choose the right kind of friends. You can ask God to help you know who loves Him and who would be a good friend. God likes to answer prayers like that—just like He answered the disciples' prayer. —C.B.

### READ MORE
Read Proverbs 13:20.
Why is it important to choose good friends?

### FUN FACT
The name Matthias is a shortened form of Mattathias. It means "gift of God."

# Praising in Prison

**Paul and Silas** were teaching people about Jesus. Some people didn't like their teaching and accused them of breaking the law. So the Roman rulers had Paul and Silas thrown into jail. The rulers told the jailer, "Guard these men very carefully!" The jailer obeyed. He put Paul and Silas in a lonely part of the jail and chained their feet to a big wooden block.

Late at night Paul and Silas were praying and singing praises to God. The other prisoners were listening. Suddenly there was an earthquake! It was so powerful that the jail shook. The chains fell off the prisoners and the doors in the jail swung open. When the jailer woke up and saw the open doors, he figured all of the prisoners had run away. He knew he would be in big trouble and wanted to die. But Paul shouted, "We are all here!"

The jailer called for a light so he could see. Shaking with fear, he went to Paul and Silas and asked, "What must I do to be saved?"

## I can praise God at all times.

"Believe in the Lord Jesus," Paul and Silas said, "and you will be saved." That night the jailer and his family became Christians.

Even though Paul and Silas were treated unfairly, they still praised God. And God used them to lead people to Jesus!

We can praise God too, even when things don't go the way we want them to. Just like God used Paul and Silas, God can use our faithfulness as an example to others. —T.M.

### FUN FACT

In 2005 two ancient prison cells were discovered in Tiberias, Israel. Small holes had been cut through the walls so family members could feed the prisoners inside.

### READ MORE

Find Philippians 1:3–11.
Paul wrote Philippians while he was in prison.
What was his attitude while he was in jail?

# The First Miracle

**Jesus was at a wedding** dinner with His mother and His disciples. The person in charge of the party had an embarrassing problem. The wine had run out before the dinner was over! "They have no more wine," Jesus' mother said to him.

Jesus had not yet done any miracles. But His mother must have known that He could do something to help. So she told the servants at the wedding, "Do whatever He tells you."

Jesus saw six big stone water jars nearby. The Jews used the water from the jars for special washings to make themselves pure. Jesus told the servants to fill those jars with water. The servants did what Jesus told them to do. They filled the jars to the very top. And then Jesus performed a miracle. He turned the water into wine!

"Take some out," Jesus said, "and bring it to the person in charge of the dinner."

> Cana in Galilee was the place where Jesus began to perform miracles. He made his glory public there, and his disciples believed in him.
> JOHN 2:11 GW

## Jesus gives me His best.

The servants brought a cup of wine to the person in charge of the dinner. He tasted the wine and was amazed at how good it was. Then he said to the groom, "Everyone brings out the best wine first. But you have saved the best for last."

The person in charge of the dinner didn't know where the wine came from. But the servants knew, and so did Jesus' disciples. This was the first of Jesus' many miracles. He showed His power as God at the wedding dinner, and His disciples put their faith in Him.

When Jesus performed miracles, He was often helping a person in need. He still helps people today. And like the wine that Jesus provided for a wedding dinner, His help will be His very best. —C.B.

**READ MORE**
Read John 4:43–54.
What was the second miracle that Jesus performed?

**FUN FACT**
The stone jars in this story probably held about 20 to 30 gallons of water (76–113 liters). Six jars would hold about 150 gallons (567 liters) of miracle wine!

> Locusts have no king,
> but they are able to
> work together.
>
> PROVERBS 30:27 ERV

# The Mighty Locusts

**Locusts are small** creatures. They are anywhere from a half-inch to three inches long (1.3 to 7.6 centimeters). You might not even notice a single locust by itself because it is so small.

But in some parts of the world, when the warm season comes and plants start growing, lots and lots of locusts come together. They move together in huge swarms with great power. Together they destroy whole fields full of plants. Locusts eat so many crops that they can cause large groups of people to starve. One small insect can't do very much by itself. But when locusts work together, they become a powerful force.

The book of Proverbs in the Bible tells us to learn from the locusts. They don't have a leader to tell them what to do. But when they work together, they can do big things. As God's people, we can also do great things by working together. Teamwork helps us to do more than we could do by ourselves. But unlike the locusts, we do have a leader to follow—Jesus!

## We can do great things when we work together.

When we work together to serve God, we achieve much more than we could on our own. Why not try the lesson of the locusts? You could invite a group of kids from your church or school to do a service project. Maybe you could come up with ideas like collecting food for others or taking gifts and cards to someone who is sick. When you work together, you will be amazed at how much God can do through you! —T.M.

## FUN FACT

A swarm of desert locusts can cover up to 460 square miles (1,200 square kilometers). That's an area larger than Hong Kong!

## READ MORE

Read Exodus 10:12–19.
What did God use locusts to do in Egypt?

# Adam's Special Helper

**On the sixth day** of creation, God formed a man from the dust of the ground. God named the man Adam. Then God put Adam in a beautiful place called the Garden of Eden. The garden was filled with all kinds of trees. A river flowed through the garden to water the ground. God gave Adam the job of taking care of the garden.

> So the man gave names to all of the livestock. He gave names to all of the birds of the air. And he gave names to all of the wild animals. But Adam didn't find a helper that was right for him.
>
> **GENESIS 2:20 NIRV**

God also gave Adam another job. He brought the animals He had made to Adam and told Adam to give them names. Do you think it would be fun to name the animals? Adam named the sheep and the lions, the donkeys and the horses. He named the sparrows and the eagles and the ravens. Adam gave names to the big animals and the little animals. He gave names to all the birds. Whatever Adam called each living creature became its name.

## Marriage is God's idea.

There were a lot of animals and birds to name! But as Adam went through all the creatures, he didn't find a helper that was right for him. So God said, "It is not good for man to be alone," and He caused Adam to fall asleep. Then God took a rib from Adam and used it to create a woman. She became Adam's wife and he named her Eve. She was created to be Adam's special helper.

Adam and Eve were the very first husband and wife. God wanted them to love each other and help each other, just like husbands and wives should today. Marriage between a man and woman is God's idea. Someday He may give you a special helper too. —C.B.

### **FUN FACT**

We call the bald eagle "bald" because of the light feathers on its head that make it look bald from a distance. Its scientific name is "sea eagle."

## **READ MORE**

Read Matthew 19:3–6.
What did Jesus say about marriage?

# Paul Chooses the Right Words

> "As I walked around, I looked carefully at the things you worship. I even found an altar with TO AN UNKNOWN GOD written on it. Now I am going to tell you about this 'unknown god' that you worship."
>
> ACTS 17:23 NIRV

**One day the apostle Paul** was walking through the city of Athens. He saw many idols and false gods. The people believed in so many false gods that someone had even built a monument to "an unknown god." Paul talked to the people about Jesus, but they didn't understand.

Many people in Athens enjoyed talking about new ideas. So some people invited Paul to a meeting where all of the smart men and deep thinkers met. "Please explain to us what you have been teaching," they said. "We want to know what it means."

Paul talked about the monument to an unknown god. He said to the people, "I will tell you who the unknown God is!" Paul told how the one true God created the world. He explained that God was too great to live in a house made by people. He told them that Jesus is God's Son who rose from the dead.

## I can help other people understand who Jesus is.

Some people laughed at Paul's teaching. But some of them listened and believed and decided to follow Jesus.

Paul was a good teacher because he talked to people in a way they could understand. He put the story of Jesus into words that made sense to others.

Sometimes you might talk to people who don't know about Jesus. They might not understand the words people use in church. But like Paul, you can talk to others in a way they can understand. The story of Jesus isn't hard. You can ask God to give you the right words to tell others about Jesus and He will help you. —T.M.

## FUN FACT

Paul preached about the "unknown god" at a place called Mars Hill. People still visit Mars Hill in Athens, Greece. A metal sign on the hill reminds tourists of Paul's sermon.

## READ MORE

Read Acts 7:48–50. Paul told the people in Athens that God was too great to live in a house made by people. According to these verses, where is God's throne?

# People Will Know

**Jesus knew** He would not be with His disciples much longer. During the years He had spent with them, Jesus taught the disciples many things. One of the most important things was to love other people.

> "All people will know that you are my followers if you love each other."
>
> JOHN 13:35 ERV

One day Jesus told His disciples, "I am giving you a new commandment: love each other." Jesus wanted His followers to love other people the way He loved them. If the disciples showed Jesus' kind of love, other people would know that they were His followers.

Did you know that's still true today? Jesus' words were not just for His twelve disciples. They are for us too! The love Jesus talked about is not the "feeling" kind of love—it's the "showing" kind of love. There are many ways you can show love to others.

## I can love like Jesus.

When you're at home, you can show love by using kind words in your family. You can show love by helping with chores and obeying your parents. If you have brothers or sisters you can play with them when they want someone to spend time with them. You can help them if they have a problem.

When you're at school, you can show love by being polite to your teachers and classmates. You can be a friend to someone who needs a friend. If a new student joins your class, you can make that person feel welcomed.

When we love others the way Jesus loves us, people will know that we are His followers. —C.B.

## READ MORE

Read Hebrews 13:1–2.
What do these verses say about welcoming visitors?

## FUN FACT

The phrase "love one another" is found twelve times in the New International Version of the New Testament.

# Joshua's Farewell Speech

> "Be very strong. Be careful to obey everything that is written in the Scroll of the Law of Moses. Don't turn away from it to the right or the left."
>
> **JOSHUA 23:6 NIRV**

**Joshua trusted God** in everything he did. He led Israel with courage, helping the Israelites defeat their enemies and move to the promised land.

The Israelites were at peace as Joshua neared the end of his life. He brought Israel's leaders together to encourage them as they took over his work. Joshua gave them important advice, telling them how to be a successful nation.

First, Joshua reminded the people of everything God did to bring them to their land. Then he said, "You must be careful to obey everything written in the law of Moses. Never turn away from it." He also said, "The Lord helped you defeat many great nations. With His help, one man from Israel could defeat one thousand enemy soldiers. The Lord your God fights for you."

Joshua finished his speech with a warning. He told the people that loving God was the most important thing they could do. Anything that took their attention away from God was dangerous. If the people worshipped anything besides God, they would bring trouble on themselves. But if the Israelites continued to follow God, He would keep His promise to bless them.

## I can choose to be a part of God's promises.

Someday you will grow up and make your own decisions. You will have a choice to follow God or follow other things. When you believe in Jesus as your Savior, you will enjoy God's faithfulness and blessing. Forever! —T.M.

### FUN FACT

The "law of Moses" is the first five books of the Bible. They are also called the Pentateuch, which means "five books."

### READ MORE

Read Joshua 1:1–9. What instructions was Joshua given when he became leader? Who gave him these instructions?

# No Ordinary Man

**The day Jesus** was crucified was no ordinary day. But that's because Jesus was no ordinary man.

It was nine o'clock in the morning when Jesus was put on the cross. He was treated like a criminal. The Roman soldiers standing nearby laughed at Him.

But while Jesus was on the cross, God showed His power. From noon until three o'clock, the sky went dark. Only God can make the sky dark in the middle of the day! And the moment Jesus died, the curtain in the temple was torn in two from top to bottom. The earth shook and rocks split apart. Tombs broke open and some of God's people who had died came out of their graves. Only God could make that happen!

> "This man was surely the Son of God!"
> MARK 15:39 NIRV

### Jesus is God's Son.

The Roman soldiers near the cross were terrified. One of the officers said, "This man was surely the Son of God!"

There is no other way to explain the things that happened that day. God showed His power, and the people were filled with fear when they saw what God could do.

Today, some people believe that Jesus was only a prophet or teacher. Some say Jesus was a good man. But Jesus is much more than a prophet or teacher. He is much more than just a good man. Jesus is the Son of God for sure!
—C.B.

## FUN FACT

Jesus was crucified at a place called Golgotha. The name comes from the Aramaic language and means "skull." In the Latin language, the name is Calvary.

## READ MORE

Read Mark 15:42–47.
Where was Jesus buried?

# Different Opinions

**Paul and Barnabas** were missionaries. They loved Jesus and worked together to tell people about Him in many different places.

After some time Paul wanted to go back to the towns he and Barnabas had already visited. Paul thought it was important to encourage the new Christians in those towns. Barnabas agreed. But when he said he wanted to take his nephew John Mark along, Paul was unhappy. John Mark had gone with Paul and Barnabas on another trip but left early, without finishing his work.

> Paul and Barnabas had a serious argument about this. They separated and went different ways. Barnabas sailed to Cyprus and took Mark with him. But Paul chose Silas and left.
>
> ACTS 15:39–40 ICB

Barnabas and Paul had an argument. When they couldn't agree, they decided the only answer was to split up. Barnabas took John Mark with him and sailed to the island of Cyprus. Paul chose a man named Silas and started his journey to Syria.

Even though Paul and Barnabas were good Christian men, they still disagreed. No matter how much two people love God, they may have different opinions. In this story, Paul and Barnabas had to stop traveling together to settle their argument. But God gave each one new friends and blessed them as they worked to share the story of Jesus.

*I can respect others, even when we disagree.*

Barnabas and Paul didn't let their argument keep them from their missionary work. And they continued to respect each other. Paul spoke kindly about Barnabas and John Mark in the letters he wrote later.

We won't always agree with others. But when disagreements happen, we can keep doing the things God has asked us to do. We can still speak kindly about others, even when we have different opinions. God can still use us to do His work. —T.M.

**FUN FACT**

Paul also took a man named Timothy on many of his trips. Paul taught Timothy to be a pastor. They became so close that Paul called Timothy his "son in the faith."

## READ MORE

Read Colossians 3:12–15.
What is Paul's advice for avoiding disagreements?

# Three Men Who Stood Up

> "If you throw us into the hot furnace, the God we serve can save us. And if he wants to, he can save us from your power. But even if God does not save us, we want you to know, King, that we refuse to serve your gods. We will not worship the gold idol you have set up."
>
> DANIEL 3:17–18 ERV

**Nebuchadnezzar,** king of Babylon, built a huge gold idol. All the rulers in Babylon came to see it. The king's official announced, "You must bow down and worship the idol when you hear music playing. Whoever doesn't bow down will be thrown into a hot furnace."

Three young men from Israel had been given positions of honor in the king's house. Their names were Shadrach, Meshach, and Abednego. But because they loved God, they would not worship the king's idol. Some other officials were jealous of the three Israelites and told the king that the young men were breaking the law. King Nebuchadnezzar was furious! He called for Shadrach, Meshach, and Abednego to come to his court.

"Is it true that you won't bow down and worship the gold idol?" he asked. "If you don't worship it, you will be thrown into the furnace. No god will be able to save you!"

Shadrach, Meshach, and Abednego said, "Our God can save us."

## God is the greatest.

Nebuchadnezzar was so angry that he made the furnace seven times hotter than usual. His soldiers tied up the three young men and threw them into the furnace. But when the king looked inside the furnace, he saw four men instead of three! An angel was with Shadrach, Meshach, and Abednego. The angel kept them from being burned.

Then King Nebuchadnezzar realized that God is real. "No other God can save His people like this," the king said. He made a new law that no one could speak against God.

The God who saved Shadrach, Meshach, and Abednego is the God we serve today. No one is greater than He is. —T.M.

### FUN FACT

The gold idol that Nebuchadnezzar built was about eighty-seven feet tall (twenty-seven meters) and almost nine feet wide (three meters).

### READ MORE

Read Isaiah 43:1–2. What promise does God make to His people in these verses?

# Sewing for God

**A woman named Tabitha** lived in the city of Joppa. Her Greek name was Dorcas. She was a follower of Jesus and enjoyed doing good things for other people. She knew how to sew, and she used her talent to make clothing for widows. She also gave money to people who were poor.

> She was always doing good things for people and giving money to those in need.
> **ACTS 9:36 ERV**

Then Tabitha became sick and died. Her friends were very sad. They washed her body and put her in a room. But when some people in Joppa heard that the apostle Peter was in a nearby town, they sent two men to find him. The men begged Peter to come with them to Joppa.

So Peter followed the men and went to the room where Tabitha's body lay. The widows were crying as they showed Peter the clothes Tabitha had made for them.

Soon Peter sent everyone out of the room. Then he knelt down and prayed to God. When he was done praying, he said, "Tabitha, stand up!" At once she opened her eyes and sat up! When Peter told Tabitha's friends to come back into the room, they saw that she was alive again. The story about Tabitha spread quickly through the city of Joppa. Many people believed in Jesus when they heard the news.

Tabitha was not an important leader in her city. It seems she lived all by herself. But God had given her the ability to sew, and she used her talent to help many people. And even when she died, God worked through Tabitha to help many people believe in Jesus.

## God can use me to help others.

We can be like Tabitha. We can use the talents God gives us to help other people and point them to Jesus. —C.B.

## READ MORE
Read Acts 9:32–35.
What was Peter doing in the town of Lydda when Tabitha died?

### FUN FACT
Some churches have a "Dorcas Society," which is a group of people with a mission of giving clothing to the poor. The society was named after Dorcas in this story.

# The Most Important Thing

LORD, teach me your ways, and I will live and obey your truths. Help me make worshiping your name the most important thing in my life.

PSALM 86:11 ERV

**We do important things** every day. Learning at school is important. It prepares you for your future. Eating healthy food is important. It gives you the vitamins and minerals you need to grow. Exercising is important. It makes your bones and muscles strong. What are some other important things that you do every day?

King David had many important things to do. As king of Israel, he was in charge of the whole country. He was over all of the people and the army. He had a lot to think about and take care of.

But when King David prayed, he asked God to make one thing the most important part of his life. David wanted the most important part of his life to be worshipping God. He wanted to learn God's ways. David knew how great God was. "My Lord, there is no God like you," David prayed. "No one can do what you have done."

David honored God with his prayer, and asked God to give him strength. David didn't mean big muscles. He wanted strength to have patience and do what was right.

## Worshipping God is the most important thing.

We can pray the same prayer that King David prayed. We can ask God to make worshipping Him the most important part of our lives. We can tell God how great He is and ask Him to give us strength. When we put God first, He will be with us in all the other important things we do. —T.M.

**FUN FACT**

The word *worship* means to honor something that is worthy. When we worship, we are saying that God is worthy—that He has great worth or value.

**READ MORE**

Read Psalm 86.
Which parts of David's prayer can you pray today?

# Two Silver Trumpets

**Have you ever** heard church bells ringing? Some churches ring bells to tell people it's time to come worship. Church bells are loud and clear. They can be heard from miles away.

> "Make two trumpets of hammered silver. Use them to call the people together and to march out of camp."
>
> **NUMBERS 10:2 ICB**

When the people of Israel were in the wilderness they didn't have churches with bells. It was hard to get more than two million people to come together at one time. So God told Moses to make two silver trumpets to call the people together.

When both trumpets were blown, everyone had to join together in front of the entrance to the meeting tent. If only one trumpet was blown, just the leaders would come. With one blast of a trumpet, tribes from the east side of the camp would start out. When the second blast was blown, the camps on the south side started to move. Only the sons of Aaron were allowed to blow the trumpets.

*Music can call me to worship God.*

The silver trumpets could also be used to warn the people of an attack. God said if that happened, He would save them from their enemies. But there were happier times for the trumpets too. God told Moses to use the silver trumpets to celebrate feasts and give offerings. The trumpets reminded the people that God was always with them.

Today most churches do not use trumpets to call people to worship. And many do not use bells. But God can use any kind of music to help you worship Him. Whether you are outside or inside a church, on Sunday or any other day, music can remind you of the silver trumpets. Music can remind you that God is always there. —C.B.

### FUN FACT

Today some churches have handbell choirs. The people in a handbell choir hold a bell in each hand and ring the bells to play the notes to a song.

### READ MORE

Read 2 Chronicles 29:25–30.
Who played trumpets? Why did they play them?

# Paul's Brave Story

Paul said, "It is not important if it is easy or if it is hard. I pray to God that not only you but that everyone listening to me today could be saved and be just like me—except for these chains I have!"

**ACTS 26:29 ERV**

**The Jewish leaders** wanted Paul to stop telling people about Jesus. They went to the new governor, a man named Festus, and told him Paul broke their laws. Festus wanted the Jewish people to like him, so he listened to the leaders' stories.

A few days later King Agrippa came to visit Governor Festus. Festus told Agrippa about Paul, and the king wanted to hear Paul's story. Paul was happy to tell him. He told Agrippa about the day he met Jesus on the road to Damascus. As Paul talked, Festus called him crazy. "Paul, you are out of your mind!" Festus said. But Paul knew this was his chance to tell King Agrippa about Jesus.

"Governor Festus, I'm not crazy," Paul said. "I know Agrippa has heard about Jesus. King Agrippa, do you believe what the prophets wrote? I know you believe!"

King Agrippa said, "Do you think it's that easy to convince me to become a Christian?"

*I can have courage to talk about Jesus.*

"It's not important if it's easy or hard," Paul replied. "I pray to God that everyone listening to me would be saved."

Paul was always excited to tell people about Jesus. It didn't matter if he was preaching a sermon, chained in prison, or talking to a king. Paul used every chance to tell others about Jesus, whether they were important officials or regular people. He knew everyone needed to trust in Jesus.

We can do what Paul did too. No matter who we meet or talk to, we can ask God for a chance to tell them about Jesus. —T.M.

**FUN FACT**

King Agrippa was related to Herod the Great, the king who wanted to kill baby Jesus. Agrippa was the last king that came from Herod's family.

**READ MORE**
Read Acts 28:30–31.
What did Paul do while he waited for his trial in Rome?

# Protect the Truth

**Timothy was a young man** who became a close friend of the apostle Paul. Timothy learned from Paul and traveled with him. Then he became pastor of the church in Ephesus.

Timothy and Paul both worked hard to tell others about Jesus. But Timothy's childhood was much different than Paul's. Timothy grew up with a mother and grandmother who were both Christians. They taught Timothy about God and Jesus. Paul knew that Timothy had that same strong faith.

Being raised in a Christian home is a special blessing and gift from God. Paul had not been raised in a Christian home. So he reminded Timothy to protect the truth he had been taught as a child. "Do not be ashamed to tell people about our Lord Jesus," Paul said. Paul reminded Timothy that the Holy Spirit would give him power to be bold when telling others about Jesus.

> Protect the truth that you were given. Protect it with the help of the Holy Spirit who lives in us.
>
> 2 TIMOTHY 1:14 ICB

## I can learn about God as I grow up.

Christian parents or grandparents can help kids learn about God and His love for them. It's wonderful when families read the Bible and pray together. But kids who don't have Christian parents or grandparents can still learn about God by reading their Bibles.

Whether you grow up in a Christian family, like Timothy, or you're from a family that doesn't know Jesus, like Paul, God wants you to know Him. Knowing and believing the truth about Jesus is like having a special treasure to protect. —C.B.

### FUN FACT

Timothy was from a city called Lystra. His mother's name was Eunice and his grandmother's name was Lois. The Bible doesn't tell us the name of Timothy's father, but says he was Greek.

### READ MORE

Read 2 Timothy 1:13–14.
What did Paul tell Timothy to do?

# The Doubting Disciple

Then Jesus told him, "Because you have seen me, you have believed. Blessed are those who have not seen me but still have believed."

JOHN 20:29 NIRV

**Mary Magdalene** was the first person to see Jesus after He rose from the dead. She ran to tell the disciples the good news. "I have seen the Lord!" she said. Later that night the disciples were together in a locked room. Suddenly, Jesus appeared! "Peace be with you," Jesus said. Then He showed the disciples His hands and His side. The disciples were very happy when they saw Jesus.

One of the disciples, named Thomas, was not with the others when they saw Jesus. They were excited to tell Thomas, "We have seen the Lord!"

But when they told Thomas, he did not believe them. "First I must see the nail marks in His hands," Thomas said. "I must put my finger where the nails were and put my hand into His side. Then I will believe."

*I will believe without seeing.*

A week later, the disciples were together again when Jesus suddenly appeared. "May peace be with you!" He said. Then He spoke directly to Thomas. "See my hands? Put your finger here. Reach out your hand and put it into my side. Stop doubting and believe."

Thomas looked at Jesus. But he didn't have to put his finger into Jesus' hands. He didn't have to put his hand in Jesus' side. Thomas just said to Jesus, "My Lord and my God!"

When Thomas saw Jesus in person, he believed that Jesus rose from the dead. But we can believe Jesus is alive even without seeing Him in person. That's what it means to have faith. —C.B.

## FUN FACT

Because of this Bible story, a person who has a hard time believing something is sometimes called a "Doubting Thomas."

## READ MORE

Read 1 Corinthians 15:3–8.
How many people saw Jesus after He rose from the dead?

# Salty People

**Do you ever add** a little salt to your food? Mashed potatoes without salt taste pretty bland. Pretzels without salt are boring. Adding salt makes your food taste better. Salt helps to bring out a food's natural flavor.

In Bible times salt was very important. It not only added flavor to food, it also kept food from spoiling. The people in those days did not have refrigerators, so they added salt to their meat to keep it from going bad. Salt is a substance that everyone needs.

When Jesus taught, He used examples from everyday life to help people understand what He was saying. Jesus told His followers that they should be like salt. Just like salt makes food taste better, believers can make the world a better place by living the way Jesus taught. And just like salt keeps food from going bad, Jesus' followers could keep others from spoiling their lives with sin and disobedience.

When you are a follower of Jesus, you can be "salty" too. Just like salt can make your mashed potatoes and pretzels taste better, the love and kindness you show to others can add joy and happiness to their lives. And just like salt keeps food from going bad, you can encourage others to make good choices.

Whenever you spend time with others, be sure to add the salt! —C.B.

> "You are the salt of the earth. But if the salt loses its salty taste, it cannot be made salty again."
>
> MATTHEW 5:13 ICB

*I can make the world a better place.*

**READ MORE**

Read Colossians 4:5-6.
How can we be like salt to people who are not Christians?

**FUN FACT**

People in Bible times collected salt by pouring sea water into pits and letting the water evaporate. Then, only salt was left.

# Praying in the Garden

> "Abba," he said, "everything is possible for you. Take this cup of suffering away from me. But let what you want be done, not what I want." *Abba* means Father.
>
> MARK 14:36 NIRV

**Jesus knew** He was going to die on the cross soon. But the disciples didn't understand. When Jesus brought them to the Garden of Gethsemane to pray, He told most of the disciples to sit near the entrance. But He took Peter, James, and John with Him in the garden. "My soul is very sad," Jesus told His closest friends. "I feel death coming. Stay here. Keep watch."

Jesus went a little farther into the garden. He kneeled on the ground to pray. Jesus knew God had sent Him into the world to give His life for people's sins. Jesus knew His death would be hard, and He asked God to keep Him from the suffering. But Jesus also prayed, "Father, let what you want be done, not what I want."

Jesus prayed all through the night. Even though Jesus told His disciples to pray too, they kept falling asleep. But Jesus kept talking to God and prepared himself to die on the cross. Jesus would do whatever God asked Him to do.

Jesus realized how painful it would be to die for the sins of the whole world. But He agreed to do it anyway. He knew His death was God's plan for the world, and He wanted to obey His Father more than anything else.

## Jesus died for me—I can live for Him!

The Bible says Jesus' death proves that God loves us. Since God showed His love for us in such a big way, we can show Him our love too. The best way we can love God is by giving Him every part of our lives. —T.M.

### FUN FACT

The Garden of Gethsemane is found at the bottom of the Mount of Olives. Scientists say the olive trees in the Garden of Gethsemane are some of the oldest ones in the world.

### READ MORE

Read Matthew 14:23, Mark 1:35, and Luke 5:16.
What did Jesus often do?
Did He do it by himself or with others?

# A Sign and a Promise

> "I will put my rainbow in the clouds to be a sign of my promise to the earth."
>
> **GENESIS 9:13 GW**

**Noah and his family** lived in the ark for many months. God kept them safe during the giant flood that wiped out every living thing on earth. When dry land finally appeared, Noah and his family came out of the ark. The animals also came out of the ark, just like they had gone in—two by two. Then Noah built an altar to the Lord and made a sacrifice. God was pleased with Noah's sacrifice.

God made a promise to Noah and his family and every living creature that was on the ark. "I will never send another flood to kill all life or destroy the earth," God said. "I am giving you a sign of my promise. It is for you and all living creatures for all generations to come."

*The rainbow is a sign of God's promise.*

The sign of God's promise was a beautiful rainbow in the sky. God said to Noah, "When the rainbow appears in the clouds, I will see it. I will remember that my promise will last forever. It is a covenant between me and every kind of living thing on earth."

The first rainbow appeared in the sky thousands of years ago. God still puts rainbows in the sky today. He is faithful and His word is true. God has never sent another flood to destroy the whole world.

The next time you see a rainbow, remember the promise that God made to Noah. That promise was also for you—and God always keeps His promises. —C.B.

## READ MORE

Read Genesis 8:22.
What other promise did God make to Noah?

## FUN FACT

Sometimes a second rainbow—called a "double rainbow"—forms behind a rainbow. The second rainbow is usually twice as wide as the first, but not as bright. And its colors are in a backward order.

# Getting Along

Here is what I'm asking Euodia and Syntyche to do. I want them to agree with each other because they belong to the Lord.

**PHILIPPIANS 4:2 NIRV**

**Have you ever** had a disagreement with your mom, or your neighbor, or your best friend? It's hard to get along with people all the time. No matter how much you love someone, you will sometimes disagree. Sometimes people get on our nerves, even when they aren't doing anything wrong. And we might say something that hurts another person's feelings, even if we didn't mean to.

In the Bible, Euodia and Syntyche were friends who disagreed. These women were both part of the church at Philippi. They had helped Paul and his missionary helpers spread the good news about Jesus. But for some reason Euodia and Syntyche were having problems with each other. Paul told the women it was important for them to get along. They belonged to God and they represented His kingdom. Paul knew Euodia and Syntyche weren't setting a good example for others.

Because God is loving and kind, it was important for Euodia and Syntyche to be loving and kind. They needed to show God's love and kindness to each other so people could see what God is like. Paul encouraged the women by saying, "Always be joyful because you belong to the Lord. I will say it again. Be joyful. Let everyone know how gentle you are."

### I can show kindness and love no matter what.

We should try to be joyful and gentle too. We can show our joy and gentleness by getting along with others. Even when we disagree or don't like the things other people do, we can still be kind and loving. When we are, we show people what God is like.
—T.M.

## FUN FACT

The church in Philippi was the first Christian church in Europe. Paul used the church as a good example of generosity.

## READ MORE

Read Romans 12:9–12.
What do these verses say about getting along with others?

# God Asks Some Questions

"Where were you when I laid the earth's foundation? Tell me, if you know."
JOB 38:4 NIRV

**Job was a man** who loved God. God had blessed Job with many good things, but then some very bad things happened. He lost almost everything he owned. He became very sick. Job's friends felt sorry for him, but they thought he had caused his own problems. They told Job that God was punishing him for his sins! Job became very tired of his troubles and questioned God's plan.

God knew what Job was thinking and asked him some questions. God said to Job, "Where were you when I laid the earth's foundation? Tell me, if you know. Who measured the earth? What was it built on? Who created the ocean and caused it to be born? I put clouds over it as if they were its clothes. I wrapped it in thick darkness. I said, 'You can come this far, but you can't come any farther. Here is where your proud waves have to stop.'"

Job listened as God said more. "Can you make the morning appear? Where does light come from? Where does the darkness go? Have you seen where the hail and snow are stored? Can you make it rain? Can you make lightning appear?"

## Sometimes things happen that we can't explain.

Job couldn't answer God's questions. He realized that he should not question God. When Job's troubles finally came to an end, God gave him even more blessings than he had before.

What can we learn from the story of Job? We may not always understand the things that happen in our lives. But God's power and wisdom are much greater than we can imagine. We can trust Him to do what's right. —C.B.

## READ MORE
Read Job 38 to see more questions that God asked Job. What does Job say in Job 40:3–5?

## FUN FACT
Job lived in a place called Uz. Nobody knows exactly where Uz was. But it may have been near Midian, where Moses lived for forty years.

# It's Good to Work

> We hear that some people in your group refuse to work. They are doing nothing except being busy in the lives of others. Our instruction to them is to stop bothering others, to start working and earn their own food. It is by the authority of the Lord Jesus Christ that we are urging them to do this.
>
> 2 THESSALONIANS 3:11–12
> ERV

**When the apostle Paul** wrote a letter to the church in Thessalonica, he gave them some advice. He had heard that some people in the church weren't doing everything they should be doing. Some people were being lazy. They weren't obeying the teaching Paul gave them when he came to see them.

Even when Paul and his helpers had visited the church to tell people about Jesus, they worked to earn money. They didn't take anything from anyone without paying for it. Paul and his team spent their whole lives traveling around to tell people about Jesus. They gave up their normal jobs and a regular life to work for God. But they made sure they set an example by working hard wherever they went.

Some people in Thessalonica didn't want to work. They started bothering others by being nosy. Paul said that was not okay! He said the other members of the church needed to help those people change their ways.

## I will work hard instead of being lazy.

Paul knew God wants us to use our talents and abilities for Him. God wants us to make the most of the life He's given us. Through our hard work, God gives us the food and clothes we need—and He also helps us provide for others who are not able to work.

God created us to do something. If we aren't busy doing something good, we might get busy doing something bad. So instead of being lazy, we can be like Paul. With God's help we can work hard and use our energy to serve Him and others. —T.M.

## FUN FACT

There's an old saying that goes, "The only place where success comes before work is in the dictionary." That's just another way of saying nobody gets where they want to go without working hard.

## READ MORE

Read Colossians 3:23–24.
What do we get when we work hard?

> "I will choose one man. His stick will begin to grow leaves. And I will stop the Israelites from always complaining against you."
>
> **NUMBERS 17:5 ICB**

# Aaron's Staff

**The people of Israel** were complaining—again. So God said to Moses, "Get twelve wooden staffs from the people, one for each tribe. The leader of each tribe must write his name on the staff. Put the staffs in the meeting tent."

Some of Israel's leaders didn't want to follow the orders of Moses and his brother Aaron. The people weren't showing Moses and Aaron the respect they should have. So God told Moses that He would show the people exactly who they should follow. The man whose staff grew buds and blossoms would be priest for the people.

So the leaders of the tribes gave Moses their wooden staffs. Moses put the staffs in the meeting tent. The next day, when Moses went into the tent, he saw that Aaron's staff had grown buds and blossoms and was covered with almonds!

## God helps the people He chooses.

Moses brought the twelve staffs out before the people. There was no doubt that God had chosen Aaron, who was from the tribe of Levi, to be the leader of the priests.

God told Moses to keep Aaron's staff in the meeting tent so the people would remember that God had chosen Aaron. As priests, Aaron and his sons would serve God in the meeting tent and teach the people the laws of God.

God chooses certain people to serve others in His work. They may be pastors or missionaries or Sunday school teachers. When God chooses people, He also helps them. Whatever God asks you to do, He will help you to do it. —C.B.

### FUN FACT

Priests had to wear special clothing that was designed by God himself. When Aaron went into the holy of holies, he wore a "breastpiece" on his chest. It contained four rows of precious stones.

### READ MORE

Read Numbers 6:22–27.
How did the priests bless the people of Israel?

# Trust and Obey

> Lord of heaven's armies, happy are the people who trust in you.
>
> **PSALM 84:12 ICB**

**Have you noticed** that things are better when you trust and obey your parents? When you trust your parents, you believe they know what is best for you—even if you don't understand or agree right now. And obeying your parents is doing what they tell you to do.

Things are better when we trust and obey God too. He wants us to trust Him because He knows what is best for us. He wants us to obey Him so we will do what is right. God is pleased when we trust and obey Him.

The Bible gives many examples of people who trusted God and obeyed Him. Noah trusted and obeyed when God told him to build the ark. Abraham trusted and obeyed when God told him to move to another country that he had never seen. Joshua trusted and obeyed God when he led the Israelites across the Jordan River. Daniel trusted and obeyed God by praying even though it was against the law. Peter trusted and obeyed when Jesus told him to throw his fishing net on the other side of the boat—even though he had been fishing all night without catching anything. Because these people trusted and obeyed God, He was very pleased with them.

Reading the Bible helps you know how to trust and obey God. Praying allows God to work in your life and help you do what He wants you to do. So read the Bible and pray every day!

Do you want to please God? Then trust and obey Him. —C.B.

## I will trust and obey God.

### FUN FACT

A song called "Trust and Obey" was written in 1887. Many churches sang it for almost a hundred years. Some churches still do!

### READ MORE

Read Psalm 37:3–6.
What do these verses tell us about trusting God?

# Be Prepared

**No soldier would** go into battle without being prepared. In Bible times soldiers wore body armor made of several different pieces. The apostle Paul used the example of a soldier's armor to teach us how to protect ourselves from our spiritual enemy.

The first piece of armor is a belt which holds everything else together. When we put on the belt of truth, we are prepared to stand up for what we believe.

The breastplate is a piece of armor that protects a soldier's heart. In the Bible, the breastplate is righteousness, which means "right living." Living the way God wants us to live protects our hearts from things that are evil.

Good shoes help a soldier stand firm. The good news of Jesus is the footwear for Christians. When we believe in Jesus, we are at peace with God.

A shield protects soldiers from the enemy's arrows. Our faith in God is like a shield that protects us against the attacks of Satan. The shield of faith helps us to stand strong against temptation.

> Stand firm then, with the belt of truth buckled around your waist, with the breastplate of righteousness in place, and with your feet fitted with the readiness that comes from the gospel of peace. In addition to all this, take up the shield of faith, with which you can extinguish all the flaming arrows of the evil one. Take the helmet of salvation and the sword of the Spirit, which is the word of God.
>
> **EPHESIANS 6:14–17 NIV**

## God's armor helps me be prepared.

Just like a helmet protects a soldier's head, our salvation protects our minds from things that could make us doubt who God is. When people are saved, they know that God is real.

The sword of the Spirit is the Word of God. It's our weapon for fighting the enemy. Knowing and speaking the Word of God will lead us to victory!

When you wear the armor of God and carry the sword of His Spirit, you are prepared for anything. —C.B.

## FUN FACT

Roman soldiers in the apostle Paul's time used a sword called the gladius. It was about twenty inches long (fifty-one centimeters) with a double-edged blade.

## READ MORE

Read 1 John 5:4.
What gives us victory?

# Not a Hometown Hero

Then Jesus told them, "A prophet is honored everywhere except in his own hometown and among his relatives and his own family."

MARK 6:4 NLT

**Jesus was traveling** with His disciples and teaching about God's kingdom. One day, they stopped in a place called Nazareth, which is where Jesus grew up.

On the Sabbath day, Jesus was teaching in the synagogue. Many of the people who listened to Him were surprised. "Where did He get all this wisdom and the power to perform miracles?" they asked each other. "He's just a carpenter. He's only the son of Mary, and His family lives right here." They didn't think Jesus was anyone special, and they refused to believe in Him.

Jesus told the people, "A prophet is honored everywhere except in his own hometown." Because they didn't believe, Jesus didn't do miracles for them. He healed a few sick people, but He didn't show all of His power. Jesus was amazed that His neighbors refused to believe. So He left and went to teach in other villages.

The people of Nazareth thought they knew who Jesus was. They thought they understood the knowledge and talents He had. They didn't think a man who worked with His hands could understand God's teachings without learning from a special teacher called a rabbi. They had already made up their minds about Jesus. They didn't believe He was able to do anything great.

## God tells me who I am.

Sometimes you might feel like people don't accept you, just like Jesus' neighbors didn't accept Him. People might think they have you all figured out, but God is the one who tells you who you are. Even though the people wouldn't listen to Jesus, He was still the Messiah. And no matter what people think about you, God thinks you're great! —T.M.

### FUN FACT

Nazareth was a town of about two hundred people when Jesus lived there. Today Nazareth has over sixty-thousand residents. A nearby town called Upper Nazareth has thousands more people.

### READ MORE

Read John 7:1–9.
Who were some other people who didn't believe in Jesus?
Did Jesus do what these people wanted Him to?

# Without Words

**When we look** at the world around us, we can see the things that God has made. We can see the blue sky and the bright sun shining during the day. We can see the soft moon and the twinkling stars glowing at night. We can watch the water in rivers and streams, flowing wherever God directs it. People who live near the mountains can see how majestic they are. People who live near the oceans can see how powerful they are.

> The heavens tell about the glory of God. The skies announce what his hands have made.
>
> **PSALM 19:1 ERV**

All of creation shows the glory and greatness of God. It shows us how creative and powerful He is. Every day the sun comes up, reminding us that God is Light. At night, the moon and stars remind us that God is watching over us as we sleep. The beauty and greatness of creation tell the world that God is its Maker. Creation's message goes out to the whole world. God's glory is always on display for everyone to see.

Psalm 19 is one of the many psalms David wrote. He loved to praise God with his words. And over thousands of years, many people have used words to praise God and tell of His power and glory. But the things of nature do not need words. The beauty of God's creation speaks for itself.

No matter where you live, you can see God's glory in the things He has made. If you look and listen, their message is loud and clear. —C.B.

## God's creation speaks.

### READ MORE

Read Psalm 19:1–6.
How do these verses describe the sun?

## FUN FACT

The earth is about 93 million miles (150 million kilometers) away from the sun. This distance changes a bit during the year because the earth's path around the sun is shaped like an oval.

# David Builds an Altar

> But King David answered Araunah, "No, I will pay you the full price. I will not take anything that is yours and give it to the LORD. I will not give offerings that cost me nothing."
>
> **1 CHRONICLES 21:24 ERV**

**King David** sinned against God because he counted all of the Israelites. That doesn't sound like a bad thing, but God didn't want David to do it.

David was proud of how great his nation was. But he had forgotten that God was the one who gave it to him. Because of the king's sin, God punished Israel. Many people became sick and died.

Right away, David realized that he had done wrong. And he wanted to make things right. So God told David to build an altar on the land of a man named Araunah. David went to Araunah and asked to buy the land. "I will pay you the full price," David said. "Then I can build an altar to worship the Lord."

But Araunah told David to take the land for free. "I will also give you cattle for the offering," Araunah said.

## I will give God my best.

"No," David answered. "I will pay the full price. I will not take something that is yours and give it to the Lord. I will not give offerings that cost me nothing."

David bought the land for around fifteen pounds of gold (seven kilograms). He built the altar and prayed. Then God stopped the punishment against the Israelites.

David knew his offering had to cost him something to mean something. He wanted to give his best gift to God to show his obedience. God gives us the best of everything. We can give Him our best to show just how much we love Him. —T.M.

## FUN FACT

One ounce of gold (about twenty-eight grams) can be stretched into a thin gold thread about five miles long (eight kilometers).

## READ MORE

Read 1 Chronicles 21:28–22:5.
What was built later at the same place where David built his altar?

# The Water and the Word

**Have you ever** picked an apple or a banana from a tree? Have you ever pulled a carrot or potato from the ground? God gives us these good things to eat!

God sends rain and snow to water the ground. When the earth gets the right amount of water, plants and trees grow and produce fruits and vegetables. That's how we get delicious foods like strawberries, corn, and beans. Water also helps wheat seeds sprout and grow into stalks. The grain that appears on the stalks can be ground into flour to make bread and pancakes and pasta. God's purpose in sending the rain and snow is to provide food for the people He created.

> "The rain and snow come down from the heavens and stay on the ground to water the earth. They cause the grain to grow, producing seed for the farmer and bread for the hungry. It is the same with my word. I send it out, and it always produces fruit. It will accomplish all I want it to, and it will prosper everywhere I send it."
>
> **ISAIAH 55:10–11 NLT**

## The seeds of God's Word can grow in me.

In the book of Isaiah, God reminds us that He gives us good things. And just like He gives us food from the earth, He also gives us His words in the Bible. The Bible is a spiritual food!

Like seeds that are planted in the ground, God's words are planted in our hearts and minds as we read the Bible. The Holy Spirit is like the rain that waters the ground. It helps the seeds of God's Word to grow inside us. And as they grow, we will understand more about God's love and how we can show our love to Him and to others.

God's purpose in giving us His Word is to help us grow in Him. —C.B.

### READ MORE

Read 2 Corinthians 9:10.
What does God give to the farmer?
What does He give to His people?

### FUN FACT

One acre of corn (4,046 square meters) needs more than 350,000 gallons of water (1,325,000 liters) to grow!

## SEPTEMBER
# 22

The yes to all of God's promises is in Christ. And that is why we say "Amen" through Christ to the glory of God.

2 CORINTHIANS 1:20 ERV

# One Answer

**Kids who go to school** have to take tests. Some tests are fill-in-the blank, and you have to write in the answer. Other tests are multiple-choice, meaning you have to pick the correct answer from a list. Then there are matching tests where you have to find two things that go together.

No matter what kind of test you take, there is usually only one right answer. You can't circle A and B on a multiple choice test. You can't write two words onto a blank made for one word. There is only one right answer to each question.

When it comes to God's promises, there is only one right answer too. The answer is the same for every single promise. The Bible tells us that Jesus is the answer! Today's verse says, "The yes to all of God's promises is in Christ." This means that all of God's promises are fulfilled in Jesus. He makes every promise true.

## Jesus is the only answer.

God promises He will take care of all our needs through the blessings of Jesus. Do you know why? Because Jesus is the perfect example of God's love and power! God showed us how big His love is by sending Jesus to earth. Jesus forgives us of our sins and gives us a relationship with God that will last forever! Nothing can take God's love away from us because of what Jesus has done.

Every promise God makes is satisfied in Jesus. Jesus is the answer to the most important questions of life! —T.M.

### FUN FACT

A "standardized" test is one that asks every student the same questions. These tests were first given in China about a hundred years after Jesus lived on earth. They covered topics like music, arithmetic, writing, and archery.

### READ MORE

Read 1 Timothy 2:5–6.
What do these verses tell us about Jesus?

# Angels Everywhere

**The king of Aram** was at war with Israel. Elisha was God's prophet for Israel, and God would tell him what the king of Aram was planning to do. Then Elisha would warn the king of Israel.

> He has put his angels in charge of you. They will watch over you wherever you go.
>
> **PSALM 91:11 ICB**

The king of Aram was very angry about that! He sent an army with horses and chariots to capture Elisha. The army arrived during the night and surrounded Elisha's city of Dothan. When Elisha's servant went out the next morning, he saw the enemy army. "Oh no!" the servant said. "What shall we do?"

"Don't be afraid," Elisha told his servant. "The army that fights for us is larger than the one that is against us." Then Elisha prayed, "Lord, open his eyes so he can see."

The Lord answered Elisha's prayer. The servant could see that the hills were filled with horses and chariots of fire. God had sent His own army of angels to protect Elisha from Aram's army! As the enemy army came closer, Elisha prayed again. "Lord, make these men blind," he asked.

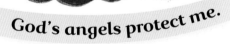

## God's angels protect me.

So God struck the soldiers of Aram with blindness. They couldn't see anything, so Elisha offered to help them. He led the army to the city of Samaria. When Elisha prayed for God to open their eyes, the soldiers saw that they were standing right in front of Elisha and the king of Israel!

Elisha told the king of Israel to show kindness to his enemies. So the king gave them some food and water and let them go. And after they left, the soldiers of Aram didn't bother the Israelites anymore.

No matter how great the enemy is, God's army of angels is greater. You can't see them, but God's angels are everywhere. —C.B.

## READ MORE

Read Genesis 19:15–17.
Who did God send His angels to protect?

### FUN FACT

Elisha led the blind soldiers about twelve miles (nineteen kilometers) from Dothan to Samaria.

# Jonathan's Secret Code

> Jonathan said to David, "I make this promise before the LORD, the God of Israel. I promise that I will learn how my father feels about you. I will learn if he feels good about you or not. Then, in three days, I will send a message to you in the field."
>
> 1 SAMUEL 20:12 ERV

**King Saul** wasn't obeying God. He was jealous of David and wanted to kill him.

Saul's son Jonathan was David's best friend. Jonathan loved David like a brother and knew God was on David's side. When David asked Jonathan, "What have I done wrong? Why is your father trying to kill me?" Jonathan didn't know. But he made a plan to find out.

David was hiding. Jonathan was going to learn what Saul was planning to do. The two friends made a secret code so Jonathan could tell David what he had found out.

"I will come back after three days and shoot arrows with my bow," Jonathan said. "My servant boy will run to pick up the arrows. If everything is fine, I will tell the boy, 'The arrows are closer to me. Come back.' But if there is trouble I will say, 'The arrows are farther away. Go get them.' If I say that, you must leave."

## I can be a helping friend.

After three days Jonathan came to the field where David was hiding and shot his arrows. As the boy ran to pick them up, Jonathan said, "The arrows are father away. Go get them." David knew this meant Saul was planning something bad. After the servant left, David came out from his hiding place and said good-bye to Jonathan.

Jonathan helped David because he knew David was serving God. When we see other people following God, we can help and encourage them. We can be loyal to them even when others are against them.

When we help people who serve God, we are serving God too. —T.M.

### FUN FACT

Arrows in Bible times had arrowheads of flint, bronze, or iron. Bows were made from wood and the string was made from the guts of oxen.

### READ MORE

Read 2 Samuel 9:1–10.
How did David keep his promise to love Jonathan's family forever?

# The Gift of Grace

> God saved you by his grace when you believed. And you can't take credit for this; it is a gift from God. Salvation is not a reward for the good things we have done, so none of us can boast about it.
>
> **EPHESIANS 2:8–9 NLT**

**Have you ever** borrowed books from a library? Library books need to be returned by a certain date. If you don't return the books on time, you'll have to pay a fine when you bring them back.

But sometimes libraries have a "day of grace." On the day of grace, people who have overdue books can return them without having to pay a fine. The debt is erased because the library has shown grace. Grace is a gift that you cannot earn. It's something that is given to you.

God saves people by His grace. We can't earn our salvation. No matter how many good works we do or how much money we give to help others, we could never earn our way to heaven.

## I am saved by God's grace.

Everyone sins. Everyone has a debt to pay. But nobody can pay the debt of their sins. That's why Jesus died on the cross. He paid the debt of sin for us.

Salvation is a free gift because of God's grace. When we believe in Jesus, our debt is erased. You never have to worry about being good enough to go to heaven. Believing in Jesus as your Savior is all it takes!

Libraries might have a day of grace once in a while. But with Jesus, every day is a day of grace. You don't have to wait until a special time to receive His grace. You can receive it today! —C.B.

**FUN FACT**

The name Grace dates back to the 1500s and is still a very popular girl's name. It comes from the Latin language and means "favor" or "blessing."

## READ MORE

Read John 1:14–18.
What do these verses tell us about Jesus (the Word)?

# The Wedding Celebration

"Here is what the kingdom of heaven will be like at that time. Ten bridesmaids took their lamps and went out to meet the groom. Five of them were foolish. Five were wise."

**MATTHEW 25:1-2 NIRV**

**The Israelites** had special wedding traditions. After two people became engaged, the groom left to prepare a house for his bride. It usually took a year for him to get everything ready. The bride didn't know exactly when he would come back—it was a surprise! So the bride and her bridesmaids were supposed to be ready for his return.

When the time came for the groom's return, his friends went through the streets letting everyone know he was coming. Many people would join the march to the bride's house. The bride and groom would then make their marriage promise to each other and a big party would begin.

Jesus told His followers a parable about a wedding. He said that ten bridesmaids were waiting for the groom to come through the streets. They carried oil burning lamps. Five of the bridesmaids were wise. They had brought extra oil to keep their lamps burning. The other five had not brought extra oil.

As the bridesmaids waited into the night, they got tired and fell asleep. Suddenly someone yelled, "Here's the groom!" The bridesmaids quickly got their lamps ready, but those who didn't have extra oil had to leave to find more. When they returned, the wedding had started and the doors were locked. Five bridesmaids missed the whole celebration.

## I will be ready for Jesus to come back.

Jesus is like the groom coming back for His bride. The bride is the church, which is all the people who love Him. No one knows just when He'll return. So we can be like the five wise bridesmaids and be prepared for Jesus when He comes. We can obey God's Word. We can ask God to help us love Him more. We can tell others about Jesus. If we're ready when Jesus comes back, we won't miss out on His great celebration. —T.M.

## FUN FACT

The Israelites' marriage celebration included a supper that lasted for seven days. There was lots of food, dancing, and music.

## READ MORE

Read John 14:2-3.
What is Jesus doing for us that grooms did for their brides during Bible times?

# Breakfast with Jesus

> Jesus said to them, "Come and have breakfast."
> **JOHN 21:12 NIRV**

**After Jesus rose** from the grave, He spent some more time on earth before going back to heaven. One day, Jesus surprised His disciples with a miracle.

Seven disciples had gone fishing at night, but they didn't catch anything. In the morning, Jesus was standing on the shore, but the disciples didn't recognize him. Jesus asked them if they had caught any fish. When the disciples answered no, Jesus said, "Throw your net on the right side of the boat and you will catch some."

The disciples did what they were told. They caught so many fish they weren't able to haul in the net! Then John said to Peter, "It's the Lord!"

Peter jumped out of the boat and splashed toward Jesus. The other disciples brought in the boat towing the net full of fish. When they all got to the shore, they saw a fire of hot coals with fish on it. There was some bread too.

### Jesus cares about His disciples.

"Bring some of the fish you have just caught," said Jesus. "Come and have breakfast."

Jesus shared a meal with His disciples, just as He had done many times before. He performed a miracle, just as He had done many times before. Jesus showed His disciples His love and care for them had not changed even though He had died and come back to life.

Jesus is the same today. He wants you to be His disciple. He loves and cares for you too. —C.B.

## READ MORE

Read Luke 24:36–42.
How did Jesus prove to His followers that He was alive and not a ghost?

## FUN FACT

When the disciples dropped their net on the right side of the boat, they caught 153 fish!

Again Jesus asked, "Simon, son of John, do you really love me?"

JOHN 21:16 NIRV

# Questions for Peter

**After Jesus** and His disciples had finished eating breakfast on the shore, Jesus asked Simon Peter a question. "Simon, son of John, do you love me more than the others do?"

"Yes, Lord," said Peter. "You know I love you."

"Take care of my lambs," said Jesus.

Jesus asked Peter again, "Simon, son of John, do you love me?"

Peter answered, "Yes, Lord. You know that I love you."

"Take care of my sheep," said Jesus.

A third time Jesus asked, "Simon, son of John, do you love me?"

It hurt Peter's feelings that Jesus asked him this question three times. "Lord, you know everything," said Peter. "You know that I love you."

"Feed my sheep," said Jesus.

## If I love Jesus I will love others.

When Jesus told Peter to take care of His lambs and sheep, He was talking about people who were Christians. Peter had spent a lot of time with Jesus, and Jesus wanted Peter to help other people to know Him. Some of the new Christians were like lambs that needed lots of care and teaching. But even people who had been Christians for a while needed to be taught and cared for. If Peter really loved Jesus, he would also love and care for Jesus' people.

Jesus is a shepherd. His people are the sheep. If we really love Jesus, we can show it by treating others with love and kindness. We can help them to know Him better. —C.B.

### FUN FACT

Sheep usually eat grass and pasture plants called forbs. A forb is a flowering plant like clover and milkweed.

### READ MORE

Read Matthew 16:17–19.
What did Jesus tell Peter in these verses?

# A Runaway Slave

**Slavery is a terrible thing.** Through much of history, some people have believed they could own other people. Some people would make their slaves work hard. During Bible times, many people in the Roman Empire had slaves.

> I pray that the faith you share will make you understand every blessing that we have in Christ.
>
> **PHILEMON 6 ICB**

The apostle Paul knew a slave owner named Philemon. Paul wrote a letter to him, saying he thanked God for Philemon in his prayers. Paul had heard about the love Philemon showed toward God's people and the faith he had in Jesus.

But then Paul talked about something else. Philemon had a slave named Onesimus who had run away. He might even have stolen some money when he left. But Onesimus had met Paul in Rome and he became a Christian.

So Paul asked Philemon to let Onesimus return to him, not as a slave but as a Christian brother! "If you think of me as your friend, then let Onesimus come back to you," Paul said. "If he owes you anything, I will pay back whatever he owes. As a follower of the Lord, please do this for me. I am writing this letter knowing that you will do what I ask."

## Christians are like brothers and sisters.

Paul knew that if Philemon really had the love of Jesus in him, he would forgive Onesimus and take him back. Onesimus would not be a slave anymore, but a friend. When Onesimus became a Christian, he became Philemon's spiritual brother.

God wants all of us to show love and forgiveness to people in the same way that He loves and forgives us. When we forgive others, it is an example of God's forgiveness for all to see. God is pleased when we forgive others, just like we are pleased when He forgives us! —C.B.

## READ MORE

Read Colossians 4:7–9 to learn more about Onesimus.

## FUN FACT

Running away was a very serious crime for Roman slaves. The law said they could be killed if they ran away!

> "The man called ten of his servants together. He gave a bag of money to each servant. He said, 'Do business with this money until I get back.'"
>
> LUKE 19:13 ICB

# Servants and Coins

**Jesus told His followers** a story about a man who traveled to another country to become a king. Before he left, he gave each of his servants a bag of money and said, "See what you can earn with this while I am gone." After he was crowned king he came back. Then he asked his servants to tell him what they had earned with his money.

The first servant said, "Sir, I have earned ten bags of money with the one you gave me."

"Well done," the king said. "Since you were faithful with small things, I will put you in charge of ten cities."

"Sir," the second servant said, "I have earned five bags of money with the one you gave me."

The king replied, "You will be in charge of five cities."

## I will work for God's rewards.

But a third servant gave back the bag of money he had been given. "I kept it hidden in a handkerchief," he said. "I was afraid because you are a hard man."

The king became angry. He ordered that the third servant's bag of money be given to the servant with ten bags. "People who use what they have will get more," the king said. "But those who do not use what they have will have everything taken away from them."

God gives each of His followers jobs and the ability to do them. When we do our jobs the best we can, other people are helped and He is pleased. God rewards us for letting Him work through our lives. —T.M.

## FUN FACT

Each bag of money in this story was called a mina. Mina was a Greek word. It stood for enough money to pay a worker for three months.

## READ MORE

Read Ephesians 6:7–8.
What attitude should we have when we work for the Lord?

# A Shiny Face

**When you look** at someone's face, you can tell if that person is happy or sad. You can tell if a person is excited or bored. The face shows others what a person is feeling on the inside.

> His face was shining because he had spoken with the LORD.
> **EXODUS 34:29 NIRV**

Moses' face showed people that he had been with God! When Moses came down from Mount Sinai after forty days with God, his face was shining. He had been meeting with God to receive a new set of stone tablets with the Ten Commandments. Moses had broken the first set when he saw the people worshipping a golden calf. Now, after getting even more instructions for the Israelites, Moses was coming back to the people. He didn't know it, but his face was so bright the Israelites were afraid to look at him.

Moses' face glowed so much that he had to wear a veil when he spoke to the people. Whenever Moses spoke with God, he would take off the veil. Then he would put it back

## I can shine for God.

on when he talked to the people. Whether Moses met with God on the mountain or in the meeting tent, his face would shine afterward.

Moses was filled with the glory of God and it showed on his face. His heart and soul were filled with love for God. If you love God with all your heart and soul, it will show on your face too. But others won't be afraid to look at you. They'll want to be near you! —C.B.

## READ MORE

Read Isaiah 60:1–5.
What happens to people who shine with God's glory?

## FUN FACT

Foods like blueberries, salmon, spinach, and tomatoes can help your skin have a healthy glow.

# Watch Your Step

The LORD directs the
steps of the godly.
He delights in every
detail of their lives.

**PSALM 37:23 NLT**

**Has someone ever told you** to "watch your
step"? Maybe you were walking along a bumpy road
or going down a flight of stairs. It's important to watch
where you are going. If you're not careful where you
walk, you could fall and get hurt.

Have you ever followed someone's footsteps as
they were walking ahead of you? Maybe you were on a
snowy sidewalk or a sandy beach. Sometimes it's a fun
game to place your feet in another person's footsteps.
And sometimes it's safer to let another person direct our
steps.

Today's Bible verse says that God will direct
our steps if we love and follow Him. These "steps"
are not where we put our feet on a bumpy road or
a sandy beach. These are the steps we take in our
lives. They are the important decisions we make.

## I will ask God to direct my steps.

Did you know you don't have to make important decisions alone? If you ask God, He
will help you with your decisions no matter how big or small they may seem. God will
help you take the right steps in your life as you make decisions to please Him.

You can ask God to help you make good friends. You can ask God to help you decide
what to be when you grow up. You can ask God how you can serve Him right now in
your church or school or neighborhood. God will help you with all of those decisions.
He will help you take the right steps. And when you follow in God's footsteps, you will
always go in the right direction! —C.B.

**FUN FACT**

In the New Living
Translation of the Bible,
Jesus says "Follow me"
twenty-two times.

**READ MORE**

Read John 8:12.
What happens when we walk in Jesus' footsteps?

# The Humble Leper

**Crowds of people** came to Jesus to be healed from their pain and sickness. One man who had leprosy asked Jesus for healing in a special way.

People with leprosy usually stayed away from healthy people. They weren't allowed to touch anyone else because their disease could spread very easily. But that didn't stop this man. He came close to Jesus, got on his knees, and begged for help. "If you are willing," the man said to Jesus, "you can heal me and make me clean."

> A man with leprosy came and knelt in front of Jesus, begging to be healed. "If you are willing, you can heal me and make me clean," he said.
>
> **MARK 1:40 NLT**

Jesus was very concerned for the man and touched him. "I am willing." Jesus said. "Be healed!" The man's leprosy went away at once!

## I will ask Jesus to do what He wants.

This man knew that Jesus had the power to heal him. He had faith that Jesus could do exactly what he asked. But he also knew that it was Jesus' choice to heal the man or not. When the man with leprosy came to Jesus saying, "If you are willing," it showed that he trusted Jesus. He was saying that what Jesus wanted was more important than what he wanted.

It's more important to ask Jesus what He wants to do, than tell Him what we want for ourselves. When we ask Jesus to do what He wants in our lives, we are being humble like the man with leprosy. We're telling Jesus that His way is more important than our way. And we trust Him to do what is best. —T.M.

## READ MORE

Read Matthew 6:7–10.
How did Jesus say we should pray about God's will?

**FUN FACT**

The words *leprosy* or *leper* occur fifty-five times in the Old Testament and thirteen times in the New Testament. Today leprosy is known as Hansen's disease.

## OCTOBER
# 4

> But Christ offered only one sacrifice for sins, and that sacrifice is good for all time. Then he sat down at the right side of God.
>
> **HEBREWS 10:12 ERV**

# Once and Forever

**Many of the things** we do every day have to be done over and over again.

Think about brushing your teeth. Once a week isn't enough—your teeth keep getting dirty so you have to brush them every day. Or when you eat breakfast, you know you'll be hungry again by lunchtime. One meal does not keep you full all day. It's the same with sleeping. One night of sleep only gives you energy for the next day. Many things have to be done over and over for us to stay healthy and happy.

That's how it was for the Israelites, too. God had told His people to offer sacrifices to pay for their sins. Because people sin every day, they had to make sacrifices over and over again. Those sacrifices couldn't take away the people's sins. They were just a payment to make up for sin. Year after year, the Israelites had to keep offering sacrifices to stay right with God.

## Jesus' death was the perfect sacrifice.

But everything changed when Jesus died on the cross. He offered His body as a perfect sacrifice to God. It was a sacrifice for the sins of the whole world! And Jesus only had to offer himself as a sacrifice one time. His death was enough to pay not only for your sins, but for everyone's sins forever.

Jesus lived a perfect life, so He was a perfect sacrifice to God. When we believe in Jesus, we don't have to keep asking God to save us. In Jesus, God accepts us once and forever. —T.M.

## FUN FACT

People should brush their teeth two or three times a day for at least two minutes each time. Some toothbrushes keep track of brushing time by sending signals to a person's cell phone!

## READ MORE

Read Hebrews 10:1–10.
Why are we made holy through Jesus' sacrifice?

# A Very Long Sermon

**Paul had spent** a week in a city called Troas. Sunday was the last day of his visit, and he was meeting with other Christians to talk about Jesus.

> On Sunday we all met together to eat the Lord's Supper. Paul talked to the group.
> ACTS 20:7 ERV

Christians in Paul's time didn't have church buildings yet. They met in people's homes. And when they got together, they spent as much time as they could praising God and learning about Jesus.

Since it was Paul's last day in Troas, he just kept teaching and preaching. It got to be midnight, but the people weren't tired of listening. They didn't want Paul to stop! So he kept preaching and teaching until it was morning. The people were happy to meet together and didn't care how long their meeting lasted. They wanted to learn as much as they could about Jesus so they could keep growing in their faith.

It's good to meet with other Christians.

Today many people meet in church buildings to praise God and listen to preaching. Most church meetings last an hour or two. If the meeting gets too long, some people get bored—or fall asleep. Kids might draw pictures or look at a book. It can be hard to sit still for a long time. But it's important to be a Christian, and it's important to meet with other Christians—no matter how long the meeting lasts.

If you have a good church to attend, you can be thankful for a place to go every Sunday. Whether you have church in a big or small building or in someone's home, God is pleased when you meet with others to learn more about Him. —C.B.

## FUN FACT

Church buildings started to appear two hundred or three hundred years after Jesus went back to heaven. As the number of believers grew, Christians wanted bigger places to meet than in people's homes.

## READ MORE

Read Acts 20:7–12. What happened to a man named Eutychus while Paul preached all night?

# God Is Good

> Taste and see that the LORD is good. Oh, the joys of those who take refuge in him!
>
> **PSALM 34:8 NLT**

**You can't know** how good something is until you try it. You have to bite into a juicy orange to know how delicious it is. You have to taste a drop of honey to know how sweet it is. You have to sip some hot cocoa to enjoy its chocolaty flavor. And you have to experience God to know how good and wonderful He is.

While Saul was king of Israel, David spent many years on the run. When Saul knew David was supposed to be the next king, he wanted to get rid of him. So David often ran to the hills or the desert or a cave to get away from Saul.

But besides running to new places, David also ran to God. He knew that God was good and would help him no matter where he was. David knew that God would protect him from his enemies, no matter how big or strong they were.

Because David knew God, he knew that God was good. David spent a lot of time talking to God and praising Him. David had many experiences with God that made him know how good God is.

We can run to God like David did. We can pray to Him when we're worried about something. We can read His Word when we need His guidance. We can praise Him in good times and bad times—just like David did. When we really get to know God, we will see that He is good. —C.B.

## I know that God is good.

### FUN FACT

People have about ten thousand taste buds when they're born. But at about age fifty, many people start losing them. An older person may only have half as many working taste buds.

### READ MORE

Read Psalm 34:1–10.
How do these verses show that God is good?

# The Patient Gardener

"So he went to the man who took care of the vineyard. He said, 'For three years now I've been coming to look for fruit on this fig tree. But I haven't found any. Cut it down! Why should it use up the soil?'"

LUKE 13:7 NIRV

**Do you know** someone who is patient? It can be hard to be a patient person. How do you feel when someone is patient with you?

One time Jesus told a parable about patience. The story was about a man who planted a fig tree in his garden. Each year he checked the tree for fruit, but it never grew any figs. After three years he said to his gardener, "I have been looking for fruit on this tree for three years, but I never find any. Cut it down! Why should it waste the ground?"

But the gardener wanted to give the tree another chance. "Master, let the tree have one more year to produce fruit," the gardener said. "Let me dig up the dirt around it and fertilize it. Maybe the tree will have fruit on it next year. If it still does not produce fruit, then you can cut it down."

## Jesus is patient with us.

Jesus told this story to help us understand how patient He is with people. He gives us many chances to live the life He wants us to live. When we believe in Jesus and grow in our love for God, others can see the good changes in our lives. They show up just like fruit growing on a healthy tree. But when people choose not to obey God, they are like a tree that doesn't have any fruit.

The gardener in Jesus' story asked his master to give the fig tree another year to grow fruit. In the same way, Jesus is patient and waits for people to accept Him—even if it takes some time. —T.M.

## READ MORE
Read 2 Peter 3:8–9.
What does God want for all people?

### FUN FACT
The ancient Romans made a dessert with figs. It was a cake called basyniai and also included walnuts, poppy seeds, and honey.

> Obey the Lord your God. Then all these blessings will come and stay with you.
>
> DEUTERONOMY 28:2 ICB

# Many Blessings

**It was almost** time for the Israelites to cross the Jordan River. They were about to enter the land God had promised to the family of Abraham, Isaac, and Jacob. God taught the people many things while they were in the wilderness. He reminded them how important it was for them to obey Him if they wanted His blessings in their new land.

Moses told the people this promise from God: "You will be blessed in the cities and countries. Your children will be blessed. Your crops and cattle will be blessed. The grain you harvest and the bread you bake will be blessed. You will be blessed no matter where you go. The Lord will help you win your battles. He will bless your barns with plenty of grain and other food. He will bless the land He is giving you. He will send rain at the right time. Then all the nations will see that you belong to Him."

## Obeying God is important.

The Israelites wanted God's blessings. They wanted to be happy in their new land. But in order to be blessed in their new land, they could not worship false gods. God had chosen them as His special people and gave them special instructions to follow.

You may never have to go to a new land, but you can learn from this story. If you believe in Jesus, you are God's special child. He wants to bless you. He wants you to be happy. It is important for God's children to follow His instructions in the Bible. And it is important that we only worship Him. —C.B.

### FUN FACT

The words *bless, blessed,* or *blessing* are used around three hundred times in the Old Testament.

### READ MORE

Read Acts 5:29–32.
What does God give to people who obey Him?

# A Different Kind of Healing

**Jesus walked** from the city of Tyre, on the Mediterranean Sea, down to the Sea of Galilee. On the far side of the Sea of Galilee was a place called the Ten Cities.

Some people brought a man to him. The man was deaf and could hardly speak. They begged Jesus to place his hand on him.

**MARK 7:32 NIRV**

While Jesus was there, some people brought Him a man who needed healing. The man was deaf, and because he couldn't hear he could hardly talk. This man's friends begged Jesus to place His hands on the man and heal him.

Jesus led the man away from the crowd. Then he did something strange. First, Jesus put his fingers into the man's ears. Then he spit on his finger and touched the man's tongue. Jesus looked up to heaven, breathed deeply, and said, "Ephphatha!" That means "Be opened!" As soon as Jesus did that, the man could hear! His tongue started working right and he could speak clearly.

The man's friends saw what Jesus had done. He told them not to tell anyone else about the miracle, but the more Jesus told them, the more they kept talking about it. The people were amazed by Jesus' power. "He has done everything well," they said. "He makes deaf people hear. And He gives a new voice to people who couldn't talk."

## God will show me His power.

Jesus healed this man differently than He healed other people. Sometimes He spoke and people were healed. Sometimes He touched people to heal them, and sometimes they touched Him for healing! Today, God may use doctors and medicine. Or He may choose to give us strength through our sickness instead of healing us. That's when God says His grace is enough to help us through our pain. Whatever He chooses to do, God is showing us His power in our lives. —T.M.

## FUN FACT

Our tongues have many important jobs. Besides helping us talk, they also help us taste and feel texture. Our tongues help our body begin digestion before food reaches our stomachs.

## READ MORE

Read Mark 5:18–20.
What did Jesus tell this man to do after he was healed? Where did the man go?

# Joshua Is Tricked

> But they did not ask the Lord what to do.
>
> JOSHUA 9:14 ICB

**People called** the Hivites were scared of the Israelites. They had heard how the Israelites had defeated Jericho, and they were afraid that they would be attacked next. So the Hivites made a plan to trick Israel's leader, Joshua.

The Hivites got some old bottles and hung them on their donkeys. They put on old clothes and sandals. They found some moldy bread and put it in their food bags. Then they went to the camp of the Israelites.

"We've come from far away," they said to Joshua. "We want to make a promise of peace with you."

"Who are you?" Joshua asked.

"We are your servants," the Hivites answered. "We came because we heard of the great power of your God. We have heard how you defeated two kings east of the Jordan River. We want to make a peace promise with you. Look at our moldy bread. Look at our old bottles and clothes. You can see we've been on a long journey."

The men of Israel thought the Hivites' story sounded true. So they didn't ask God what to do. They made a peace promise with the Hivites and said they would never hurt them. Later, the Israelites found out the truth, but they honored their promise not to hurt the Hivites. The Hivites lived with the Israelites as servants.

## I will ask God to show me what to do.

God wants us to ask for His wisdom in all the decisions we make. We can do that by praying for His help and by reading the Bible. We can also talk to other Christians who are wise and ask for their help too.

It's easy to be tricked by the enemy. That's why it is so important to ask for God's wisdom in everything you do. —C.B.

### FUN FACT

The Hivites were a family group that came through Noah's son Ham and Ham's son Canaan.

### READ MORE

Read Psalm 37:1–9.
What do these verses say about trusting God?

# Remember Your Creator

Young people, it's wonderful to be young! Enjoy every minute of it. Do everything you want to do; take it all in. But remember that you must give an account to God for everything you do.

**ECCLESIASTES 11:9 NLT**

**King Solomon** gave us some great advice in the books of Proverbs and Ecclesiastes. As the wisest man who ever lived, he had important things to say.

Did you know that some of Solomon's advice is just for young people? At the end of Ecclesiastes, Solomon gave special instructions that are perfect for kids. "It's wonderful to be young! Enjoy every minute of it," Solomon said. "Do everything you want to do; take it all in. But remember that you must give an account to God for everything you do."

Solomon encouraged young people to have lots of fun. It's good to enjoy the life God has given you! You can play hide-and-seek with your friends. You can explore God's creation and discover sticks and bugs and flowers. You can laugh and sing silly songs and spend time doing all the things that you enjoy. You can let everything around you put a smile on your face. But Solomon says that as you play and laugh and smile, it is important to remember your Creator.

*I will remember God while I enjoy being a kid.*

Our happiest living comes when we enjoy the things God wants us to enjoy. We can read His Word and talk to Him in prayer and serve the people that He has created. These are all very good things.

But it's easy to want other things more than the things God wants for us. We might want things that other people have. And it can be tempting to enjoy things that do not please God. That's why Solomon said it was important to remember God while we are young. Remembering our Creator when we are kids will help us make good choices throughout our whole lives.
—T.M.

### FUN FACT

Did you know Solomon enjoyed animals? Visitors brought him horses and mules, and he sent ships around the world to bring back apes and peacocks!

### READ MORE

Read Psalm 119:9–11.
How can you remember God while you are young?

# A Woman's Faith

> Then Jesus answered, "Woman, you have great faith! I will do what you asked me to do."
>
> MATTHEW 15:28 ICB

**Jesus and His twelve disciples** were Jewish. One time they left their home area of Galilee where many Jews lived and met a woman who was not Jewish. She called out to Jesus, "Lord, Son of David, please help me! My daughter has a demon inside of her and is suffering very much."

Since the woman was not a Jew, the disciples didn't think she should be following Jesus. And at first Jesus did not answer her. His followers said, "Tell her to go away. She keeps crying out and is bothering us."

But the woman did not give up. She bowed down before Jesus and said, "Lord, please help me!"

Jesus saw that the woman's faith was real. So He said to her, "Woman, you have great faith. I will do what you have asked me to do." And at that moment the woman's daughter was healed.

*Jesus loves people from every nation.*

Some people thought Jesus should only love Jewish people. They believed that only Jews should get to know about God's kingdom. But Jesus came for all people, including the woman in this story.

Jesus taught that everyone who loves Him is welcome in God's kingdom. No matter what country you live in, or what family you come from, you can be part of God's kingdom too. Anyone can worship Jesus. Anyone can ask Him for forgiveness and be saved. All who have faith in Jesus will be a part of God's kingdom. —C.B.

### FUN FACT

During the time Jesus lived on the earth, it was not proper for a woman to call out to a man. This mother's boldness showed how much she believed Jesus could heal her daughter.

### READ MORE

Read Matthew 8:28–34. How do these verses show that Jesus has power over demons?

# Celebration on the Wall

**When the Israelites** finished rebuilding the wall of Jerusalem, Nehemiah planned a special celebration. People came from all over to sing and play music on many different instruments. They all wanted to praise God for helping them complete the project.

The priests helped the people become clean and pure so they could worship God. Then they made the city gates and the wall clean as a way to worship God.

Nehemiah told all the leaders of Judah to walk on top of the wall with two big choirs. The choirs sang songs of thanks to God and all the people shouted for joy. The shouting was so great it could be heard far away. And the people brought gifts and offerings that the priests placed in storehouses. They did this to obey God's law.

Nehemiah knew it was important to thank God for His help in finishing the big building project. He knew that everything the Israelites had belonged to God—even the wall that protected their city.

> The wall of Jerusalem was set apart to God. For that occasion, the Levites were gathered together from where they lived. They were brought to Jerusalem to celebrate that happy occasion. They celebrated the fact that the wall was being set apart to God. They did it by singing and giving their thanks to him. They celebrated by playing music on cymbals, harps and lyres.
>
> NEHEMIAH 12:27 NIRV

## I will praise God for helping me do good work.

The celebration was a way of honoring God. The Israelites obeyed Him by making every part of the city holy.

When we finish big and important jobs, it's good for us to thank God too. We honor Him when we realize that everything we do—even our ability to work—comes from Him.

God gives you strength to do the things you do. You can praise Him with a shout of joy. You can tell God that every good thing in your life belongs to Him. —T.M.

## FUN FACT

The walls that surround Jerusalem today are not the walls that Nehemiah built. The current walls were built by the Ottoman Empire in the 1500s, on top of the older walls from Bible times.

## READ MORE

Read Psalm 9:1–2.
How did David say he would give thanks to God?

> Jesus said to the father, "Why did you say 'if you can'? All things are possible for the one who believes."
>
> MARK 9:23 ERV

# If You Can

**Have you ever** had a problem that you just couldn't fix? Maybe the chain came off your bike and you didn't know how to put it back on. Or maybe it was a much bigger problem—like someone you loved getting sick.

A man in the Bible had a big problem, and he came to Jesus asking for help. "Teacher, my son has an evil spirit. He throws himself on the ground and grinds his teeth. He becomes very stiff. I asked your followers to help him but they could not do it."

Jesus said, "Bring the boy to me." When the boy came, he fell on the ground and rolled around. "How long has this been happening?" Jesus asked.

"Ever since he was very young," said the father. "If you can do anything, please help us."

"Why did you say 'if you can'?" asked Jesus. "All things are possible for the one who believes."

Right away the father shouted, "I do believe! Help me to believe more!"

## Jesus can do what I can't.

Jesus saw that many people were watching to see what would happen. He spoke to the spirit and said, "You evil spirit that makes this boy deaf and stops him from talking—I command you to come out and never enter him again!" And that is what happened!

Jesus' disciples could not heal the boy, so his father didn't know if Jesus could help the child either. You might feel helpless too sometimes. You might wonder, "Who can I talk to about this big problem?" But Jesus can do anything, because He is God. And just like the boy's father in this story, we can always ask Him to help us believe more. —C.B.

### FUN FACT

Ohio, one of the fifty states in the United States of America, gets its state saying from this Bible story. Ohio's official motto is, "With God, all things are possible."

### READ MORE

Read Mark 9:2–10. What happened to Jesus just before He healed the boy in this story?

# Like a Water Fountain

**A water fountain** is a great place to go when you're thirsty. You can push a button or turn a knob and water squirts from the spout. The water doesn't stop until you turn it off.

> "Anyone who believes in me may come and drink! For the Scriptures declare, 'Rivers of living water will flow from his heart.'"
>
> JOHN 7:38 NLT

Did you know that people who love Jesus are like water fountains? We don't have buttons or knobs, but Jesus said that "living water" will flow out of us. The living water is God's Holy Spirit, who comes into our lives when we believe in Jesus.

Jesus was in Jerusalem celebrating a special event called the Feast of Shelters. On the last day of the feast, the Jews would take water from a well and pour it out before God. On this day, Jesus shouted to the crowd, "Anyone who is thirsty may come to me! Anyone who believes in me may come and drink! For the Scriptures declare, 'Rivers of living water will flow from his heart.'"

*The Holy Spirit is a gift from God.*

Jesus was saying that He gives us the Holy Spirit when we decide to follow Him. The Spirit is like a fountain of water that never stops flowing. He is always there to help us with whatever we need. The Spirit helps us to know right from wrong and gives us courage when we feel afraid. He helps us obey God and love Him more. The Holy Spirit is the way God takes care of us.

Whenever we need a drink, we can find a water fountain. Whenever we need help, the Holy Spirit is always there for us. —T.M.

## READ MORE

Read Isaiah 44:2–4.
What did Isaiah compare God's Spirit to?

## FUN FACT

In different places, water fountains are also called "drinking fountains" or "bubblers."

> "No eye has seen, no ear has heard, no mind has imagined what God has prepared for those who love him."
>
> 1 CORINTHIANS 2:9 NLT

# Can't Imagine!

**Have you ever seen** a falling star or streaks of lightning? Have you ever seen an eagle soar through the sky or a deer run through the woods? Have you ever seen a newborn baby? Those are amazing things to see!

What is the most amazing thing you have ever heard? Have you listened to birds chirping or frogs croaking? Maybe you have heard the sound of the ocean or a thunderstorm. It's fun to listen to different sounds.

What are some things you have imagined? Have you ever daydreamed that you were an astronaut walking on the moon, or a scuba diver swimming in the sea? Maybe you've imagined what you will be when you grow up. You can use your mind to picture many different things.

## God loves me more than I can imagine.

No matter what you have seen or heard, no matter what you can imagine, it's not nearly as amazing as God's love for you. If you love Jesus and trust in Him, God's love is the greatest thing you will ever know. And God will help you to become all that He wants you to be.

You might not walk on the moon or scuba dive in the sea, but God has wonderful things that He wants you to do. You might become a missionary. You might write stories to change people's lives. You might sing or play an instrument to help people praise God.

God loves you and wants to use you—more than you can imagine! —C.B.

### FUN FACT

If you like lightning, you should visit the Catatumbo River in Venezuela. People who live there can see lightning about three hundred nights a year.

### READ MORE

Read Psalm 63:3–5. What should we do because we know God loves us so much?

# Words on a Scroll

**God had a message** for the people of Judah. God wanted to warn them that if they didn't stop sinning against Him, He was going to bring a disaster on them.

Jeremiah was God's prophet at that time. Jeremiah asked a man named Baruch to write down the words as he spoke the message from God. Baruch wrote the message on a scroll and read it at the temple. When some of the king's officers heard what Baruch had done, they sent for him. "Bring us the scroll that you read to the people," they said.

> "Jeremiah, get a scroll. Write on it all the words I have spoken to you about Israel and Judah and all the nations."
>
> **JEREMIAH 36:2 ICB**

Baruch brought the scroll to the officers and read it. The men became afraid and said, "We must tell the king!"

The officers asked Baruch where the words had come from. "Jeremiah spoke and I wrote down the words," he said. "You and Jeremiah must go and hide," the officers answered.

## God's words help us to know what is right.

When the officers told the king about God's warnings, the king asked a servant to read the scroll out loud. As the man was reading, the king would cut off pieces of the scroll and throw them in the fire! He had no respect for God's Word.

When people are disobeying God, they usually don't want to hear His words. They don't want to be told what trouble their bad choices may bring. But the words of God bring us peace and hope and life. They help us to know what God wants us to do. They make us wise and good and more like Jesus.

We can be thankful that God loves us so much that He gave us the Bible! —C.B.

### FUN FACT

Most books of the Bible were first written on papyrus or parchment. The papyrus plant is a reed that grows near the Nile River. Parchment was made from treated leather.

### READ MORE

Read 2 Chronicles 7:14.
What promise does God make in this verse?

# Storm Warning

"Obey the Lord by
doing what I tell you.
Then things will go
well for you. And your
life will be saved."

JEREMIAH 38:20 ICB

**Storm warnings** help people to stay safe in bad weather. If a regular storm is coming, the warning tells people they need to get home as quickly as possible. But if hurricane is coming, people should leave their homes for safer places. Storm warnings can save lives when people listen to them.

God's prophets gave the Israelites many warnings. They weren't warnings about the weather though. They were warnings about the bad things that would happen if the people didn't listen to God. When Zedekiah became king of Judah, he did not listen to the words God spoke through the prophet Jeremiah. Some of Zedekiah's officials threw Jeremiah into an old muddy well because they didn't like his warnings.

One day, King Zedekiah sent for Jeremiah to ask if he had received any other messages from the Lord. Jeremiah said, "Yes, King, you and your people will be handed over to the king of Babylon. Everyone who stays in Jerusalem will die, but everyone

### I will listen to God.

who surrenders to the Babylonians will live." Jeremiah was speaking the truth of God. But when the Babylonians came, Zedekiah did not surrender. He tried to run away and things ended badly for him.

We do not need prophets today because we have the Bible. God gives us many words of both warning and encouragement in the Bible. The most encouraging message in the Bible is the story of God's love for all people. He sent Jesus to die on the cross so that anyone who believes in Him could be part of God's family. And when He takes us to heaven, there are no more storms! —C.B.

### FUN FACT

Jeremiah was a prophet in Judah for about forty years. During his years of being a prophet, five different kings ruled over Judah.

### READ MORE

Read Jeremiah 38:1–13 to find out how Jeremiah got out of the muddy well.

# Living Stones

> You also are like living stones, and God is using you to build a spiritual house. You are to serve God in this house as holy priests, offering him spiritual sacrifices that he will accept because of Jesus Christ.
>
> **1 PETER 2:5 ERV**

**Long ago,** a cornerstone was a large, square stone used to start the foundation of a building. The foundation is very important because it holds up everything built on top of it. And the cornerstone was very, very important, because it kept the foundation straight and sturdy. All of the other stones or bricks were laid based on where the cornerstone was placed.

Did you know that Jesus is called the cornerstone of the church? That means He is the starting point for the whole big family of God. When Jesus died on the cross and rose again, He became the cornerstone for everyone in the church. Everyone who believes in Jesus is like another stone that lines up with the cornerstone. These are the "living stones" that today's verse talks about. Every Christian gets to be part of the wonderful building Jesus started!

### I am like a stone used to build a house for God.

As more and more people follow Jesus, they are like other stones, stacked one on top of another to make a building. And it's the most amazing building ever! It's a beautiful place of worship that pleases God.

Sometimes it's hard to explain just how special it is to be part of God's family. That's because there is nothing else in whole world like this building made up of living stones. Everyone who believes in Jesus can be a part of His wonderful house of worship. —T.M.

### READ MORE

Read Acts 4:8–12.
When Peter was on trial, what did he call Jesus?

### FUN FACT

Today a cornerstone is usually a decoration on the outside of a building. Many times, the date the building was finished is written on the cornerstone.

# Better Than Silver or Gold

Peter said, "I don't have any silver or gold, but I do have something else I can give you."

**ACTS 3:6 ERV**

**One day** Peter and John went to the temple at three o'clock in the afternoon. It was time for the daily prayer service.

At the temple, Jesus' two disciples saw a man who had been crippled his whole life. The man's friends brought him to the temple every day. They put him by a place called the Beautiful Gate, where he begged for money. Today the man asked Peter and John for money.

"I don't have silver or gold to give you," Peter replied. "But I have something else. By the power of Jesus Christ from Nazareth—stand up and walk!"

Peter took the man's hand and lifted him up. And right away the man's feet and legs became strong. He jumped up and began walking around and praising God. All the people knew who he was. They had seen him begging at the Beautiful Gate for a long time. But now they saw him walking and praising God. They didn't understand how that could happen!

## Jesus' power is better than anything.

"Why are you surprised?" Peter asked the people. "It wasn't our power that made this man walk. God is the One who did this! He is the One who gave glory to Jesus. This man was healed because we trusted Jesus. It was Jesus' power that made him well. You saw it with your own eyes!"

Peter and John could only do miracles by the power of Jesus. It was Jesus who helped them heal people. Jesus has that kind of power because He created the whole world. The whole universe runs the way it does because Jesus keeps it going! Isn't it amazing that Jesus has that kind of power? You can be confident in Him. —C.B.

### FUN FACT

When the Israelites rebuilt the walls of Jerusalem under Nehemiah, they worked on gates called the Sheep Gate, the Fish Gate, the Horse Gate, the Valley Gate, and the Water Gate.

### READ MORE

Read Colossians 3:16–17.
**What do these verses say about the way we should live?**

# A Humble Servant

**Have you ever** had to do a job you didn't want to do? Maybe you wished somebody else would do it. Or maybe there was something else to do that seemed more important.

One time Jesus did a job that nobody expected Him to do. After He had eaten the last supper with His disciples, Jesus took off His coat and wrapped a towel around His waist. He poured water into a bowl and began washing His disciples' feet. Then He used the towel to dry their feet off.

> "I am your Lord and Teacher. But I washed your feet. So you also should wash each other's feet. I did this as an example for you. So you should serve each other just as I served you."
>
> JOHN 13:14–15 ERV

When He was finished, Jesus sat down at the table and said, "Do you understand what I did for you? You call me 'Teacher.' And you call me 'Lord.' That is what I am. But I washed your feet." In Bible times, foot-washing was usually done by servants. It was the lowest kind of service. Because Jesus was the disciples' leader, He could have made them wash His feet. But Jesus turned things upside down. He showed them that to be like Him they had to become humble servants.

*I can be a humble servant like Jesus.*

Being humble means you don't think you're better than other people. You don't demand your own way. When Jesus washed the disciples' feet, He showed humbleness. Then He told His disciples to serve each other like He had served them.

Depending on where you live, you may not ever serve others by washing their feet. But you can be a humble servant in other ways. You can let someone go ahead of you when you're standing in a line. You can share your dessert with your brother or sister or friend. You can even do a job you don't want to do, like taking out the trash.

When you become a humble servant, others will see Jesus in you. —T.M.

## READ MORE

Read Philippians 2:5–8.
Besides washing His disciples' feet,
how did Jesus show humility?

### FUN FACT

During Bible times, most people wore sandals. The sandals were made with leather or wood soles and fastened with leather straps. Since the shoes were open, people's feet would get very dirty.

# A Special Seat

> The Son made people clean from their sins. Then he sat down at the right side of God, the Great One in heaven.
>
> **HEBREWS 1:3 ERV**

**What do you do** after you've finished a hard job? Do you clap your hands and shout for joy? Do you celebrate with a yummy snack? Sometimes when we finish an exhausting job that takes a lot of energy, it feels good to sit down. It's nice to relax when we know our hard work is finished!

After Jesus came to earth and died on the cross, He rose from the dead. He spent some time with His disciples and told them what they needed to do after He left. Then Jesus went back to heaven. When His job on earth was finished, He sat down in the place of honor next to God. Jesus got to sit down because He had finished everything He came to earth to do.

When Jesus defeated sin on the cross, He won the victory forever. His death covered the cost of all His people's sins for all time. He got to sit down because the job was completed. There was nothing else He had to do to make us right with God.

When we confess our sins and believe in Jesus, we become a part of His completed work. Our sin is forgiven forever—there is nothing else we have to do to be made right with God. We can be sure that we are a part of God's family because we know Jesus is sitting next to God in heaven. One day we will see Jesus sitting on His throne. And we will join all of those who love Him and sing praises to Him forever! —T.M.

## Jesus finished the work of paying for my sin.

## FUN FACT

In ancient kingdoms, sitting at the right side of a king was an honor. When a king placed someone at his right side, that person was able to act with the king's power.

## READ MORE

Read Luke 22:66–69.
When Jesus was on trial before the Jewish priests, where did He say He was going next?

# The Vineyard Workers

> "God's kingdom is like a man who owned some land. One morning, the man went out very early to hire some people to work in his vineyard."
>
> MATTHEW 20:1 ERV

**Jesus told a story** about a man who owned a vineyard. That's a place where grapes are grown.

The man went out early one morning to hire people to work in his vineyard. He agreed to pay the workers one silver coin if they worked the whole day. The workers agreed and started picking grapes.

Around nine in the morning the vineyard owner went into town and saw some people standing around. "Work in my field and I will pay you what is right," he told them. They agreed. At twelve o'clock and three o'clock, the owner went out and hired even more workers for his vineyard. Then at five o'clock he hired some more.

At the end of the day, the owner was ready to pay the workers. The people who started working at five o'clock, three o'clock, twelve o'clock, and nine o'clock were all paid one silver coin. Then the workers who were hired first were also paid one silver coin!

## God will do what is right.

"The workers you hired last only worked for an hour," they complained. "You paid them the same as us and we worked all day in the hot sun!"

The owner said, "You agreed to work all day for one silver coin and that is what I gave you. I can give the others the same pay if I want to."

If you believe in Jesus when you're a child, you will serve God for many years. Other people may believe in Jesus much later in life and serve Him for only a short time. But everyone who believes in Jesus will enjoy the good things of heaven. God is always fair. He will give each of us what is right.
—C.B.

**FUN FACT**

Of all the plants in the Bible, the grapevine is mentioned most. People would eat grapes fresh off the vine, dry them for raisins, press them for wine, or make them into vinegar.

## READ MORE

Read Ephesians 6:7–8.
What do these verses tell us about the work we do?

# Be Filled

> Like babies that were just born, you should long for the pure milk of God's word. It will help you grow up as believers.
>
> 1 PETER 2:2 NIRV

**How often** do you like to eat? Did you know that many newborn babies eat every two hours?

Babies need to eat more often than older kids. Because babies grow so fast, their bodies need nutrition to give them energy. When they drink milk, they get the energy they need to grow big and strong. Milk helps their brains grow so they become smarter and learn how to do things. Without milk, a baby couldn't become a healthy adult.

Just like milk helps a baby grow strong, the Bible helps Christians grow strong. The apostle Peter said we should "crave" or "long for" the Scriptures. That means we should want the truth of the Bible so badly that we won't be happy until we get it.

Babies usually cry when they're hungry. Once their mothers start feeding them, the crying stops. When babies taste the yummy milk and know they're getting what they need, they are happy and peaceful. Peter said it should be the same way for us. If we have trusted in Jesus, then we know that God is good. Now that we've had a taste of His goodness, we should want to be filled with His goodness.

We eat food every day so our bodies will grow strong. In the same way, reading the Bible every day will help us grow in our faith. As we get our spiritual nutrition, we become smarter and stronger in our love for God. Be sure to fill up on Scripture every day so you can keep growing! —T.M.

## I will crave God's Word.

### FUN FACT

A baby's brain gets almost twice as big in the first year. That growth is part of what makes a baby hungry so often!

### READ MORE

Read Psalm 19:7–10.
What did King David compare the Scriptures to?

# Joseph Forgives

**Jacob died** when he was a very old man. Jacob's twelve sons, Joseph and his brothers, buried him in their homeland and returned to Egypt where they had been living. But when they got back, Joseph's brothers were worried.

The brothers had been mean to Joseph when they were younger. They sent him away because they didn't like him. But because of God's plan, Joseph was now one of the most important people in the world! Now that their father was gone, the brothers thought Joseph would hold a grudge and be unkind to them. So they sent him a message saying, "Before your father died, he said, 'Tell Joseph to forgive his brothers for the bad things they did to him.' So Joseph, we beg you, please forgive us. We are servants of God, the God of your father."

When Joseph heard the message, he cried. His brothers came into his palace and bowed down to show him respect. They told Joseph they would be his servants. But Joseph said, "Don't be afraid. I am not God! I have no right to punish you. I will take care of you and your children." The brothers were happy when they heard Joseph's kind words.

> After Jacob died, Joseph's brothers were worried. They were afraid that Joseph would still be mad at them for what they had done years before. They said, "Maybe Joseph still hates us for what we did."
>
> **GENESIS 50:15 ERV**

## I can choose to forgive people who hurt me.

Even though Joseph had a reason to be angry, he chose to keep forgiving his brothers. He refused to hold a grudge and made sure his brothers knew that he loved them. Joseph showed how important it is to let go of the hurtful things people do. Sometimes we must choose to forgive people over and over. But when we love people the way Joseph did, it's an example of God's love and forgiveness toward us. —T.M.

## READ MORE

Read 2 Corinthians 2:5–8.
What did Paul say will happen to people if we don't forgive them?

## FUN FACT

Forgiveness is good for your body. When you forgive someone, your blood pressure lowers and your heart rate slows down.

# Everyone Will Bow

At the name of Jesus everyone in heaven, on earth, and in the world below will kneel and confess that Jesus Christ is Lord to the glory of God the Father.

**PHILIPPIANS 2:10–11 GW**

**Depending on** where you live, you may not see people bowing to each other very often. But did you know that a long time ago bowing was very common? Regular people would bow to kings and other important officials. When they bowed, people were saying they were less important than the person they bowed to. Bowing was a way of showing respect and admitting that one person had more power than the other.

Christians know that Jesus is the one true King. We know He has more power than anyone else. So it's good for us to praise Him for being more important than we are. When we worship Jesus for His greatness, it's like we're bowing before Him.

But not everyone sees Jesus the way we do. Some people do not accept Jesus as God's Son. Some people don't know that He offers everyone forgiveness for their sins. They don't bow before Jesus by worshipping Him.

### Everyone will bow before Jesus someday.

When people around us don't love Jesus the way we do, it can be hard to worship Him the way we should. It's even harder if people make fun of us for being Christians. But the Bible says that one day every person will bow before Jesus. Everyone will know His greatness and say out loud that Jesus is the one true King.

Have you ever felt alone when you worshipped Jesus? You can remember today's verse. Jesus is glad when you choose to honor Him now instead of waiting until later!
—T.M.

## FUN FACT

When people bow it's kind of like what animals do in nature. A weaker animal lowers itself to a stronger animal as a sign of defeat.

## READ MORE

Read Isaiah 45:22–23.
What promise did Jesus make before He ever came to earth?

# Water from the Rock

**The Israelites** were thirsty as Moses led them through the wilderness. There wasn't enough water so they complained to Moses and Aaron. "Why did you take us out of Egypt and bring us to this bad place? There is no grain. There are no figs, grapes, or pomegranates. There's no water to drink!"

Moses and Aaron went to the meeting tent to ask God what to do. "Bring your staff," God told Moses. "Take Aaron and the people and go to that big rock. Speak to the rock in front of the people. Then water will flow from the rock and the people can drink."

> But the LORD said to Moses and Aaron, "You did not trust me enough to honor me and show the people that I am holy. You did not show the Israelites that the power to make the water came from me. So you will not lead the people into the land that I have given them."
>
> NUMBERS 20:12 ERV

Moses, Aaron, and all the people went to the rock. "You people are always complaining," Moses said. "Now listen to me. I will cause water to flow from this rock."

But Moses didn't speak to the rock like God had said. Instead, He hit it with his staff twice. Water came out of the rock even though Moses disobeyed God's instructions. The people and their animals drank from it. But God knew Moses hadn't listened to Him.

## God wants me to obey Him.

God told Moses and Aaron that they had not allowed Him to show His power. Moses and Aaron had done things their own way instead. Because they disobeyed, God said they wouldn't get to lead the Israelites into the promised land.

God wants people to obey Him. When we disobey God, there are consequences. When we're tempted to disobey, we can remember that God blesses obedience. God loves us so much He will help us to do what's right when we ask Him. —T.M.

## **READ MORE**

Read James 1:22–25.
What happens to us when we obey God?

### FUN FACT

The place where Moses struck the rock was named Meribah, which means "argument." That's because the people argued with God.

# The Way to Pray

**Have you ever** made a wish? Kids like to make wishes. Many times, parents put candles on their children's birthday cakes to make the celebration even more fun. The kids who are celebrating their birthday make a wish before blowing out the candles. They might wish for a puppy or a new toy. They might even wish for their mom or dad to get a new job. Sometimes wishes come true, but sometimes they don't.

Some people think that praying is like making a wish. They hope that if they tell God what they want, He will give them what they ask for. But God loves us so much that He doesn't always give us what we want. He gives us what's best for us!

Sometimes what God thinks is best isn't the same as what we think is best. Sometimes it takes a while before we understand why God said no when we asked for something. And that can make it harder to pray. But we can always count on one thing—that God hears us when we pray. And if our prayer matches the good things He wants for us, He will give us what we ask.

So the next time you want something, you can tell God how you feel. You can even tell Him what you would like to see happen. But then you can ask Him to do what He wants. When you pray that way, you are trusting God to listen and to do what is best. —T.M.

**God listens to my prayers and does what is best.**

## FUN FACT

Ancient Jewish families did not celebrate birthdays. The only birthday parties mentioned in the Bible are for the Egyptian Pharaoh and King Herod!

## READ MORE

Read John 14:12–14.
Whose name has power when we pray?

# The Evil King

**Israel's king Ahab** did many things to disobey God. He was evil, and so was his wife, Jezebel.

> So Ahab went home angry and upset because Naboth told him, "I will not give you my family's land." Ahab went to bed, turned away from everyone, and refused to eat.
>
> **1 KINGS 21:4 ERV**

Ahab had a neighbor named Naboth who owned a vineyard. One day the king said to Naboth, "Give me your vineyard. I want to make it a vegetable garden. I will give you a better vineyard in its place, or I will pay you for it."

But the vineyard was very special to Naboth. "I will never give my land to you," he told the king. "This land belongs to my family."

King Ahab went home upset that he didn't get his way. Then he pouted.

When his wife, Jezebel, heard what happened, she wrote letters in the king's name and put the king's seal on them. She sent the letters to leaders in Naboth's town and told them to bring Naboth to a meeting. The leaders found two people to lie about Naboth, and say that he had cursed God and the king. After the liars told their story, Jezebel gave orders to kill Naboth. When Naboth was gone, Ahab took over his vineyard.

## Nothing is hidden from God's sight.

God sent Elijah to tell Ahab he would be punished for his sin. And Ahab was punished later. He was killed in a battle.

God sees everything people do, even if they think it's a secret. Nothing is hidden from His sight, whether it's bad or good. Like Ahab, we can't hide our bad actions from God. But Jesus said that God sees every good thing we do too—and He will reward us for those. —T.M.

### READ MORE
Read Isaiah 3:10–11.
What happens to the righteous?
What happens to people who do evil?

### FUN FACT
Many times in the Bible, a person's name told others where they came from or what they did. Naboth's name means "fruit" because his family owned a vineyard.

# Coming True

"While you heard these words just now, they were coming true!"

LUKE 4:21 ICB

**The prophets** in the Old Testament carried God's messages. God would tell them what to say to the people. The prophets told the people about things that would happen soon, but they also told about things that would happen after many years.

The prophets often talked about the Messiah who would come to earth. The Messiah would be someone who would save people from sin. He would come from the tribe of Judah and be born in Bethlehem. The Messiah would speak in parables and be praised by children. He would be called a Nazarene and would teach in Galilee. He would be treated badly and die the death of a criminal. His hands and feet would be pierced. He would rise from the dead and be a sacrifice for sin.

All of these things were written in the Old Testament many years before Jesus was born. The Jewish leaders in Jesus' day could read those prophecies to know what the Messiah would be like.

One Sabbath day Jesus read a prophecy about the Messiah from the book of Isaiah. When He finished reading He said, "While you heard these words just now, they were coming true." Jesus was telling the people that He was the promised Messiah! Many people did not understand. And even after Jesus died on the cross, they still did not understand. But some people believed that Jesus was the Messiah. They knew He had come to save people from sin.

## Jesus is the Messiah God promised to send.

Today we have both the Old Testament and the New Testament. We can read the prophets' messages from long ago, and also the stories of Jesus to see how they fit together. We can know that Jesus is the Messiah. And we can be happy that all of God's words are true. —C.B.

### FUN FACT

People who study the Bible as a job are called "theologians." Theologians believe there are three hundred to four hundred Old Testament prophecies that Jesus fulfilled.

### READ MORE

Jesus read the words from Isaiah 61:1–2. Read the verses to find out what He said.

> The people of Israel
> did what was evil in
> the sight of the LORD.
> They forgot the
> LORD their God.
>
> JUDGES 3:7 NIRV

# The First Judge

**After Joshua died,** the Israelites turned away from God. Younger people didn't know what God had done for Israel. They began praying to false gods, and they did what the Lord said was wrong. God had warned the people what would happen if they turned away from Him. Because they chose to disobey, He didn't protect the Israelites like before. He let their enemies attack them and take their possessions. He allowed another king to rule over them for eight years. Then the people cried out to God for help.

God heard the people's prayers and chose a man named Othniel to help them. He became their first judge. The Spirit of the Lord was with Othniel. God helped him defeat the king who was ruling over the Israelites. After that, the land had peace for forty years.

The Israelites were supposed to tell their children and grandchildren about the mighty things God had done. The younger people were supposed to know how God had led them through the Red Sea and guided them for forty years in the wilderness. God wanted the children to know how He helped the people cross the Jordan River and

## Children need to know about God.

enter the promised land. But as the older people died, many of the younger people grew up without knowing God.

Othniel was the nephew of Caleb. Caleb and Joshua were the two spies who were allowed to enter the promised land because of their faith. Maybe Othniel learned about God from his uncle Caleb. Somehow Othniel knew the great things God had done.

Someday you may have children. If you do, you can tell them about God and all He has done for you. Right now you can say "thank you" to God if you have a mom, or dad, or grandma, or grandpa who has told you about His love. That is a special blessing!
—C.B.

## READ MORE

Read Judges 3:12–15.
Why did Israel need a second judge after
Othniel died? What was his name?

## FUN FACT

The king that
Othniel defeated
was named
Cushan-Rishathaim!

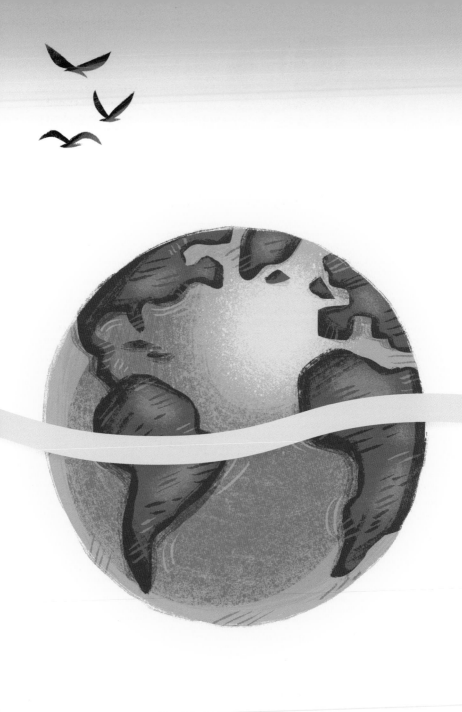

> "I am the Alpha and the Omega. I am the First and the Last. I am the Beginning and the End."
>
> **REVELATION 22:13 NIRV**

# The Beginning and the End

**Did you know** that Jesus was with God at the time of creation? When the moon and stars and the land and sea were created, Jesus was right there. He came to earth as a baby later. But He has always been alive as God.

While He was on earth, Jesus healed many people who were sick. He performed many miracles and taught people about God's kingdom. Many people followed Jesus, but many were against Him. The Jewish leaders did not agree with the things He was saying. When Jesus said He was God, they were very upset. That's when they made plans to kill Him.

When Jesus died on the cross, most people thought that was the end of Him. But then Jesus rose from the dead and spent more time with His followers before He went back to heaven!

## Jesus has always been alive.

Jesus is alive today just like He was at creation. Jesus is alive today just like He was when He walked on earth. Jesus will always be alive! Someday Jesus is coming back to earth, and everyone who loves Him will be able to be with Him forever.

We don't know when Jesus will return, but it will be the greatest day ever! Until that day comes, we can just keep loving Jesus and loving others. We can pray and read the Bible. When we do, God will remind us that Jesus is alive. He is the beginning and the end! —C.B.

### FUN FACT

Alpha (A) and omega (Ω) are the first and last letters of the Greek alphabet. Saying Jesus is the "Alpha and Omega" is like saying He's everything from A to Z.

### READ MORE

Read Revelation 1:4–8.
What do these verses tell us about Jesus?

# A Special Meal

When it was time to eat the Passover meal, Jesus and the apostles were at the table. Jesus said to them, "I've had a deep desire to eat this Passover with you before I suffer."

LUKE 22:14–15 GW

**Just before Jesus died,** He shared a special meal with His disciples. It was time to remember the Passover, and they were all together in the upstairs room of a house.

As the men sat around a table, Jesus took a loaf of bread and said a prayer of thanks. Then He broke pieces off the bread and gave them to His disciples. "This is my body, which is given for you," Jesus told them. "Eat this to remember me." After supper was over, Jesus took a cup of wine. Before He passed it to His disciples He said, "This cup shows that God has a new agreement with His people. My blood will pay for your sins."

Jesus said these things to help the disciples understand what was about to happen. Jesus knew He would soon die on the cross. He used this last supper as an example, to explain to the disciples what His death would mean for the world. The broken bread was a sign that Jesus would give up His body for all people. The cup of wine was a sign that Jesus' blood would pay the price for the sins of everyone who would believe in Him. The disciples didn't understand everything He said, but Jesus was telling them how God was going to forgive people of their sins through Him.

## The Lord's Supper tells how Jesus saves His people.

When you go to church, you may hear someone read this story during a communion service. Most churches celebrate communion, or the "Lord's Supper," because Jesus told us to break bread and drink from the cup to remember Him. When we do this, we tell the story of how God saves people, just like Jesus told His disciples. —T.M.

### FUN FACT

In some churches the Lord's Supper is called the Eucharist. This word means "to give thanks."

### READ MORE

Read 1 Corinthians 10:16–17.
What did the church at Corinth do as part of its worship?

# No Trade Backs

**Have you ever** made a trade? Maybe at lunch you traded your grapes for your friend's cookie. Or maybe you traded a toy with your neighbor or switched beds with your brother or sister. It's fun to take something you have and trade it for something new.

Sometimes when kids make a trade they say, "No trade backs!" That means that once the trade has been made, it can't be undone. You can't give or get back what you traded.

> Christ didn't have any sin. But God made him become sin for us. So we can be made right with God because of what Christ has done for us.
>
> 2 CORINTHIANS 5:21 NIRV

Did you know that God wants to make a trade with you? When Jesus came to earth, He was perfect and He lived without sinning. But when Jesus died on the cross, God put everyone's sins on Jesus. He let Jesus take every single sin from every person who has ever lived—or who will ever live in the future. And then God said He would make a trade.

*God trades my sin for Jesus' perfection.*

Since Jesus has taken our sins, God gives us the chance to have Jesus' goodness. The Bible calls that His "righteousness." Since Jesus was perfect, God will let us have Jesus' perfection instead of our sin. It's the most important trade you can ever make!

All we have to do to finish the trade is say yes to God's offer. The best part is, once we agree to the trade there are no trade backs. It can't be undone. We are right with God forever! —T.M.

### READ MORE
Read Galatians 3:13–14.
What else do we receive as a part of God's trade?

### FUN FACT
For more than a hundred years, "trading cards" have been popular. Baseball cards are some of the most common trading cards in the United States, Canada, Cuba, and Japan.

# Losing a Friend

**When David came back** from fighting a battle he got some bad news. A man arrived from King Saul's camp where there had been another battle. David could tell something bad had happened. The man had dirt on his face and his clothes were torn. He bowed before David.

"What happened?" asked David.

"King Saul's army fled from the battle and many of the soldiers were killed," he said. "Saul and his son Jonathan died too."

The news made David so sad that he tore his clothes. The men around him tore theirs too. They cried and didn't eat anything until evening.

Even though King Saul had been an enemy of David, his death still made David sad. And Saul's son Jonathan was David's best friend. David was heartbroken to lose people who were so important to him. He honored Saul and Jonathan by writing a song. Today's Bible verse is part of that song.

## God comforts me when I am sad.

Whether someone has died or just moved away, it's hard to lose someone you care about. It's okay to be sad and to think and talk about people who aren't with us. It's even okay to cry like David did. We can honor people like David did too. You can remember them in special ways. You can write a song or poem like David did. You can draw a picture or fill a box with things that remind you of that person.

It's never easy to lose someone you love, but God will comfort you and be your friend when you are lonely.
—T.M.

## FUN FACT

In ancient Israel, people would wear "sackcloth" when someone they loved had died. It was a tough, scratchy cloth made from goat hair. People would also put ashes on themselves to show their sadness.

## READ MORE

Read 2 Samuel 1:19–27.
What are some of the things David said about Saul and Jonathan in his song?

# An Heir to the King

> For his Spirit joins with our spirit to affirm that we are God's children. And since we are his children, we are his heirs. In fact, together with Christ we are heirs of God's glory.
>
> **ROMANS 8:16–17 NLT**

**You may have heard** people use the word heir when they talk about kings and royalty. The dictionary says an heir is a person who has the right to become a king or queen when the current king or queen dies. Heirs will have all the same rights and honors as the person who was ahead of them.

Not anyone can become an heir. You might be very smart and a good leader, but you can't just ask to be an heir. Usually a person can only be an heir if he or she is born into the ruling family. An heir has to be a son or daughter of the king or queen.

God is King of the whole universe. Since Jesus is His Son, that means Jesus is God's heir. He receives all the good things and honor that God has. Do you want to know something amazing? The Bible tells us that we get to be heirs with Jesus too!

## I am an heir to the King of the universe.

When we ask Jesus to forgive our sins, we become part of God's family. The Holy Spirit is a witness that we are children of God through Jesus. And because we are God's children, that means we are His heirs. Like Jesus, we get to receive the good things God has!

Have you ever wondered if you are important or if you will ever do important things? If you ever feel that way, you can remember today's Bible verse. You are the son or daughter of the King! And all that He has is yours. —T.M.

### READ MORE
Read Galatians 4:4–7.
What were we called before we became heirs?

### FUN FACT
The Prince of Wales, Charles, is heir to the throne of the United Kingdom. He is the son of Queen Elizabeth II.

# Happy or Sad

> **Be happy with those who are happy. Be sad with those who are sad.**
>
> ROMANS 12:15 GW

**Everyone wants** to be understood. When you are sad, you want someone to make you feel better. When you are happy about something, you want the person you tell to be happy too.

The way we'd like to be treated when we are happy or sad is the same way we should treat others. If you have a friend who is sad because his dog ran away, you can be sad with him. If you have a friend who is happy because she won a race on the playground, you can be happy with her.

Jesus cared about people that way. When His friend Lazarus died, Jesus saw how sad Lazarus's sisters were. Jesus was sad with them. But when Jesus told His followers how much God loved them, He wanted them to be full of joy like He was.

Even when Jesus was dying on the cross, He still cared about others. Jesus looked down from the cross and saw his mother, Mary, standing next to John. John was one of Jesus' disciples who followed Jesus everywhere. He was Jesus' closest friend. Jesus knew His mother and John were sad. So in the last few moments of His life He showed how much He cared for them. Jesus told John that Mary was now his mother, and he told Mary that John was now her son. Jesus knew they would help each other through the sad days after His death.

## I can be happy or sad with others.

We can follow Jesus' example and care about others whatever they're going through. When someone is sad, be sad with them. When someone is happy, be happy too! —C.B.

### FUN FACT

Scientists say that when you see a friend smile, the muscles in your face make the same expression. You start smiling without even being aware of it!

### READ MORE

Read Revelation 21:3–4.
What do these verses tell us about heaven?

# Have Hope

> May the God of hope fill you with all joy and peace as you trust in him, so that you may overflow with hope by the power of the Holy Spirit.
>
> **ROMANS 15:13 NIV**

**People hope** for many things. When kids try out for a sports team, they hope to be chosen. Kids who like to act hope to get a part in a play. Kids who like to sing hope to be part of a choir.

Adults hope for things too. They hope to get good jobs. They hope to have children. They hope to have good health. Sometimes, if they're planning an outside activity, they hope for good weather!

Have you noticed that people always hope for good things? No one would hope for bad things. To hope means we want something good to happen. But sometimes the things we hope for don't turn out the way we want them to.

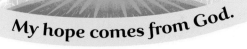

## My hope comes from God.

When the apostle Paul taught people about Jesus, he said our hope comes from God. When Jesus came to earth, many of God's promises came true. That gives us hope that the rest of God's promises will come true too. God promises that people who believe in Jesus will go to heaven. He promises that He will always be with us. He promises to help us in times of trouble. And He promises that Jesus will come back someday.

We hope for these things to happen. But we can also know they will come true. —C.B.

**READ MORE**

Read Psalm 33:18–22.
Why can we have hope?

**FUN FACT**

"Every cloud has a silver lining," is a saying from the 1800s. It means we can hope for good to come out of our problems.

# Elijah Goes to Heaven

They kept walking along and talking together. Suddenly a chariot and horses appeared. Fire was all around them. The chariot and horses came between the two men. Then Elijah went up to heaven in a strong wind.

2 KINGS 2:11 NIRV

**Most people** don't know when their life on earth will end, but the prophet Elijah did. God had told people the exact day Elijah would go to heaven.

Elijah's student, Elisha, was sad when he thought about Elijah leaving. As Elijah traveled to say good-bye to friends, Elisha would not leave his side.

Finally, Elijah said good-bye to Elisha. "What can I do for you before I'm taken away?" Elijah asked.

Elisha wanted to have God's power like Elijah had. So Elisha said, "Please give me a double share of your spirit."

"You have asked for something I can't give you," Elijah said. "Only the Lord can give it."

Suddenly, a chariot and horses appeared. But it wasn't a regular chariot and horses—they had fire all around them! The chariot and horses drove right between Elijah and Elisha, and Elijah was taken to heaven in a strong wind!

Elijah was taken so quickly that his coat flew off and fell to the ground. Elisha picked up the coat and went to the Jordan River. When he hit the water with the coat, God gave Elisha the power Elijah had. The water split apart so Elisha could cross the river.

## God uses people as examples in my life.

Elisha learned from Elijah. He wanted to be like him. God used Elijah to help Elisha become a great prophet. Did you know that God has put people in your life as good examples too? When you see good things in the people around you, you can ask God to help you learn from them. You can be like Elisha! —T.M.

### FUN FACT

Today, we say someone who sets a good example is a "role model." The term was first used in the late 1950s.

### READ MORE

Find 1 Kings 19:19–21.
What did Elisha do when he met Elijah?

# Good News

**If you had** good news to share, you would want to tell as many people as you could. You would never be ashamed or embarrassed to share your good news. You would be happy and excited to share your good news to anyone who would listen.

> I'm not ashamed of the Good News. It is God's power to save everyone who believes.
>
> **ROMANS 1:16 GW**

The apostle Paul was a great teacher and missionary. He was a follower of Jesus and he wanted everyone to know the good news about Jesus. Paul wanted everyone to know and believe that Jesus was the Messiah God had promised to send to earth. Jesus came into the world to die on the cross for our sins. And because Jesus died and rose from the dead, all who believe in Him are forgiven and saved from the punishment of sin forever. That is good news!

Paul told people, "As a man, Jesus was born from the family of David. But through the Holy Spirit, Jesus was shown to be God's powerful Son when he rose from the grave."

*I can be proud to share the good news.*

Paul believed that God had given him a special job. Paul's whole life was about telling people of all nations about Jesus so they could believe in Him. Paul traveled to many cities and countries so he could tell the good news to as many people as possible. When he was writing a letter to the Romans Paul said, "I am not ashamed of the good news. It is the power God uses to save everyone who believes in Jesus. The good news shows how God makes people right with Him by faith."

Just like Paul, you can be proud to share the good news about Jesus. It's the best news anyone can share. —C.B.

## READ MORE

Read Acts 20:22–24.
What was Paul's purpose in life?

### FUN FACT

In older translations of the Bible, the word *gospel* is used instead of "good news." But the meaning of gospel is "good news"!

# Jesus Helps Many People

Jesus replied, "We must go on to other towns as well, and I will preach to them, too. That is why I came."

**MARK 1:38 NLT**

**One day Jesus,** James, and John went to the home of Simon Peter and Andrew. Peter's mother-in-law was there, and she was sick with a fever. Right away Jesus helped her. He held her hand and helped her to get up. When she stood, her fever was gone! She began making food for Jesus and the others who were in the house.

That night, many sick people were brought to Jesus. Everyone in the town of Capernaum gathered at the door of the house. The people had many different sicknesses, but Jesus healed all of them. He even made demons come out of people.

The next morning Jesus got up early. He went to a quiet place where He could be alone to pray. Before long, some of Jesus' followers went out to look for Him. When they found Him they said, "Many people are looking for you!"

But Jesus said, "It's time to go to other towns. I want to tell God's message to those people too. That is why I came."

Jesus loved everyone who followed Him. He wanted to heal their sicknesses, but He also wanted them to know how they could be forgiven of their sins. He wanted to heal their spirits as well as their bodies. That's why Jesus traveled to different places, so more and more people could learn about God's love.

## Jesus wants to help everyone.

You can tell others about God's love just like Jesus did. No matter where you live, there are people who need to hear God's message. —C.B.

### FUN FACT

There were two sets of brothers among Jesus' twelve disciples. Simon Peter and Andrew were brothers. James and John were also brothers.

### READ MORE

Read Matthew 4:23–25.
What do these verses tell us about Jesus' ministry?

# Emergency Exit

**Have you ever** flown on a big airplane? Before a plane takes off, flight attendants tell passengers how to be safe during the flight. They also explain what to do if something bad happens and the passengers need to get off the plane.

Depending on the size of the plane, there are several emergency exits people can use if they need to escape. The exits are marked with signs that light up so everyone can see them. Glowing arrows on the floor point people toward the exits if the plane is dark inside. Flight attendants tell passengers to find their closest exits before the plane takes off. That way they'll know where to go if an emergency happens.

Escaping temptation is a lot like looking for an emergency exit. Because we live in a sinful world, we will all be tempted. It happens to everyone, so we shouldn't be surprised when it happens to us. But God promises that when we are tempted to disobey, He will give us a way out. Just like an emergency exit on a plane, God has given us a way to escape danger. We just have to go in the right direction.

> The only temptations that you have are the same temptations that all people have. But you can trust God. He will not let you be tempted more than you can bear. But when you are tempted, God will also give you a way to escape that temptation. Then you will be able to endure it.
>
> 1 CORINTHIANS 10:13 ERV

## When I feel tempted, God gives me a way out.

God's Word is like the exit sign that lights up. It shows us where to go when we're tempted. Prayer is like the glowing arrows on the floor. It helps us know what to do when we are turned around.

The next time you feel tempted to disobey God, just look for the way out. God will show you where to go.
—T.M.

### **FUN FACT**

The international emergency exit sign is a green and white image of a man running through a door. It was created by a Japanese designer in the 1970s.

### **READ MORE**

Read Hebrews 2:17–18.
Who can help us find the way out of temptation?

# The Promised Land

There has never been
another prophet like
Moses. The Lord knew
Moses face to face.

DEUTERONOMY 34:10 ICB

**Do you remember** how Moses disobeyed God by hitting a big rock with his stick instead of speaking to it? When that happened, God told Moses that he would not be allowed to lead the people of Israel into the promised land. But before Moses died, God let Moses see the promised land from the top of a mountain.

Moses climbed up to the top of Mount Nebo. From there he could see across the Jordan River. God showed Moses all the land the Israelites had been promised. Moses could see where the tribes of Naphtali, Ephraim, and Manasseh would live. He could see the land where the tribe of Judah would live, all the way to the Mediterranean Sea. God showed Moses the southern desert and the whole valley around Jericho.

"This is the land I promised to Abraham, Isaac, and Jacob," God said to Moses. "I said to them, 'I will give this land to your descendants.' I have let you see it, Moses, but you cannot cross over."

## God is full of love and kindness.

Then Moses died and God buried him. Moses had lived to be 120 years old and he was still strong with good eyesight. The Israelites cried for Moses for thirty days. Then Joshua became the new leader.

Because God is holy, He had to discipline Moses for disobeying. But God is also full of love and kindness. He wanted Moses to see the land where the Israelites would soon be living. God wanted Moses to know that He keeps His promises.

There are consequences to disobeying God. But God's love is greater than our sin. He will forgive us when we ask. He always shows kindness to the people who love Him. —C.B.

**FUN FACT**

Parts of the promised land were named after the sons of Jacob. Joseph didn't have land named after him, but his two sons, Ephraim and Manasseh, did. The family of Levi, where the priests came from, lived in special cities throughout the land.

## READ MORE

Read Psalm 145:8–9.
What do these verses tell us about God?

# Give Thanks to God

> Give thanks as you enter the gates of his temple. Give praise as you enter its courtyards. Give thanks to him and praise his name.
>
> PSALM 100:4 NIRV

**When many people** hear the word thanksgiving, they think of a holiday with pilgrims, turkey, and pumpkin pie. Americans celebrate Thanksgiving each November to remember all of their blessings. Several other countries have a holiday like Thanksgiving too. It's good to think about all the wonderful things in our lives.

Taking time to be thankful goes back to the days of the Old Testament. King David wrote a special song called "A Psalm for Giving Thanks." All through this psalm David tells us to remember the great things God does. He wrote, "Shout to the Lord with joy, everyone on earth. Worship the Lord with gladness. Come to him with songs of joy."

David wanted God's people to realize that God rules over everything. David reminds us that God made us and we belong to Him, just like sheep belong to a shepherd. As we take time to worship God, it's good to thank Him. We can praise God's name. Because God is so good, His love will never stop. He will always be faithful to us.

## I can thank God any time.

We don't have to wait for a special holiday to thank God. We can give Him our thanks any time. Think of all the things today that you are thankful for. They can be things you can see, like your clothes and your food. They can be things that you can't always see, like God's love and peace. Everyone has something to be thankful for. And God is pleased when we thank Him! —T.M.

### FUN FACT

Almost every language has a way of saying "thank you." Here are just a few: gracias (Spanish), merci (French), arigato (Japanese), dank u (Dutch), spasibo (Russian).

### READ MORE

Read Psalm 111.
How long should we praise God?

> "We do not ask these things because we are good. We ask because of your mercy."
>
> DANIEL 9:18 ICB

# Daniel Prays for God's People

**Daniel in the lions' den** is a cool story of how Daniel prayed to God even when the king said it was against the law. Kids love the part when Daniel spent the night in the lions' den and God kept him safe.

But that's not the only story in the Bible about Daniel praying. Today's Bible verse is part of a long prayer that Daniel said to God. Daniel was sad about everything that was happening to the Israelites. He was sad that they had sinned and turned away from God. He was sad that the people had been taken away from Jerusalem and that their city had been ruined.

So Daniel prayed. He told God that he was sorry for his sins and the sins of God's people. He asked God to help them and to do good things for them. He asked God to forgive them. But Daniel didn't ask God for good things because he thought the Israelites deserved them. Daniel knew the people did not please God by the way they were living. He knew they deserved to be punished. Daniel asked for kindness instead because of God's mercy and forgiveness. Daniel knew that God is full of love and gentleness. He knew that God would listen to his cry for help.

## I can pray to God like Daniel did.

Did you know that God will listen to us in the same way? We can ask God to help us do what is right. We can ask God to help us please Him. But when we don't do the right thing, we can ask God to forgive us. He is full of love and mercy. —C.B.

### FUN FACT

Daniel in the lions' den is one of the top three Old Testament stories in children's Bible storybooks today. The other top stories are the creation of the world and Noah's ark.

### READ MORE

Read Psalm 32:1–2.
How do people feel when their sins are forgiven?

As the sun went down that evening, people throughout the village brought sick family members to Jesus. No matter what their diseases were, the touch of his hand healed every one.

LUKE 4:40 NLT

# Healing Hands

**Jesus healed** sick people in different ways. Sometimes He just spoke and people were healed. But many times Jesus used His hands to heal. He touched deaf ears so they could hear. He reached out to lepers to cure their skin disease. He touched tongues so people could speak. He wiped the eyes of the blind so they could see. When people were sick in bed, Jesus took them by the hand and helped them to stand up after they were healed.

Jesus loves people and wants to help them. When He was on earth, He was the Son of God in a human body. But He didn't act like He was more important than other people. Jesus healed people with His hands to show how much He cared about them. Even though Jesus is a King, He acted like a servant.

## Jesus' hands are healing hands.

Many people brought their children to Jesus so He could place His hands on their heads and bless them. Jesus used His hands to perform miracles that fed thousands of people. He used His hands to break the bread and pour the wine that He shared with His disciples. And Jesus' greatest act of love was when His hands were nailed to a cross so He could heal the world of sin.

Next time you fold your hands to pray, think of how Jesus used His hands to heal and bless people. Then thank Him for caring for you today. —C.B.

### READ MORE

Read Luke 24:50–53.
What was the last thing Jesus did before going back to heaven?

### FUN FACT

Did you know your fingers do not have muscles? The muscles that control your fingers and thumb are located in the palm of your hand and your forearm.

# A Sun and Shield

> The LORD God is like the sun that gives us light. He is like a shield that keeps us safe. The LORD blesses us with favor and honor. He doesn't hold back anything good from those whose lives are without blame.
>
> **PSALM 84:11 NIRV**

**Because the sun** is the star closest to earth, it looks like it's the brightest. But do you know just how bright the sun is?

We measure weight in pounds, and we measure distance in feet. But scientists measure light in units called lux. When the sun is overhead, it gives off about one hundred thousand lux. To help you understand how bright that is, think about a sports field lit up at night. Those bright lights that help players and fans see give off about five hundred lux. The sun is more than two hundred times brighter—and it's ninety-three million miles away!

The sun's brightness helps us see everything we do. It lights our way when we're outside. It gives us direction. The Bible tells us that God is like the sun. He gives us direction and helps us see where we should go.

## God is my sun and shield.

The Bible also says that God is like a shield. During Bible times, soldiers sometimes carried a shield as big as a door. It was made from wood and covered in leather. The shield was big enough to protect a soldier's whole body. The soldier could hide behind the shield and find safety. The enemy's arrows would hit the shield and not the soldier. That's what God does for us. He protects us from Satan's attempts to hurt us, just like a shield would.

No matter what you're doing today or where you're going, God is your sun and shield. He helps you know where to go, and He protects you. When you know that, you can have courage every day! —T.M.

### FUN FACT

Sirius is the brightest star in the nighttime sky. But because it's so much farther away, it doesn't seem as bright as the sun. If Sirius and the sun were placed right beside each other, Sirius would look many times brighter than the sun.

### READ MORE

Read Isaiah 60:19–20. Who will be the source of light in heaven? What will happen to the sun?

# A God Who Sees

**In Bible times** many people had servants because there was so much work to do. Sarah and Abraham had a servant girl named Hagar.

> From heaven
> the LORD looks down
> and sees everyone.
>
> PSALM 33:13 NIRV

Sarah and Hagar weren't getting along very well, so one day Hagar ran away. She went into the desert and stopped to rest by a spring of water. Then an angel of the Lord came and spoke to her. The angel said, "Hagar, where have you come from and where are you going?"

"I'm running away from my owner, Sarah," Hagar replied.

The angel said to Hagar, "Go home to your owner and obey her. You are going to have a son. You will name him Ishmael because the Lord has heard your cries."

Hagar said to the angel, "You are a God who sees." Then she returned home.

## God always sees me.

Did you know that God can see everyone all over the world at the same time? It's hard for us to understand how that can be. But with God it's possible. That means He sees when you're happy and He sees when you're having a bad day. He sees when you have a problem and He sees when you have a need.

God also sees when you do the things that please Him. Your teacher might not see when you help a friend on the playground, but God sees. You parents might not see when you put the dishes away or pick up your games, but God sees. He sees everything all the time. He is a God who sees. —C.B.

## READ MORE

Read Genesis 21:14–21.
How did God care for Hagar and Ishmael in the desert?

**FUN FACT**

The well where Hagar met the angel was called Beer Lahai Roi. The name means "the well of the Living One who sees me."

# The Mind of God

Our Lord is great
and powerful.
There is no
limit to what
he knows.

PSALM 147:5 ERV

**Do you know** what the word omniscience means? It means to know everything. So when we say that God is omniscient, it means He knows everything there is to know. God knows everything that has ever happened, and He knows everything that is going to happen. He knows every person, and He knows everything about every person. There is nothing in the whole world that God doesn't know.

When the apostle Paul wrote to people at the church in Corinth, he told them that his own wisdom and knowledge came from God. It was only through the Holy Spirit that Paul was able to understand and teach things about God.

When we believe in Jesus, He fills us with His Holy Spirit. The Holy Spirit helps us to understand more about God and the Bible. As Christians, we will understand some spiritual things that confuse people who don't follow Jesus. But even with the Holy Spirit giving us wisdom and knowledge and understanding, we will never know everything God knows.

## God knows everything.

When Paul was teaching the Corinthians these things, he shared some words from the book of Isaiah: "Who has known the mind of the Lord and who has been able to teach Him?" Paul knew the Holy Spirit was helping him to learn and understand many things, but he would never know as much as God does. And Paul said he would never understand everything about God.

Some people are pretty smart. They know a lot of things about a lot of things. But no one knows as much as God does. That's why He sent the Holy Spirit to teach us. When we listen to Him, we'll know just what God wants us to know. —C.B.

### FUN FACT

The IQ test measures a person's intelligence compared to everyone else. An average score is 100. IQ stands for "intelligence quotient."

### READ MORE

Read Psalm 139:1–6.
What do these verses tell us about God's knowledge?

# What Will People Think?

**When Peter came to the city** of Antioch, Paul was disappointed because Peter did something that wasn't right.

God had told Jesus' followers that His salvation was for all people, not just the Jews. At first it was hard for some of the disciples to accept this idea. It was different from what they had been taught before. But they obeyed God and began teaching non-Jewish people about Jesus too. Jesus' followers invited the non-Jewish people into God's family.

During the first part of Peter's stay in Antioch, he spent time with the non-Jewish people. He ate meals with them, even though Jewish leaders had taught that this was wrong. But Peter knew it was okay because of what God had told him.

But later when some Jewish people came to Antioch, Peter stopped spending time with the non-Jewish people. He wouldn't eat with them because he was afraid of what the Jewish people would think. These Jews had not believed God's new promise or accepted Jesus as the Messiah. When Paul saw how Peter was acting, he spoke up in front of everyone. Paul let Peter know that what he was doing was wrong.

> When Peter first came to Antioch, he ate and associated with the non-Jewish people. But when some Jewish men came from James, Peter separated himself from the non-Jews.
>
> GALATIANS 2:12 ERV

## I will please God instead of people.

Peter made a mistake that is easy to make. He was worried about what other people thought about him. Peter wanted to please people instead of God.

It can be hard to do the right thing when other people disagree or make fun of you. But just like Paul was watching Peter, other people are watching us. The choices we make will let others know who we want to please the most.

You can be a good example and choose to obey God, no matter what others think or say. When people see you doing the right thing, they will know who is most important in your life. —T.M.

### FUN FACT

In Bible times, there were about sixteen places named "Antioch." Two of them are mentioned in Scripture, including the place where followers of Jesus were first called "Christians."

### READ MORE

Read Galatians 1:10.
Who was Paul trying to please?

# God's Song

**Celebrating birthdays** is fun! When it's your birthday, people find special ways to honor you. They might give you a present wrapped in shiny paper. They might make you a cake and decorate it with yummy frosting. They might give you a card that tells you the things they like about you. Someone might even sing "Happy Birthday to You"!

It's fun to have people sing to you. It makes you feel loved and special. It's a way for others to show you how much they care about you.

Did you know the Bible says God will sing over His people? It won't be for birthdays, but it is a special way He shows His love. A prophet named Zephaniah told the people of Israel that God would have so much joy over them that He would sing happy songs.

## God promises to sing over His people with joy.

When Jesus comes back and the world is made right, God will live with us and we will live with Him. His presence will be so perfect and wonderful that He will calm us with His love. We won't be afraid anymore. We will live in perfect peace. And as we delight in this peace, we will hear God's beautiful song of love for His people.

We can look forward to the day when we will live in a perfect world with God. Until then we can have joy in the many promises of His love and care. The music will be sweet to our ears! —T.M.

## FUN FACT

The tune of "Happy Birthday to You" was written around 1893, and the words were printed with the music by 1912. According to the *Guinness Book of World Records*, it is the most recognized song in the English language.

## READ MORE

Read Isaiah 62:3–5.
How does Isaiah describe the way God delights in His people?

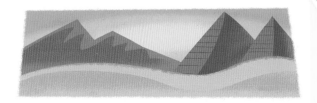

> Faith is being
> sure of what we
> hope for. It is being
> certain of what
> we do not see.
> HEBREWS 11:1 NIRV

# Joseph's Final Words

**Joseph was the eleventh son** of Jacob. As his father's favorite, he was hated by his brothers. They sold him as a slave, but God made Joseph a great ruler in Egypt.

Joseph's father and brothers came to Egypt during a famine in their homeland of Canaan. Joseph helped them with food and brought them to the king of Egypt. Pharaoh invited Joseph's whole family to live in Egypt. So they made their home in a place called Goshen.

Joseph continued to live in Egypt too. He knew he would die there, but he believed that someday God would lead his family back to the promised land of Canaan. He called his brothers together.

"I am about to die, but God will take care of you," Joseph said. "He will lead you out of this land. He will lead you to the land of Abraham, Isaac, and Jacob." Then Joseph asked the men in his family to make a promise. "Promise me you will carry my bones with you out of Egypt," he said.

## I have faith in God.

When he was 110 years old, Joseph died. God had used him to save his whole family, even though his brothers had treated him badly. God had used Joseph to explain dreams that no one else could understand. God had used Joseph to provide food for the entire land of Egypt during a famine. God had used Joseph because Joseph always trusted God.

Joseph didn't know when or how the Israelites would finally leave Egypt, but he knew it would happen. Joseph had faith in God's promise.

Having faith means we believe God is real. It means we believe in His promises, just like Joseph did. It means we believe God will do what He says He will do. —C.B.

## READ MORE
**Read Exodus 13:19.**
**Who kept the promise made to Joseph?**

## FUN FACT
The Israelites left Egypt 144 years after Joseph died.

# Rich and Poor

God chose the poor in the world to be rich with faith. He chose them to receive the kingdom God promised to people who love him.

JAMES 2:5 ICB

**When Jesus lived** on earth, He showed love to everyone. It didn't matter if someone was old or young, or rich or poor. If people wanted to follow Him, or if they showed faith in Him for healing, Jesus accepted them. He never looked at the way a person was dressed. He didn't care how much money a person had. Jesus never thought that some people were more important than others. He loved everyone the same.

One day when Jesus was teaching, He spoke some words from the book of Isaiah. "The Spirit of the Lord is in me," Jesus said. "This is because God chose me to tell the good news to the poor. God sent me to tell the prisoners of sin that they are free, and to tell the blind that they can see. God sent me to free those who have been treated unfairly, and to announce the time when the Lord will show kindness to all people."

## We are all the same in Jesus.

God wants us to treat others the way Jesus did. We should not treat anyone in a special way just because she's wearing nice clothes. And we should never ignore someone just because he might be poor.

God loves everyone the same. Anyone who follows Jesus and becomes part of God's family receives all of God's riches. God's riches are far better than the world's. And God's riches last forever! —C.B.

## FUN FACT

Jesus quoted the words of Isaiah 61:1–2. Isaiah wrote those words about Jesus seven hundred years earlier!

## READ MORE

Read James 2:1–5.
Why should we be careful in the way we treat others?

> Asa did what was right in the eyes of the LORD. That's what King David had done.
>
> 1 KINGS 15:11 NIRV

# King Asa

**Asa was the** great-great-grandson of King David. David was a great man, but Asa's father and grandfather were not good men. They did evil things and disobeyed God. They didn't lead the people the way God commanded. They were not righteous like King David was. But God let them rule over the kingdom of Judah because of the promise He had made to David.

When Asa became king, he had a choice to make. He could disobey God and do the evil things his father and grandfather had done, or he could follow God. If he followed God, Asa could change the kingdom and make things better.

Asa decided to do what was right. He chose to be the kind of king that David had been. He followed God, and he got rid of all of the idols his father and grandfather had made. He threw out the men of Judah who had been doing evil things. Asa even took

## I can choose to be a person who obeys God.

away his grandmother's job as "queen mother" because she had been worshipping false gods! Asa brought expensive gifts to God's temple as an offering. He committed his whole life to God.

King Asa didn't let the sins of his family keep him from obeying God. He made his own choice to obey God and be a good king. There might be people near you, even in your own family, who do not obey God. It can be hard to do things differently than they do, but you can choose to obey God like Asa did. It doesn't matter what kind of family you come from. You can always decide to do the right thing. —T.M.

### FUN FACT

A "change agent" is a person who brings change. Most people use the phrase to describe a person who works in business. But it can describe someone who changes a family too.

### READ MORE

Read 1 Kings 22:41–43.
Who was Asa's son? What kind of king was he?

# For Kids Too!

> Open my eyes
> so that I can see the
> wonderful truths
> in your law.
>
> PSALM 119:18 NIRV

**Kids are not** allowed to drive a car until they reach a certain age. Most kids can't go to college until they are older. Teenagers and adults get to do things that younger kids are not ready to do. But no matter how old you are, God has given you the Bible. And you can learn from it!

God's Word is for kids as well as adults. God wants you to read the Bible to learn more about Him. Some of the verses and stories might be hard to understand, but you can ask God for help—and He will make them clear as you learn more and more about the Bible. But there are many verses in the Bible that kids can read and learn right now. Here are just a few:

In the beginning God created the heavens and the earth (Genesis 1:1 NLT).

O LORD of Heaven's Armies, what joy for those who trust in you (Psalm 84:12 NLT).

"Let the children come to me. Don't stop them! For the Kingdom of God belongs to those who are like these children" (Luke 18:16 NLT).

Children, obey your parents because you belong to the Lord, for this is the right thing to do (Ephesians 6:1 NLT).

Let us continue to love one another, for love comes from God (1 John 4:7 NLT).

See? These verses are not hard to understand. And there are many more verses in the Bible that you can read and learn. So just keep reading God's Word every day. He will help you understand many wonderful things! —C.B.

## I can ask God to help me understand the Bible.

### FUN FACT

Psalm 119 is the longest chapter in the Bible. It has 176 verses!

### READ MORE

Read Psalm 117—the shortest psalm in the Bible. What do you think these verses mean?

> "Everyone who lifts himself up will be brought down. And anyone who is brought down will be lifted up."
>
> LUKE 18:14 NIRV

# Two Prayers

**Jesus told a story** to teach people how to please God. The story was about a Pharisee—a proud religious person—and a tax collector. Most people hated tax collectors.

"One day a Pharisee and a tax collector went to the temple to pray," Jesus said. "The Pharisee stood away from the tax collector and prayed out loud. He said, 'God, I thank you that I am not as bad as other people. I am not like men who steal or cheat or do evil things. I thank you that I am better than this tax collector. Two times a week I skip eating to pray, and I give one-tenth of everything I earn.'

"The tax collector stood alone too. But when he prayed he would not even look up to heaven. He prayed with sadness and said, 'Oh God, show kindness to me. I am a sinner.'"

## God is pleased when I'm humble.

Then Jesus explained His story. "The tax collector's prayer made him right before God. But the proud Pharisee, who thought he was so good, was not right with God. People who are proud and think they're important will be humbled. But those who are humble—like the tax collector—will be made great."

There are always people who think they're better than others. Many people think they are doing everything right. They think they're very good people. But God wants everyone to be humble. He wants us to realize that no one is perfect and that we all need His forgiveness.

God's kindness is great, and He will make humble people great. —C.B.

## READ MORE

Read Psalm 25:4–9.
Who shows humble people how to do what is right?

# Never Forget

But the Lord says, "Can a woman forget her baby? Can she forget the child who came from her body? Even if she can forget her children, I cannot forget you. I drew a picture of you on my hand. You are always before my eyes."

ISAIAH 49:15–16 ERV

**It's easy to forget** some things, like where you put your shoes or when your school project is due. It's hard to remember phone numbers or your grandmother's birthday. Sometimes people make lists to help them remember the things they know they'll forget!

But some things are easy to remember, like your eye color and your favorite food. You don't have to write a note to remember your own name or your family members. You don't wake up one day and forget who you live with or the people who take care of you. And your parents can't forget you either.

## God will never forget me.

That's what God had in mind when He told the prophet Isaiah about the love He has for His people. It seems impossible for a mother to forget her child. Because mothers love their children so much, they can't stop thinking about them. But God's love is so much greater. He says that even if a mother could forget her child, He could never forget us. God loves you so much, it's like He's drawn a picture of you on His hand! He can't forget you because you are a part of Him. He sees you all the time and He loves you more than you can understand.

When we become a part of God's family, He promises never to leave us. Even if others forget about you, God never will. —T.M.

**FUN FACT**

One way to really remember something is to write it over and over. The more you write something down, the better it stays in your brain.

## READ MORE

Read Jeremiah 31:33–34.
What does God write on our hearts?

# The Sheep Gate

**Sheep are not** very smart. They spend most of their days just eating grass. They don't even look up very often to see where they're going. When they wander around, they can get lost. And they don't know how to find their way back to the flock.

> So Jesus said again, "What I'm about to tell you is true. I am like a gate for the sheep."
>
> JOHN 10:7 NIRV

Since sheep need so much help, shepherds have to pay close attention to their flocks. During Bible times shepherds had to protect their sheep, guide their sheep, and always make sure their sheep weren't getting into trouble.

When a shepherd gathered his sheep at night, he would put them into a pen to keep them safe. Sometimes he would build a pen out of rocks by stacking them on top of each other. The shepherd would leave an opening in the rocks to let the sheep walk in or out. Then he would lie down in front of the opening. The shepherd acted like a gate. He made sure the sheep didn't get out and that wild animals didn't get in.

Jesus told His followers that He was like a gate for sheep. He is the only way that people can get to God. Just like a shepherd lets sheep into the pen, Jesus lets us into God's family when we believe in Him.

When we become part of God's family, Jesus cares for us like a shepherd taking care of his sheep. We don't have to worry about getting lost or falling into trouble. Jesus will guide and protect us like a shepherd watching over his sheep. —T.M.

## Jesus is the gate to God's family.

### READ MORE

Read Ephesians 2:18–19.
How can we come to God?
When we do, what do we become?

### FUN FACT

In Bible times, some sheep pens were big enough to hold several flocks at night. In the morning the shepherds would call out to their sheep. The sheep knew the voice of their own shepherd.

# Wild Animals

> People can tame every kind of wild animal, bird, reptile, and fish, and they have tamed them. But no one can tame the tongue.
>
> JAMES 3:7–8 ICB

**Most of the wild animals** in a zoo are kept in large cages. People shouldn't go into the cages because the animals are dangerous. Wild animals can attack and really hurt someone who comes too close.

But most animals can be tamed. People have tamed tigers, bears, and even lions. When an animal is tame, it's not afraid to be around people. A tame animal does not attack people because it knows its own life is not in danger.

The Bible's book of James talks about taming wild animals. It says that every kind of animal can be tamed—but no one can tame a person's tongue. Our tongues are like wild animals because the words we say can attack and hurt other people. When we call a person a bad name or tell a lie about someone, it can cause great harm. When our words are cruel instead of kind, people get hurt.

## My tongue can say kind words to others.

It's important to tame our tongues. When we have God's Holy Spirit in us, we can ask Him to help us control what we say. We can pray for the Holy Spirit to fill us with love so that our words will be kind and gentle. When we have control over our tongues, we can praise God and say good things about others. We can use polite words like "please" and "thank you," and we can respect others in the way we talk.

Don't let your tongue be like a wild animal. Let God help you tame it. —C.B.

## FUN FACT

Your tongue is a group of muscles. These muscles push and pull in different directions to help you talk, eat, and swallow.

## READ MORE

Read James 3:3–5.
What does James compare a person's tongue to?

# Food from an Angel

**Queen Jezebel** was angry when she heard that Elijah had defeated the prophets of Baal. She sent Elijah a warning. "May the gods strike me and even kill me," Jezebel said, "if by this time tomorrow I have not killed you just as you killed them."

The message scared Elijah and he ran away. He traveled to a town called Beersheba and went into the desert alone. Elijah was tired and afraid. He sat under a tree and prayed. "I've had enough, Lord," Elijah said. "Take my life, for I am no better than anyone who has already died."

Elijah lay down and went to sleep. But he woke up when an angel touched him! "Get up and eat!" the angel said. So Elijah sat up and found a hot loaf of bread and a jug of water. He ate and drank and went back to sleep.

The angel came back to Elijah and said, "Get up and eat some more, or the journey ahead will be too much for you." Elijah ate and drank some more. Then he traveled forty days to Mount Sinai where God told him what to do next. So Elijah continued his work as a prophet.

> Elijah was afraid and fled for his life. He went to Beersheba, a town in Judah, and he left his servant there. Then he went on alone into the wilderness, traveling all day. He sat down under a solitary broom tree and prayed that he might die.
>
> **1 KINGS 19:3–4 NLT**

## God is always with me and will help me.

Elijah faced a hard challenge. Even after a big victory against the prophets of Baal, he was afraid. And because of his fear, he ran away. But God took care of Elijah and helped him finish his work.

Sometimes you might go through a hard time right after a good time. Life always has ups and downs, but God is with you every day. You don't have to be afraid. God will help you no matter what. —T.M.

## **READ MORE**

Read James 1:2–4.
What is a good thing that can come out of hard times?

### FUN FACT

The tree Elijah slept under was called a broom tree. It's a desert shrub with lots of twigs. In the wet season it will have small leaves and flowers.

# Rock of Safety

From a place far away I call out to you. I call out as my heart gets weaker. Lead me to the safety of a rock that is high above me.

PSALM 61:2 NIRV

**Imagine a sailor** alone at night on a stormy sea. As the wind howls and the waves crash against his boat, he is scared. The waves grow larger until they splash over the side of his boat. The boat starts to lean into the waves. Suddenly a big wave slams into the boat and tips it over!

The sailor is knocked deep into the water and swims with all his strength to get back to the surface. When he comes up, he gasps for air. He looks around for something to hold onto as waves crash over his head. Then he sees a huge rock poking out of the water. He knows if he can get on top of that rock, he will be safe above the storm.

The story of this sailor is like a psalm King David wrote. During a hard time, David cried out to God. Like a sailor alone in the middle of the sea, David felt alone. His heart was getting weaker. He said to God, "Lead me to the safety of a rock that is high above me." David saw God like a rock that is above the dangerous sea water. He knew he would be safe in God's presence. God was high above the struggle David faced.

## God is my rock of safety.

God is our rock of safety too. He is strong in the middle of all the hard things we go through. He might not take away our problems, but we can stand on Him like a rock above a storm. We can get through our hard times with God. —T.M.

### FUN FACT

There is a famous, high rock called "El Arco" in Cabo San Lucas, Mexico. It is an arched rock formation in the Pacific Ocean.

### READ MORE

Read Psalm 18:1–3.
What are some other things David says about God?

> "You see the things that are happening now. But you don't know their meaning."
>
> MATTHEW 16:3 ICB

# Show Us a Sign

**We don't always** need a weather report to know what the weather will be like. Sometimes you can just look at the sky and know that it's going to rain. Long ago, farmers, fishermen, and shepherds learned the signs of the weather. A red sky in the morning usually means the weather is going to be bad. But if the sky is red at night, good weather is coming.

One day some Jewish leaders asked Jesus to show them a sign. They said they wanted Him to do a miracle to prove that He had come from God. But Jesus knew what was in their hearts. They were really trying to trick Him and make Him look bad. They had already seen Jesus do many miracles that showed He was the Son of God. But they still didn't believe in Him.

## The Bible says Jesus is the Son of God.

So Jesus said to them, "You see the signs in the sky and you know what they mean. In the same way, you see the things that are happening now. These are signs, but you don't know what they mean." Then Jesus left them and went away.

There are many people today who don't believe that Jesus is the Son of God. Some are waiting for proof. Some just don't understand. But God has given us the Bible. Everything we need to know about Jesus has been written down for us. We have plenty of proof and plenty of signs. All we need to do is believe!

—C.B.

**FUN FACT**

People have created a little rhyme that is usually true in parts of the world where winds blow west to east: "Red sky in morning, sailors take warning. Red sky at night, sailors' delight."

**READ MORE**

Read John 10:36–38.
What did Jesus say His miracles proved?

> "I led them with kindness and love. I did not lead them with ropes. I lifted the heavy loads from their shoulders. I bent down and fed them."
>
> **HOSEA 11:4 NIRV**

# Kindness and Love

**Oxen were some** of the most valuable animals in ancient Israel. Since they were strong and obedient, people used them for heavy jobs. Farmers used oxen to plow fields at planting time. Oxen were also used to pull wooden carts carrying people or things.

When two oxen worked together, they had even more power. At those times, the master placed a yoke around the oxen's necks. The yoke was a heavy wooden beam. It had a slot for each ox to put its head through. When the yoke was locked in place, it kept the oxen together so they moved in the same direction. The oxen's masters trained their animals very carefully to do what was needed. The masters would poke the oxen with sticks and use ropes to lead them and make sure they went where they needed to go.

## God is gentle and kind.

As God spoke to the prophet Hosea, He said He didn't treat the Israelites like a master treated oxen. God didn't give His people heavy loads, like a yoke on the shoulders of an ox. Instead, God helped His people and carried their problems for them. God wasn't harsh with His people like a farmer pulling on oxen's ropes. Instead, God was gentle and kind, like a tender owner bending down to feed his animals.

God is kind and gentle with us too. Even though He is our master, He treats us with love. We can always trust God and thank Him for His kindness. —T.M.

## FUN FACT

Horses, donkeys, mules, and water buffalo can also be yoked together to do jobs. And even though they don't wear yokes, dogs can be teamed together to pull sleds through the snow.

## READ MORE

Read Nehemiah 9:16–17. How did God treat the Israelites when they disobeyed Him?

# Staying Pure

**When Joseph worked** in Potiphar's house, he faced a tough situation. Potiphar's wife kept pushing Joseph to do something that wasn't right. Joseph didn't want to sin. He wanted to obey God. One day when Potiphar's wife wouldn't stop bothering him, Joseph just ran out of the house!

> How can a young person stay pure? By obeying your word.
>
> PSALM 119:9 NLT

Potiphar's wife was so mad that she made up a lie about Joseph. Because of her lie, Joseph went to prison for several years. But he kept trusting God and obeying Him. God had great plans for Joseph. After a while, Joseph was out of jail and ruling over the whole land of Egypt!

More than anything else, Joseph wanted to honor God. Since he wanted to please God, he lived a pure life. We can follow Joseph's example.

## I can live a pure life by obeying God's Word.

When we read and learn the Bible, it helps us make the right decisions when we are tempted to sin. At times your friends may want you to do something wrong, but having God's Word in your heart will remind you to say no. Even when it's hard, you can always ask for God's help.

Joseph is a Bible hero because he did the right thing. Do you want to live a pure life like Joseph did? Then you can read your Bible, learn what it says, and ask God to help you obey it. You can even memorize special verses to help you when you're tempted.

When you live a pure life, you follow the best path God has for you. —T.M.

## READ MORE

Read Psalm 37:30–31.
What do these verses say about righteous people?

### FUN FACT

The name *Potiphar* has a similar meaning as the name *Theodore*. Potiphar means "he whom Ra (the Egyptian sun god) gave." Theodore means "gift of God."

# A Good Name

> You should want a good name more than you want great riches. To be highly respected is better than having silver or gold.
>
> PROVERBS 22:1 NIRV

**Many people** want to have good things in life. They want a family and friends. They want to have a good job and a nice place to live. Those are good things to hope for.

Some people want to be rich or important just to please themselves. But do you know what's better than having a lot of money or being important? The Bible says having a good name is better. Do you know what it means to have a good name? It means you are honest and that people respect you. It means you can be trusted. When people hear your name they say, "That's a good person." Another way to say "good name" is "good reputation."

When you are kind to others at school, it helps you to have a good name. When you listen to your teachers and your parents, it helps you to have a good name. When you live the way God wants you to live, it helps you to have a good name too.

Some of the people in the Bible had good names. What do you think of when you hear the names of Noah, Abraham, and Moses? They were good men who obeyed God and helped other people. How about Mary the mother of Jesus, John the disciple, and Paul the great missionary? Those are good names too. Because they loved Jesus and served Him, they have a good reputation.

## Having a good name is important.

You can follow Jesus just like any of these people in the Bible did. You can help others too. If you do these things, you will have a good name. And that's better than silver or gold! —C.B.

### FUN FACT

Some of the Bible's "good names" are still popular today— names like Aaron, David, Hannah, Jacob, Noah, Rebekah, and Sarah.

### READ MORE

Read Philippians 2:6–10.
Why is Jesus' name greater than any other name?

# The Faith Hall of Fame

**If you're a sports fan** you've probably heard about the "hall of fame." In the United States, almost every sport has its own hall of fame. Other nations have halls of fame too, and they're not only for athletes. There are halls of fame for musicians, inventors, magicians, and cowboys!

Do you know what a hall of fame is? It's a place that honors people who did great things in their careers. A group of judges decides who gets to be in the hall of fame. Pictures or statues of important people are put into a special building, and they are honored for the rest of their lives—and even after they die.

> All these people were known for their faith, but none of them received what God had promised. God planned to give us something very special so that we would gain eternal life with them.
>
> HEBREWS 11:39-40 GW

Did you know there's a part of the book of Hebrews we call the Faith Hall of Fame? It doesn't honor athletes or musicians, but people who were heroes for believing in God. This part of the Bible talks about people like Noah and Abraham, who followed God by faith even when it didn't make sense. Other people honored include Isaac, Jacob,

## I can have faith through Jesus.

Joseph, Moses, Rahab, Gideon, David, and Samuel. They all did great things because they trusted God. Through their faith, God used each one for His plan and purpose.

All of these heroes lived before Jesus came to earth, so they didn't have His example to follow. But since we know Jesus and have the Holy Spirit to help us, we have even greater reasons to live by faith.

Jesus brings people with true faith together. We can follow the example of the faith heroes. And through Jesus, we too can someday shine in heaven's hall of fame. —T.M.

### FUN FACT

One of the first halls of fame in the world is called the Walhalla. It is located near Regensburg, Germany, and honors German scientists, artists, and politicians. The Walhalla was built from 1830 to 1842.

### READ MORE

Read Hebrews 11. How many of the names in the Faith Hall of Fame do you recognize?

Give thanks to the
Lord because he
is good. His love
continues forever.

**PSALM 136:1 ICB**

# God's Love Is Forever

**The people of Israel** were God's special people. He loved them no matter what. But sometimes they did not love or obey God. They would sin against Him over and over again. They would grumble and complain. They even prayed to other gods that weren't real.

Sometimes bad things would happen to the Israelites because of their sins. Then God would send leaders or prophets or judges to tell them to turn back to God. Over and over again, the people would tell God they were sorry for their sins and turn back to Him. Over and over again God would forgive them. God's mercy and forgiveness have no end because His love has no end!

If you love Jesus, you are God's special person too. It's important to do what is right. It's important to show God that you love Him by obeying His commands. When you do, it pleases God very much.

## I know God will love me forever.

But there may be times when you do something that does not please God. When that happens, you don't have to be afraid that God will punish you. Just tell God you are sorry and He will forgive you. Then ask Him to help you do what is right.

God sees what is in your heart. If you truly love Him, He knows. God's love and mercy and forgiveness are for you just like they were for the Israelites. God will never stop loving you, no matter what. His love continues forever and ever! —C.B.

### FUN FACT

In Psalm 136, the phrase, "His love continues forever" is repeated twenty-six times. In some versions of the Bible it says, "His love endures forever" or "His mercy endures forever."

### READ MORE

Read Psalm 135:13.
Besides God's love, what else will last forever?

# Jesus' Family

**Jesus' mother** was named Mary. His earthly father was Joseph. Jesus also had brothers and sisters in the town of Nazareth.

Many people knew Jesus' family and where they were from. One day when Jesus was meeting with His disciples, His mother and brothers came to see Him. They waited outside the house and sent someone in to ask Jesus to come out. People said to Jesus, "Your mother and brothers are waiting for you outside."

"Who is my mother?" Jesus asked. "Who are my brothers?" Then He looked around the room at all the people with Him. "Here are my mother and my brothers," Jesus said. "Anyone who does what God wants is my true brother and sister and mother."

> "My true brother and sister and mother are those who do the things God wants."
>
> MARK 3:35 ICB

### I can be in Jesus' family.

Jesus was saying that there are two kinds of families. We all have the family we live with—with a mom or dad and maybe a brother or sister or grandparents. But we can also belong to the family of God. When we believe in Jesus as our Savior, we become part of God's family. We're a part of all the believers called the body of Christ.

It doesn't matter what family you were born into or what family you live with. You can be part of Jesus' family! He wants you in His family.

Jesus wants to be your Savior, but He also wants to be your brother. And Jesus is the best brother anyone could ever have! —C.B.

### 𝐑EAD MORE

Read John 1:10–13. What do these verses say about being God's children?

### 𝐅UN 𝐅RCT

Jesus had four brothers. Their names were James, Joseph, Simon, and Judas. He also had sisters but the Bible doesn't tell us their names.

> "You will celebrate this festival to the LORD for seven days each year. This law will continue forever."
>
> LEVITICUS 23:41 ERV

# A Family Tradition

**Family traditions** are special. Many family traditions take place during holidays. Some families sing carols on Christmas Day. Other families eat grapes and make wishes on New Year's Eve. Traditions can be passed down from your grandparents to your parents to you. And then maybe you'll pass them down to your own kids someday!

Did you know the Israelites in the Bible had a family tradition that they passed down? God told the Israelites to celebrate a holiday every year called the Feast of the Shelters. The feast lasted a whole week. God gave His people special instructions for those seven days. The first day was a day of rest and the people were not allowed to work. God also told the people to bring sacrifices and food offerings to Him during the week. But the most interesting thing about the festival is that God told the Israelites to build shelters to live in during the week.

God told the people to stay and eat in their shelters, which were kind of like tents. God wanted to remind the Israelites of how their families lived when they left Egypt.

## Remember God's goodness.

It was a way for the people to remember the hard times their families had gone through and all that God did to save them.

God wanted the Israelites to remember this so they would keep worshipping Him. It's easy to forget all the good things God did in the past if we don't make a way to remember them. Maybe you can find a special way to remember the good things God does for your family too. You don't have to live in a shelter, but you can make your own family tradition! —T.M.

### FUN FACT
Jewish people still celebrate the Feast of Shelters every year. It takes place during September or October.

### READ MORE
Read Deuteronomy 31:10–13. Why did Moses tell the people to read God's law during the feast?

"Then join the two sticks together. In your hand, they will be one stick."

EZEKIEL 37:17 ERV

# One Kingdom

**Ezekiel was a prophet** to the people of Judah who had been taken away from their homes to Babylon. The people of Israel had already been captured by the Assyrians. The two kingdoms had been divided ever since Solomon's son Rehoboam had become the king. The tribes of Benjamin and Judah stayed with Rehoboam and called their country Judah, while the other ten tribes had become the House of Israel under King Jeroboam.

God told Ezekiel to get two sticks and write a message on each one. On the first stick Ezekiel wrote, "This stick belongs to Judah and his people." On the second stick he wrote: "This stick belongs to Ephraim, the son of Joseph, and the people of Israel."

God told Ezekiel, "Hold the two sticks together in your hand. They will look like they are one stick. When the people ask you what it means, tell them that I will take the stick of Ephraim and put it with the stick of Judah, and in my hand they will become one stick. Tell them that I will gather the people together and make them one nation.

## Jesus will be the king of all nations.

They will no longer be two kingdoms. One king will rule over them. They will no longer worship false gods. I will be their God and they will be my people."

The message God gave to Ezekiel was especially for Israel and Judah. But one day, by God's power, all the nations of the world will come together as one kingdom. The king will be Jesus, the Son of God! The people of Jesus' kingdom will be all the people who believe in Him. When you believe in Jesus, you can be in that kingdom too! —C.B.

## READ MORE

Read Ezekiel 37:27–28.
What promise did God give to His people?

## FUN FACT

God spoke these words to Ezekiel almost six hundred years before Jesus was born.

# Come Close to God

> Come close to God, and he will come close to you.
>
> JAMES 4:8 GW

**Do you have a friend** or relative who lives far away? There are many ways to stay connected with a person you love.

Even though that special person may be in a different city or even a different country, you can still feel close to each other. You can send letters to each other through the mail or pictures by e-mail. You can talk over the phone to hear each other's voices. Maybe you can video chat so you can see each other while you talk. And when you pray for each other, you will feel close too.

*I can come close to God because He is close to me.*

Did you know you can also feel close to God? Even though you can't really see Him, He is always close to you. The more you spend time with Him, the closer you will feel to Him. You can read the Bible to know God's thoughts. You can sing songs or listen to music to praise Him. You can look at the things God created to enjoy His power and His beauty. And when you talk to Him in prayer, you can know that He listens to every word you say.

God is always close to you. When you spend time with Him and think about Him, you will feel close to Him too. God wants you to come close to Him because He loves you. —C.B.

## FUN FACT

Before telephones were invented, some people would hire a messenger on horseback to deliver a message to someone who lived far away.

## READ MORE

Read Psalm 145:16–19.
What do these verses tell us about God?

# No Hiding

**Kids like to play** the game hide-and-seek. It's fun to hide. And it's fun to seek! Kids can hide in some places where it's very hard to be found. But no one can hide from God.

Adam and Eve tried to hide from God. But that is impossible. God is everywhere and He sees everything. Do you remember when God told Adam and Eve that they could eat from any tree in the Garden of Eden except one? They had more delicious food than they needed, but they chose to disobey God. Adam and Eve both knew they had sinned when they ate the fruit God told them not to eat.

> Nothing in all the world can be hidden from God. He can clearly see all things. Everything is open before him. And to him we must explain the way we have lived.
>
> **HEBREWS 4:13 ERV**

Later in the day Adam and Eve heard God in the garden. They got behind some trees and tried to hide from God. God knew where Adam and Eve were, but He called out to them, "Where are you?"

Adam said, "I heard you walking in the garden. I was afraid because I was naked, so I hid." But Adam had not fooled God.

Sometimes people seem to get away with the bad things they do. Some people steal from stores. Some kids cheat on tests. Some people lie to keep from getting in trouble. People might do these things without getting caught by other people. But God sees and knows everything.

## God sees everything I do.

Knowing that God is watching can help us be honest and do what's right. And when we do the right thing, we know that God sees that too. God is everywhere. We can't hide from Him. And that should make us feel safe and happy. He is always with us wherever we are. —C.B.

## **READ MORE**
Read Psalm 139:7–12.
What do these verses tell us about where God is?

# Write It Down

Do not let kindness and truth leave you; bind them around your neck, write them on the tablet of your heart.

**PROVERBS 3:3 NASB**

**Have you ever** used a sticky note? They are fun to peel and stick, and they're very useful!

Sometimes you need to write something down so you don't forget it. With a sticky note, you can write down a reminder and stick it to your notebook, or the refrigerator, or even your bathroom mirror. Writing a note can help you to remember something important.

In the Bible, the book of Proverbs tells us something important we should remember. We should always be kind and tell the truth in everything we do. And today's Bible verse says we can "write" that down in our minds. Think of your mind like it's a pad of paper. When you make a special note in your mind, it will help you to remember to be kind and truthful at home, at school, or anywhere you go.

Remember to be kind and truthful.

*I will try to be kind and truthful in everything I do.*

It's so important to be kind. God wants us to treat others the way we want to be treated. When we are kind to others, it makes them happy and it pleases God. And it's important to tell the truth. When we are honest, people will trust us. It's important to be a person who is truthful because God is always truthful.

Can you remember to be kind and truthful? If you think you might forget, you can write it on a sticky note!
—C.B.

## FUN FACT

Post-it notes, also called sticky notes, happened almost by accident. In 1968, a scientist in the United States was trying to develop a super-strong glue. Instead he created a sticky substance that could be reused. Later, someone put it on paper to create the Post-it note.

## READ MORE

Read Proverbs 3:3–4.
What will happen if you remember to be kind and truthful?

# The First Bundle

"Speak to the people of Israel. Tell them, 'When you enter the land I am going to give you, bring an offering to me. Gather your crops. Bring the first bundle of grain to the priest.'"

**LEVITICUS 23:10 NIRV**

**God told the Israelites** to celebrate important festivals and holidays. One of these special festivals came when the people harvested their crops.

When the people were gathering their crops, God wanted them to bring the first bundle of grain to the priest. The priest would take the grain and wave it in front of God as an offering. On the same day, the people made other sacrifices and offerings to worship God. God told the Israelites not to eat bread made from the new grain until they had offered the first part of the harvest to Him.

By giving God the first of their crops, the people were reminded that their food came from Him. By giving God the first of everything, the people were thanking God for His care for them. And by offering their grain to God before they used any for themselves, the people were giving Him the best of what they had. It was a way of telling God how very important He is.

## God provides for me.

God still wants us to thank Him for what He provides for us. It's important for us to remember just where our food comes from. You might not gather crops from a field, but you can worship God like the Israelites did. Before you eat a meal, you can thank God for giving you food. If you get an allowance, you can give the first part of it to your church. Whenever you enjoy something good, you can worship God by thanking Him. —T.M.

## READ MORE

Read Leviticus 23:12–13.
What else did God ask the people to offer Him?

## FUN FACT

A bundle of wheat is called a sheaf. Two or more are called sheaves. The original Hebrew word was *omer*.

> May those who love the LORD be like the sun when it rises in all its brightness.
>
> JUDGES 5:31 GW

# Rise and Shine

**Have you ever seen** a sunrise? If you have, then you know how beautiful it is.

After a night of darkness, it's nice to see the sun come up in the morning. The sun gives us hope and joy for a new day. It gives us light so we can see. It sends warmth to the earth. On a clear day, we enjoy the sun for many hours. It is bright and glowing. Sometimes it's so bright that you have to wear sunglasses!

God is the One who created light. Then He put two bright lights in the sky to separate the day from the night. God made the sun and the moon to give light to the earth. The moon is a smaller light, and it reflects the sun's light during the nighttime. The brightest light is the sun, which God made to rule the day.

The Bible says that people who love the Lord are like the morning sun. People who know and love Jesus can bring joy and hope to their friends and family. Their love and kindness can make others feel happy and warm inside. They can comfort people who are sad. They can give bright and cheery smiles that will make others smile too.

## I can shine like the sun.

If you love Jesus, you can shine like the morning sun. You can let His light shine so brightly through you that people nearby might need to wear sunglasses! —C.B.

### FUN FACT

In 1929, Sam Foster began selling inexpensive sunglasses in Atlantic City, New Jersey. Sunglasses became very popular in the United States through the 1930s.

### READ MORE

Read Psalm 59:16–17.
What is something we can do in the morning?

# A Promise Comes True

**God gave Abraham** a special promise. Even before Abraham had a son, God told Abraham that he would be the father of a great nation. God said that Abraham's grandkids and great-grandkids and great-great-grandkids would be too many to count. Abraham's family would grow and grow to be like the stars in the sky and the grains of sand on the seashore. God chose Abraham because he loved and obeyed God.

But God promised Abraham more than just a big family that would become a nation. When God said that all the nations of the earth would be blessed through Abraham, He was talking about Jesus. King David came from the family of Abraham, and Jesus came from the family of David!

Jesus' family history is shown in the first chapter of the book of Matthew. You can read the names of the fathers and sons from Abraham to Jesus. What God promised Abraham, way back in the book of Genesis, came true about two thousand years later when Jesus was born.

## God's promise to Abraham came true with Jesus.

Abraham was part of God's plan to save people from their sins. Jesus, the Savior of the world, came through Abraham's family. But you don't have to be from the family of Abraham or David to be saved. Anyone from any nation can be forgiven of sin when they believe in Jesus. That is how all nations of the earth are blessed through Abraham! —C.B.

## READ MORE

Read Matthew 1:1–16. How many names do you recognize in the family line of Jesus?

## FUN FACT

There are more than seven billion people in the world today. They live in almost two hundred nations.

# The Angel's Visit

**A young woman** named Mary lived in the town of Nazareth. She was engaged to marry a man named Joseph. He was related to King David.

One day an angel came to visit Mary in her home. "Greetings!" said the angel. "The Lord is with you. He has blessed you."

Mary didn't understand what the angel meant.

"Don't be afraid, Mary," the angel said. "God is pleased with you. You will become pregnant and have a baby boy. You will name him Jesus. He will be great. The people will call him the Son of the Most High God. The Lord will give Him the throne of David, and He will rule forever!"

"How can this be?" Mary asked. "I'm not married."

"The Holy Spirit will come upon you," the angel answered. "Your baby will be the Son of God. Nothing is impossible for God."

### I will let God use me for His purpose.

"I am the Lord's servant," said Mary. "Let these things happen to me as you say."

Hundreds of years before the angel talked to Mary, the prophet Isaiah said these things would happen. "The Lord himself will give you a sign," Isaiah wrote. "The virgin will be pregnant. She will have a son and she will name him Immanuel." Isaiah also wrote about this very special son: "He will rule as king on David's throne and over David's kingdom. He will rule it forever and ever."

Jesus' birth was part of God's plan to save the world from sin. Mary trusted God and let Him use her life in His good plan. When people love and obey God, He can use them for His special purpose.
—C.B.

**FUN FACT**

The name Jesus means "Jehovah [God] is salvation." Jesus was also called Immanuel because it means "God is with us."

## READ MORE
Read Genesis 49:10.
**From which tribe of Israel would the Messiah come?**

# Mary Visits Elizabeth

**After Mary learned** she was going to have a special baby, she went to visit her relative Elizabeth. Elizabeth was going to have a baby too. When Mary said hello, Elizabeth was filled with God's Holy Spirit. She was so happy that Mary had come to see her! In a loud voice, Elizabeth told Mary that she and her baby were blessed.

"When I heard your voice, the baby inside me jumped with joy," Elizabeth said. "Great blessings are yours because you believed what the Lord said to you! You believed this would happen!"

This made Mary so happy that she sang a song of praise to God. Mary stayed with Elizabeth for about three months and then went home.

> "God has blessed you more than any other woman. And God has blessed the baby you will have. You are the mother of my Lord, and you have come to me! Why has something so good happened to me?"
>
> **LUKE 1:42–43 ERV**

## God uses our friends who love Him to encourage us.

God used Elizabeth to encourage Mary. The angel had given Mary some very surprising news. Mary wasn't planning to have a baby when the angel told her about Jesus. But she was obedient to God, even though she knew other people might not understand God's plan.

When Elizabeth was filled with the Holy Spirit, she knew Mary's news even before Mary told her. Elizabeth's excitement showed Mary that God would continue to be with her as she followed His plan. When God is doing something important in our lives, He can use our Christian friends to encourage us and help us as we obey Him. And when we let Him, God can use us to encourage and help others too!
—T.M.

### READ MORE

Read Luke 1:46–55.
**Did Mary think of herself as important?**
**What are some of the words she used to describe God?**

### FUN FACT

Mothers can usually feel their babies moving inside the womb after about sixteen weeks of being pregnant.

# Joseph Has a Dream

**Joseph and Mary** were engaged to be married. When Joseph found out that Mary was going to have a baby, he was probably sad and confused. He didn't understand that the baby inside her was a miracle. Joseph was a good man and he loved Mary. He did not want to cause her shame, so he decided to end their engagement in secret.

While Joseph was thinking about this, an angel of the Lord spoke to him in a dream. "Don't be afraid, Joseph," the angel said. "You can take Mary to be your wife. The baby inside her is from the Holy Spirit. She is going to have a son. You will name him Jesus because He will save His people from their sins."

When Joseph woke up, he knew he had seen more than a dream. Joseph knew the angel's message was true. He did not have to break his engagement. Joseph took care of Mary and loved her very much.

Some people who knew Joseph and Mary probably did not understand what was happening. Friends and even people in their family might have said things that hurt Mary and Joseph's feelings. It must have been hard when other people didn't understand what God was doing.

## People might not understand God's plans for me.

But Mary and Joseph believed God and trusted Him. They knew God had chosen them for a very special purpose.

Sometimes when you trust and follow God, your friends and family might think you're wrong. But if you know you are doing what God wants, you can trust Him to make everything right. —C.B.

### FUN FACT

Some people think Joseph was much older than Mary. One reason is that the Bible doesn't mention Joseph after Jesus turned twelve years old. They think Joseph may have died sometime after that.

### READ MORE

Read John 6:37–40.
Why did Jesus say He came to earth?

# Trip to Bethlehem

**As Mary waited** for the birth of her baby, she learned she would have to take a long trip with Joseph. The emperor of Rome, called Caesar Augustus, ordered everyone to go back to their hometown as part of a census. A census is when government leaders count all the people who live in their country.

Because Mary was planning to marry Joseph, she had to go to his hometown to be counted as part of his family. They traveled about a hundred miles (160 kilometers) to Bethlehem because Joseph was from King David's family. While Joseph and Mary were in Bethlehem, the time came for Jesus to be born.

Hundreds of years earlier, the prophet Micah had said that the Messiah would be born in Bethlehem. "You, Bethlehem, are the smallest town in Judah," Micah wrote. "Your family is almost too small to count, but the 'Ruler of Israel' will come from you to rule for me."

> So Joseph left Nazareth, a town in Galilee, and went to the town of Bethlehem in Judea. It was known as the town of David. Joseph went there because he was from the family of David.
>
> **LUKE 2:4 ERV**

## God's promises about the Messiah came true.

Jesus was born in Bethlehem because God had promised the Messiah would come from King David's family. Bethlehem was the town that David came from many years before. God planned everything perfectly. Even though Joseph and Mary lived far to the north, they went to Bethlehem just in time for Jesus to be born.

God kept all of His promises about Jesus' birth. And He will keep all of His promises to us. When we see God's power to make things happen just like He said, we know we can believe everything He tells us. —T.M.

### READ MORE

Read 1 Samuel 16:4–13.
What important event happened in Bethlehem many years before Jesus was born?

### FUN FACT

Walking from Nazareth to Bethlehem could have taken eight to ten days.

# Jesus Is Born

She gave birth to her firstborn son. She wrapped him in strips of cloth and laid him in a manger because there wasn't any room for them in the inn.

LUKE 2:7 GW

**Bethlehem was crowded** when Joseph and Mary were there. Many families were in the city to be counted for the census. People had come from many different towns, so the inns and guest rooms were full.

The time came for Mary to have her baby. But since she and Joseph couldn't find a room to stay in, they spent the night in a stable or barn. That's where the Lord Jesus was born! After Jesus was born, Mary wrapped Him in strips of cloth and placed Him in a manger. A manger is a food box for animals. But that night the manger became Jesus' bed.

Jesus came from His beautiful home in heaven to a humble place on earth. He left His happy home with God to come to a sinful world. But God had a plan and purpose for sending His Son to earth. Jesus was the promised Messiah. He would forgive people of their sins and make them right with God.

## Jesus' birth was humble.

Jesus is the Son of God, the Messiah, and the King of all kings. Most kings are born in a palace—but not Jesus. He did not receive special treatment. That was not how most people expected the Messiah to be born.

But it was God's perfect plan. The King of the world was placed on a bed of straw. He would give up many nice things and do many hard things while He was on earth. Jesus did all of that because He loves you! —C.B.

## FUN FACT

In Bible times most mangers were made from clay mixed with straw or from stones held together with mud. Sometimes they were carved out of a rock.

## READ MORE

Read Hebrews 1:3–4.
What do these verses tell us about Jesus?

# Angels in the Sky

**As Mary and Joseph** welcomed baby Jesus into the world, there were some shepherds in a field nearby. They were watching over their sheep during the night when an angel suddenly appeared. The bright light of God's glory shone around the shepherds. They were terrified!

> "May glory be given to God in the highest heaven! And may peace be given to those he is pleased with on earth!"
>
> LUKE 2:14 NIRV

But the angel said to the shepherds, "Don't be afraid. I bring you good news of great joy. It's for all people. Today in the town of David a Savior has been born. He is Christ the Lord. Here is how you will know I am telling you the truth. You will find a baby wrapped in strips of cloth and lying in a manger."

Then a huge army of angels appeared in the sky. They were all praising God. "May glory be given to God in the highest heaven!" the angels shouted. "And may peace be given to those He is pleased with on earth!"

The army of angels, shining bright with God's glory, showed the greatness of Jesus. But the way God announced Jesus' birth showed what kind of king Jesus is. God didn't

Jesus came for everyone.

tell kings or powerful people in Bethlehem that Jesus had come. God shared the birth of His Son to a few poor shepherds.

Shepherds were just regular people in Bible times. Others didn't pay much attention to them. They lived simple lives and didn't make much money. But God wanted them to be the first to know that Jesus had come to earth.

There may come a time when you feel like you're not important. But that's not true at all. Every one of us is important to God, whether we're a king or a shepherd.
—T.M.

## FUN FACT

Often in Bible times, the youngest boy of the family took care of the sheep. When the prophet Samuel met the sons of Jesse to see who would be king after Saul, David—the youngest of eight boys—was out watching the sheep.

## READ MORE

Read Luke 15:10.
What is another time when angels rejoice?

# Run to the Manger

> As the shepherds returned to their flock, they glorified and praised God for everything they had seen and heard. Everything happened the way the angel had told them.
>
> LUKE 2:20 GW

**After they told** the shepherds about the birth of Jesus, the angels went back to heaven. Then the shepherds said to each other, "Let's go to Bethlehem and see what the Lord has told us about."

The shepherds went quickly, running to Bethlehem to see the baby. When they got there, the shepherds saw Mary and Joseph. Then they saw baby Jesus lying in a manger. Everything was just like the angels had told them!

As the shepherds left they told everyone they met how the angels visited them in the field. People were amazed at the shepherds' story. The shepherds returned to their sheep, praising God for everything they had seen and heard. Mary kept all these wonderful things as a good memory in her heart.

We can be excited about Jesus' birth, just like the shepherds who ran to find Him. The angels told the shepherds that the Savior had been born for all people. That means us too! As we celebrate Christmas each year, we tell the story of Jesus' birth like the shepherds did. And as we tell the story we can be like Mary and remember the great things God did that day. We can keep the miracle of Jesus' birth in our hearts and remember how important it is.

## The miracle of Jesus' birth is exciting!

As you think about Christmas Day, you can be excited about Jesus' birth. And you can think about the miracle of Jesus every day of the year. —T.M.

### FUN FACT

The angels told the shepherds they would find Jesus in strips of cloth called "swaddling clothes." They are wrapped around a baby to keep it warm and safe.

### READ MORE

Read John 20:3–9. What did Peter and John see lying in Jesus' tomb? How was this different from the swaddling clothes for baby Jesus?

> Every good present and every perfect gift comes from above, from the Father who made the sun, moon, and stars.
>
> JAMES 1:17 GW

# The Perfect Giver

**Christmas is** a time for presents! It's a time for giving gifts to show others that you care about them. It's a time for receiving presents too.

You might get an art set from your parents or a new toy from your friend. Your grandma might give you a cool pair of shoes that you've been wanting. When people give you a gift, it shows they care about you. Whenever you receive a gift, it's important to say thank you.

Do you know who the best gift giver is? The Bible tells us that every good present and every perfect gift comes from God. Think of all the good things you have in your life. Do you have food to eat and water to drink? They are gifts from God. Do you have a place to live and a bed to sleep in? Those are gifts too! These gifts don't come in fancy bags or boxes with bows, but they are still presents from God.

## God is the giver of every good thing.

The most exciting things in your life and the most ordinary things you use every day are all gifts from God. From the broccoli on your plate to your bicycle outside, God gives you everything you have. Remember to thank God for all the good gifts He gives you. He is the perfect gift giver. —T.M.

## 𝕽EAD MORE

Read Genesis 9:1–3.
What did God give to Noah and his family when they came out of the ark after the flood?

## FUN FACT

One name for God in the book of Genesis is Jehovah Jireh. This name means "the Lord will provide."

# Simeon Sees Jesus

**When Jesus was** just a few weeks old His parents took him to the temple in Jerusalem. God's law said that the first boy born into a family should be taken to the temple. The law helped people remember that it was God who gave them good things.

> "I have seen with my own eyes how you will save your people. Now all people can see your plan. He is a light to show your way to the other nations. And he will bring honor to your people Israel."
>
> LUKE 2:30–32 ERV

At the temple, Mary and Joseph met a man named Simeon. He was a man who loved and obeyed God. Before Jesus was born God had given Simeon a very special message. The Holy Spirit told Simeon that he would not die before he saw the Messiah! The Jewish people had been waiting for their Savior for many, many years, and Simeon would have the honor to meet Him. Simeon took Jesus in his arms and praised God.

"I have seen with my own eyes how you will save your people," Simeon prayed. "Now all people can see your plan. He is a light to show your way to the other nations. And He will bring honor to your people Israel." Mary and Joseph were amazed at what Simeon said.

As soon as he saw Jesus, Simeon knew that He was the Messiah. Jesus was still only a baby. He hadn't performed any miracles or taught others with His wisdom or shown that He was powerful. But God showed Simeon that Jesus had been born for a special purpose.

## Jesus was born as the Messiah.

Simeon told people in the temple what Jesus' purpose was—to save His people from their sin. When you know Jesus, you can be like Simeon. You can tell people that Jesus came to save them too. —T.M.

### FUN FACT

There were five men in the Bible named Simeon, including one of Jacob's twelve sons. The Simeon who met baby Jesus is mentioned only this one time in the book of Luke.

### READ MORE

Read Luke 2:36–38.
Who else saw baby Jesus at the temple?
What did she do?

# Wise Men Search for Jesus

**After Jesus** was born in Bethlehem, some wise men came from the east to Jerusalem. They asked people, "Where is the child who has been born to be the king of the Jews? We saw His star and have come to worship Him."

The ruler of the land, King Herod, was worried when he heard this news. He didn't want someone else to be king! So Herod called a meeting with the Jewish priests and teachers. Herod asked them where the Messiah was supposed to be born. They told Herod that the prophets had said the Messiah would come from Bethlehem.

> After the wise men heard the king, they left. They saw the same star they had seen in the east, and they followed it. The star went before them until it stopped above the place where the child was.
>
> MATTHEW 2:9 ERV

Herod called the wise men to a secret meeting. He asked them exactly when they saw the star. "When you find the child come back and tell me where He is so I can worship Him too," Herod told the wise men. But that wasn't the real reason Herod wanted to know where Jesus was. Herod wanted to get rid of Jesus!

**I will search for Jesus like the wise men did.**

When the wise men saw the star again, they followed it to the place where Jesus was. Inside the house, they found Mary with Jesus. They bowed down and worshipped Jesus. They gave Him expensive gifts of gold and frankincense and myrrh. Before they left, God spoke to the wise men in a dream. He warned them not to go back to Herod. So they went home another way.

The wise men searched for Jesus until they found Him. God led them to Jesus by showing them a special star. The wise men are an example for us. We don't have a star to follow, but we have the Bible as our guide. We can know Jesus as our King. God will help us along the way! —T.M.

## READ MORE

Read Isaiah 60:6–7.
What gifts did Isaiah say would one day
be brought to the Messiah?

## FUN FACT

Frankincense and myrrh are both made from the sap of trees. They are known for their great smell.

# Baby Jesus Goes to Egypt

> After the wise men left, an angel from the Lord came to Joseph in a dream. The angel said, "Get up! Take the child with his mother and escape to Egypt."
>
> MATTHEW 2:13 ERV

**After the wise men** went back to their homes, Mary and Joseph had to run away from theirs.

The wise men had told King Herod about a baby born in Bethlehem. They called Him the king of the Jews. King Herod didn't want to lose his kingdom. He didn't want anyone else to be the king. So he decided he would kill this baby to keep Jesus from ever becoming king. Since Herod didn't know exactly where Jesus was, he ordered that all the baby boys in Bethlehem be killed!

God sent an angel who spoke to Joseph in a dream. "Get up!" the angel said. "Take the child with His mother and escape to Egypt. Stay in Egypt until I tell you to come back." Joseph obeyed the angel. That night he took Mary and Jesus and left Bethlehem to go to Egypt. They stayed in Egypt until King Herod died.

## No one can stop God's plan.

Herod was a king and had a lot of power. But he couldn't stop God's plan of saving people through Jesus. No matter how mean and evil King Herod was, God's love and power were greater.

People make their own plans and try to take control of things—but nothing can stop God from doing what He wants. God is bigger than anything people try to do to change His plan. You can trust that God will save you through Jesus. You can always trust in God's power and love to protect you. —T.M.

**FUN FACT**

King Herod began ruling over Jerusalem about thirty years before Jesus was born. During his time as king, he built many forts, theaters, and aqueducts— giant water pipes through the desert.

**READ MORE**

Read Proverbs 19:21.
What happens when people make plans?

# Jesus Goes to Nazareth

> Jesus became wiser and stronger. He also became more and more pleasing to God and to people.
>
> LUKE 2:52 NIRV

**While Joseph, Mary, and Jesus** were safe in Egypt, King Herod died. Then an angel of the Lord came to Joseph in a dream.

"Get up!" the angel said. "Take the child and His mother and go to the land of Israel. The people who were trying to kill Jesus are now dead."

So Joseph got ready to take Mary and Jesus back to Israel. But when Joseph heard that King Herod's son was the new king in Judea, he was afraid to go there. After having another dream from God, Joseph took Mary and Jesus to the area of Galilee. Instead of going back to Bethlehem in Judea, they made their home farther north in Nazareth of Galilee. The prophet Isaiah had said many years earlier that the Messiah would be called a Nazarene. This was another sign that Jesus was the Messiah.

*Jesus is my example.*

The Bible doesn't tell us much about Jesus as a boy. It does say that Jesus obeyed His parents. It says that He grew up just like other kids. It says that He became wiser and wiser. And as Jesus grew up and got older, He pleased both God and the people around Him.

Even though Jesus was God in a human body, He still had to grow and learn. As a boy, He obeyed His parents and listened to teachers. He never did anything wrong! None of us can be exactly like Jesus, because He was the perfect person. But with God's help we can follow Jesus' example. We can become wiser by reading the Bible. We can please God and other people by doing what's right. We can grow to become more and more like Jesus. —C.B.

## READ MORE

Read John 8:28–29. What did Jesus say about pleasing God?

## FUN FACT

The fact that Jesus was taken to Egypt fulfilled another prophecy. Hosea 11:1 (ICB) says, "When Israel was a child, I loved him. And I called my son out of Egypt."

# Kingdom Work

Jesus said to them, "Why were you looking for me? Didn't you realize that I had to be in my Father's house?"

LUKE 2:49 GW

**When Jesus was twelve** years old His parents took Him to Jerusalem. They went to the temple for Passover. After the festival, Jesus' family started traveling home with a big group of people.

Mary and Joseph didn't notice at first, but Jesus had stayed in Jerusalem. After a day on their journey, Jesus' parents started looking for Him. They thought He was with some relatives, but when they couldn't find Him they were scared. So they rushed back to Jerusalem to look for Jesus.

Three days later they finally found Him. Jesus was outside the temple listening to the teachers. He paid close attention to them and asked them questions. His understanding amazed everyone.

When Jesus' parents found Him, Mary said, "Son, why have you done this to us? Your father and I have been very worried looking for you!"

"Why were you looking for me?" Jesus asked. "Didn't you know that I had to be in my Father's house?" But Mary and Joseph didn't understand what Jesus meant.

## Working for God's kingdom is the most important job.

Jesus came to earth to teach others about God and His kingdom. Even as a young boy, Jesus knew this was the reason he was born. His family didn't understand it right away, but Jesus spent every day doing His Father's work. He helped others learn about God and showed them God's love. We can follow Jesus' example. As the Holy Spirit helps us teach others about God and show them His love, we are working for God's kingdom too. It's the most important work we have to do! —T.M.

### FUN FACT

Because so many people traveled to Jerusalem for Passover each year, it took many months to get the city ready. Special ovens were even set up to cook the sacrifices people made.

### READ MORE

Read John 11:55–57.
Who looked for Jesus in Jerusalem many years later during the Passover? Why?

# The Greatest Prophet

**In the Old Testament,** we read about many prophets that God used to take His message to the Israelites. God chose each prophet for a special purpose. Sometimes God would give the prophet a message in a dream or vision. Sometimes God would speak out loud to His prophet. Real prophets always carried a message from God to His people.

> In the past, God spoke to our people through the prophets. He spoke at many times. He spoke in different ways. But in these last days, he has spoken to us through his Son.
>
> **HEBREWS 1:1–2 NIRV**

Prophets had a hard and lonely job. They often warned the people that God would punish them for not living the way He wanted them to live. Many times people didn't believe their message. Many times people didn't like what the prophets said. Many times the prophets were treated badly. They were often alone without friends to help them. But God was always with the prophets.

After Jesus came into the world, God didn't use prophets to deliver His message. God used Jesus himself. Many times people didn't believe Jesus' message. Many times people didn't like what Jesus said. Many times Jesus was treated badly. But Jesus became God's messenger to all people forever.

## Jesus' messages are from God.

Jesus is greater than any prophet because He is God. He has always been alive and He will be alive forever. Jesus knows what is in people's minds and hearts. He knows if you love Him and want to please Him. Jesus not only warns us about sin, He made the way for sin to be forgiven.

We can trust everything Jesus says because He is God. When we hear and obey His message, we please God! —C.B.

## FUN FACT

Prophets were people who spoke for God, repeating His messages to the people. In Hebrew, the language the Old Testament was written in, the word for prophet could mean "to bubble forth, like from a fountain."

## READ MORE

Read John 6:14–15. What did people say after Jesus fed more than five thousand people with one boy's lunch? What did the people want to do with Jesus?

# Coming Soon

"Listen! I am coming soon! I will bring rewards with me. I will repay each one for what he has done."

**REVELATION 22:12 ICB**

**After Jesus went** back to heaven His disciples traveled to many places to tell people about Him. John was taken away to the island of Patmos as punishment for preaching about Jesus. While he was there, God gave John a vision that showed him many things that are going to happen.

John even got to see some of heaven! He wrote about it in the last book of the Bible, called Revelation. An angel showed John a river of water flowing from the throne of God. It flows down the middle of the street in God's city. By the river is the "tree of life." It grows fruit every month!

"The throne of God and of Jesus the Lamb will be in the city." John said. "God's servants will worship Him and see His face. It will never be night. People will not need the light of a lamp or the sun. The Lord God will give them light. And they will rule like kings forever and ever."

**Jesus is coming back someday.**

Then Jesus spoke. "I am coming soon!" He said. "I will bring rewards with me to pay back each person for what he has done. I have sent my angel to tell you these things for the churches. All of this is true. I am coming soon!"

Because He said it, we can believe Jesus is coming back to earth. Then all who believe in Him as their Savior will be with Jesus forever. He will reward each one of us for the good things we did for Him. But Jesus himself is the best reward! —C.B.

## FUN FACT

John was the brother of James, who was also a disciple of Jesus. They were the sons of Zebedee and Salome. Jesus gave John and James the nickname "Sons of Thunder."

## READ MORE

Read Acts 1:9–11.
What did two angels tell the disciples about Jesus?

# Celebrate!

**On New Year's Eve** people all over the world celebrate. Many people have parties with their family and friends. Many people stay up late and play games. Some people go to see fireworks at midnight. And some people wear silly hats and blow paper horns!

They tell of the power of your awesome works—and I will proclaim your great deeds. They celebrate your abundant goodness and joyfully sing of your righteousness.

**PSALM 145:6–7 NIV**

People celebrate on New Year's Eve because it's the last day of the year. They stay up until midnight so they can cheer for the beginning of a brand-new year.

However you celebrate New Year's Eve, remember to say thank you to God for His many blessings—both in the year that's ending and the new year that's starting. From day to day and year to year God pours out His love on us. He gives us things we need like food and clothes. He gives us our families and our friends. He gives us many promises in the Bible to help us when we have problems.

## I will celebrate God's goodness all year long.

The book of Psalms is full of praise and thanksgiving to God. It shows us how to celebrate God by praising Him for His greatness and power and goodness. We can celebrate God by thanking Him for His wonderful love that lasts forever.

As you celebrate the end of the year by thanking and praising God, ask Him to guide you and bless you in the coming year. God is pleased when you trust Him. He wants to show you the plans He has for you. So praise God and thank Him. Trust God and follow Him. That's the best way to celebrate any time of year! —C.B.

### FUN FACT

In Spain, when the clock strikes midnight on New Year's Eve, people try to eat twelve grapes very quickly—one grape with each chime of the clock. Some people even practice beforehand to increase their speed.

### READ MORE
Read Psalm 145 to celebrate the greatness of God!

# GLOSSARY

*Angel:* A good being who does God's work. In the Bible, angels often carried messages for God. They also protect God's people. (See September 23.)

*Apostle:* A follower of Jesus who was sent out to spread the good news about salvation. Peter, John, and Paul were some of Jesus' apostles. (See August 28.)

*Blessing:* Kind words or a special gift from an important person. In the Bible, fathers would give a blessing to their children. God also has many blessings for the people who love and serve Him. (See July 25.)

*Christian:* A person who believes in Jesus and follows Him. (See July 12.)

*Demon:* An evil being who does the devil's work. During Bible times, demons would sometimes get inside people and cause them to suffer. Jesus would heal the people who came to Him for help by making the demons leave. (See October 12.)

*Disciple:* A person who follows a leader. In the Bible, Jesus called twelve disciples who followed Him, learned from Him, and told others about Him. (See July 6.)

*Favor:* The kindness and help that God shows to His children. (See August 8.)

*Forgiveness:* Giving up anger toward someone who has hurt you; not making someone pay for doing wrong toward you. (See June 23.)

*Grace:* The help and love God gives even though we don't deserve them. (See February 11.)

*Holy/hallowed:* Set apart as very special. God is holy, and so is His name. That means they deserve a lot of respect. (See August 5.)

*Holy Spirit:* One of the three "persons"—along with God the Father and Jesus—who are God. There is only one God, but He lives as one "Trinity." The Holy Spirit is the person of God who lives inside us when we believe in Jesus as our Savior. (See March 24.)

*Immanuel:* A name that means "God is with us." It is a name the prophet Isaiah gave to Jesus about seven hundred years before Jesus was born. (See December 16.)

*Israel:* The name of a person and two nations in the Bible. God changed Jacob's name to Israel after Jacob wrestled with God at the Jabbok River. The great nation that came from Jacob's twelve sons was called Israel. When the nation of Israel split into two kingdoms after Solomon died, the northern kingdom kept the name Israel to show it was different from the southern kingdom, called Judah. (See July 25.)

*Israelites/Jews/Jewish:* God's specially chosen people. In the first part of the Bible, God's people were usually called Israelites. Later in the Bible, they are often called "Jews" or "Jewish"—from the name of Jacob's son Judah. (See July 22.)

*Judah:* One of the twelve tribes of Israel, which were named after the twelve sons of Jacob. The tribe of Judah lived in the southern part of the promised land. Many years later, when the nation of Israel split into two kingdoms, the southern kingdom called itself Judah. (See December 9.)

# GLOSSARY, continued

**Lord:** A person who has power and authority over others; a master. The Bible uses the word *Lord* for both God the Father and Jesus. (See August 2.)

**Mercy:** God's gentle forgiveness. By showing mercy, God does not punish people in the way their sins deserve. (See February 11.)

**Messiah:** A word meaning "anointed one," or the one specially chosen by God. Jesus is the Messiah, the one chosen by God to die on the cross to save people from their sins. (See June 10.)

**Parable:** A simple story with a special truth hidden inside. Jesus liked to tell parables when He taught. (See February 17.)

**Pharisee:** A proud religious person in Jesus' time. Pharisees thought they would make God happy by following many rules. They didn't realize that God is pleased when people believe in Jesus. (See November 25.)

**Promised land:** A place that God promised to Abraham and the family that would come from him—his son, grandsons, great-grandsons, and all of those following. In Abraham's time, the promised land was called "Canaan." Later it was called "Israel." (See November 12.)

**Priest:** Men from the family of Moses' brother, Aaron, who served God at the meeting tent (or tabernacle) and the temple. They offered sacrifices to God for the people, and taught the people God's Word. (See August 1.)

**Prophet:** A person chosen by God to carry His messages to other people. Bible prophets included people like Elijah, Daniel, Isaiah, and Jeremiah. (See October 18.)

**Righteousness:** Living by faith in a way that pleases God. (See September 17.)

**Satan:** A beautiful angel who became proud and wanted to become more powerful than God. God threw Satan, also called the devil, out of heaven. Now Satan causes trouble for God's people. But God has planned Satan's defeat at the end of time. (See April 26.)

**Savior:** Someone who rescues another person from trouble or danger. Jesus is the Savior of the world, because He made a way for everyone who believes in Him to become part of God's family. (See April 21.)

**Sin:** The wrong things people do; disobedience to God's laws. The Bible says the payment for sin is death, but God offers eternal life through Jesus. (See April 16.)

**Temptation:** The feeling that you want to do something that you know is wrong. Temptation can come from outside us (the devil) or inside us (our own desires). Temptation by itself is not wrong, but doing what temptation says is wrong. (See April 26.)

**Trust:** Believing that God is real, honest, good, and able to help you . . . even when those things seem hard to believe. (See September 16.)

**Worship:** Telling God that He is good, powerful, and worth our love. We can worship God in our prayers, singing, giving, and the way we serve other people. (See October 26.)

# INDEX OF TOPICS

# INDEX OF TOPICS, continued

# SCRIPTURE PERMISSIONS

Scripture quotations marked ERV are from the HOLY BIBLE: EASY-TO-READ VERSION © 2014 by World Bible Translation Center, Inc., and are used by permission.

Scripture quotations marked GW are from *GOD'S WORD*. © 1995 God's Word to the Nations. Used by permission of Baker Publishing Group. All rights reserved.

Scripture quotations marked ICB are from the International Children's Bible®. © 1986, 1988, 1999 by Thomas Nelson. Used by permission. All rights reserved.

Scripture quotations marked MSG are from *The Message*. © by Eugene H. Peterson 1993, 1994, 1995, 1996, 2000, 2001, 2002. Used by permission of Tyndale House Publishers, Inc.

Scripture quotations marked NASB are from the New American Standard Bible®, © 1960, 1962, 1963, 1968, 1971, 1972, 1973, 1975, 1977, 1995 by The Lockman Foundation. Used by permission. (www.Lockman.org)

Scripture quotations marked NIV are from the Holy Bible, New International Version®, NIV®. Copyright © 1973, 1978, 1984, 2011 by Biblica, Inc.™ Used by permission of Zondervan. All rights reserved worldwide. www.zondervan.com. The "NIV" and "New International Version" are trademarks registered in the United States Patent and Trademark Office by Biblica, Inc.™

Scripture quotations marked NIRV are from the Holy Bible, New International Reader's Version®, NIrV® © 1995, 1996, 1998 by Biblica, Inc.™ Used by permission of Zondervan. All rights reserved worldwide. www.zondervan.com. The "NIrV" and "New International Reader's Version" are trademarks registered in the United States Patent and Trademark office by Biblica, Inc.™

Scripture quotations marked NKJV are from the New King James Version®. © 1982 by Thomas Nelson. Used by permission. All rights reserved.

Scripture quotations marked NLT are from the *Holy Bible,* New Living Translation, © 1996, 2004, 2007, 2013 by Tyndale House Foundation. Used by permission of Tyndale House Publishers, Inc., Carol Stream, Illinois 60188. All rights reserved.

Scripture quotations marked NLV are from the New Life Version. © 1969 by Christian Literature International.

# ABOUT THE AUTHORS

**Crystal Bowman** is a bestselling, award-winning author of more than eighty books for children including *The One Year Book of Devotions for Preschoolers*, *My Grandma and Me*, and *J Is for Jesus*. She also writes lyrics for children's piano music and stories for *Clubhouse Jr.* magazine. She is a mentor and speaker for MOPS (Mothers of Preschoolers) and teaches workshops at writers' conferences. She enjoys writing books for kids of all ages and wants them to know that God loves them and cares about them very much. Crystal is a mother and grandmother. She and her husband live in Florida where she likes to walk on the beach.

**Teri McKinley** grew up in the world of publishing, attending book signings and book conventions with her mother, Crystal Bowman. She began writing stories in elementary school and her love for writing grew in college while attending Baylor University. In addition to writing greeting cards for Discovery House Publishers and articles for national magazines, Teri has co-authored several books including *M Is for Manger* and *My Mama and Me*. She has a master's degree in interior design from Arizona State University and enjoys mentoring college students. Teri and her husband live in Texas.

Illustrator **Luke Flowers** spent countless childhood hours drawing sports heroes and comics at his grandfather's drawing desk. His love of art led him to Rocky Mountain College of Art and Design, where he earned a BFA in illustration. After ten years working for Young Life in the Creative Services Department, he launched Luke Flowers Creative, a company that seeks to "bring the illumination of imagination" to every project. Luke has won fourteen gold and silver Addy Awards for illustration and design.